The
OXFORD

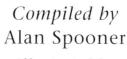

Illustrated

Junior
Thesaurus

Compiled by
Alan Spooner

Illustrated by
Peter Visscher

OXFORD
UNIVERSITY PRESS

OXFORD
UNIVERSITY PRESS

Great Clarendon Street, Oxford OX2 6DP

Oxford University Press is a department of the University of Oxford.
It furthers the University's objective of excellence in research, scholarship,
and education by publishing worldwide in

Oxford New York

Athens Auckland Bangkok Bogotá Buenos Aires Calcutta
Cape Town Chennai Dar es Salaam Delhi Florence Hong Kong Istanbul
Karachi Kuala Lumpur Madrid Melbourne Mexico City Mumbai
Nairobi Paris São Paulo Singapore Taipei Tokyo Toronto Warsaw

with associated companies in Berlin Ibadan

Oxford is a trade mark of Oxford University Press
in the UK and certain other countries

British Library cataloguing in Publication Data available

The Oxford Illustrated Junior Thesaurus is based on the text of *The Oxford Junior Thesaurus*

ISBN 0-19-910583-9 (hardback)
ISBN 0-19-910584-7 (paperback)
3 5 7 9 10 8 6 4 2

Typeset by Pentacor PLC, High Wycombe
Printed in Great Britain by Butler and Tanner, Frome

Do you have a query about words, their origin, meaning, use, spelling,
pronunciation, or any other aspect of the English language? Then write to
OWLS at Oxford University Press, Great Clarendon Street, Oxford, OX2 6DP.

All queries will be answered using the full resources of the
Oxford Dictionary Department

This thesaurus contains two main types of entry.

1 There are entries which give *synonyms* for the common words in a child's vocabulary. Where appropriate, opposites are also given. Example sentences or phrases put each word in a meaningful context.

2 There are *topic entries* which give lists of words which are not synonyms but which are related to the headword. For example, various kinds of animal are listed under **animal**; musical terms are given under **music**; and so on. These entries will be helpful to individual children who just need a jog to the memory to find the word they were looking for; they also provide opportunities for them to explore and discuss the vocabulary of a particular topic.

The arrangement of the thesaurus is simple and user-friendly. Each entry is self-explanatory: there are no abbreviations or cryptic devices. The headwords, which comprise all the words children are likely to look up as starting-points for a word-search, are arranged in simple alphabetical sequence, avoiding the need for a separate index (a common but awkward and confusing feature of some other thesauruses). The more discussable entries - topic entries, and entries for headwords with a particular complex range of senses or usages - are boxed in a blue outline. This will encourage young readers to browse.

The English language is infinitely variable and adaptable. Ultimately, children's awareness of this variety and adaptability will come not from a book like this, but from their experience of language in use. I hope, therefore, that they will be encouraged to see the thesaurus not just as a book to refer to, but as a book which raises questions about vocabulary - and about language in general - which they will want to discuss with teachers, parents, and other experienced users of our language.

The headword list in this thesaurus is derived from that of *The Oxford Illustrated Junior Dictionary*, to which this book will make an ideal companion volume.

Alan Spooner

USING THIS THESAURUS

A thesaurus helps you find words to make your language more interesting, and to help you say exactly what you want to say. It gives you words which have the same meaning as the word you thought of. These are called *synonyms*.

It may give you words which mean the *opposite* of the word you thought of.

It will often give you words which are useful when you are talking or writing about a particular *topic*.

Remember that a thesaurus does not give you explanations or definitions of what words mean. If you want to know what a word means, you need to look it up in a dictionary like *The Oxford Illustrated Junior Dictionary*.

IN THIS THESAURUS YOU WILL FIND...

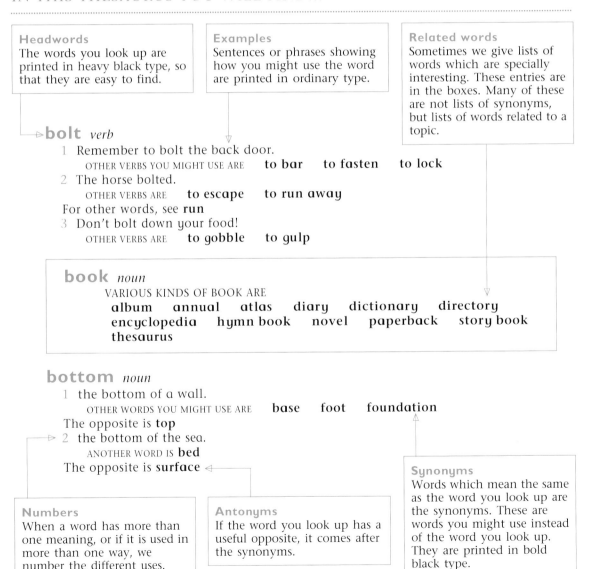

Headwords
The words you look up are printed in heavy black type, so that they are easy to find.

Examples
Sentences or phrases showing how you might use the word are printed in ordinary type.

Related words
Sometimes we give lists of words which are specially interesting. These entries are in the boxes. Many of these are not lists of synonyms, but lists of words related to a topic.

bolt *verb*
1 Remember to bolt the back door.
OTHER VERBS YOU MIGHT USE ARE **to bar to fasten to lock**
2 The horse bolted.
OTHER VERBS ARE **to escape to run away**
For other words, see **run**
3 Don't bolt down your food!
OTHER VERBS ARE **to gobble to gulp**

book *noun*
VARIOUS KINDS OF BOOK ARE
album annual atlas diary dictionary directory encyclopedia hymn book novel paperback story book thesaurus

bottom *noun*
1 the bottom of a wall.
OTHER WORDS YOU MIGHT USE ARE **base foot foundation**
The opposite is **top**
2 the bottom of the sea.
ANOTHER WORD IS **bed**
The opposite is **surface**

Numbers
When a word has more than one meaning, or if it is used in more than one way, we number the different uses.

Antonyms
If the word you look up has a useful opposite, it comes after the synonyms.

Synonyms
Words which mean the same as the word you look up are the synonyms. These are words you might use instead of the word you look up. They are printed in bold black type.

Aa

a b c d e f g h i j k l m n o p q r s t u v w x y z

abandon *verb*
1 It's cruel to abandon a pet.
    OTHER VERBS YOU MIGHT USE ARE **to desert**   **to forsake**   **to leave**
2 We abandoned the game when it rained.
    OTHER VERBS ARE **to cancel**   **to give up**   **to postpone**

able *adjective*
1 Are you able to play tomorrow?
    OTHER WORDS YOU MIGHT USE ARE **allowed**   **free**
2 Jo is an able tennis player.
    OTHER WORDS ARE **capable**   **clever**   **skilful**   **talented**

abolish *verb*
I wish they would abolish tests.
    OTHER VERBS YOU MIGHT USE ARE **to end**   **to get rid of**   **to remove**

accept *verb*
1 Please accept this gift.
    OTHER VERBS YOU MIGHT USE ARE **to receive**   **to take**
2 I accept that it was my fault.
    OTHER VERBS ARE **to admit**   **to agree**   **to believe**

accident *noun*
1 OTHER WORDS YOU MIGHT USE ARE **collision**   **crash**   **mishap**
WORDS YOU MIGHT USE FOR A VERY SERIOUS ACCIDENT ARE **calamity**   **catastrophe**   **disaster**
2 We met by accident.
    OTHER WORDS ARE **chance**   **coincidence**

accompany *verb*
Dad accompanied us to school.
    A PHRASE YOU MIGHT USE IS **to go with**

account *noun*
Jo wrote an account of the match.
    OTHER WORDS YOU MIGHT USE ARE **description**   **report**   **story**

accurate *adjective*
1 Is your watch accurate?
    OTHER WORDS YOU MIGHT USE ARE **correct**   **right**
2 Give me an accurate account of what happened.
    OTHER WORDS ARE **exact**   **precise**   **true**

ache *verb* and *noun*
For other words, see **pain**

achievement *noun*
It was a great achievement to win by four goals.
    OTHER WORDS YOU MIGHT USE ARE **accomplishment**   **feat**   **success**

act *verb*

1 She acted quickly to put out the fire.
PHRASES YOU MIGHT USE ARE **to do something** **to take action**

2 Jo likes to act in plays.
OTHER VERBS YOU MIGHT USE ARE **to appear** **to perform**
To act without using words is **to mime**

3 He was acting like an idiot.
ANOTHER VERB IS **to behave**

action *noun*

1 The film was full of action.
OTHER WORDS YOU MIGHT USE ARE **activity** **excitement**

2 It was a kind action to dig Mr Brown's garden.
OTHER WORDS ARE **act** **deed**

active *adjective*

1 Our puppy is very active.
OTHER WORDS YOU MIGHT USE ARE **energetic** **lively**

2 Mum is active in charity work.
OTHER WORDS ARE **busy** **involved** **working**

activity *noun*

1 What activities do you enjoy?
OTHER WORDS YOU MIGHT USE ARE **hobby** **job** **project** **task**

2 The shops are full of activity when the sales are on.
OTHER WORDS ARE **action** **bustle** **excitement**

actual *adjective*

Is that the actual tree Robin Hood lived in?
OTHER WORDS YOU MIGHT USE ARE **genuine** **real**

add *verb*

1 Add the milk and the sugar.
OTHER VERBS YOU MIGHT USE ARE **to combine** **to mix** **to put together**

2 We added the numbers together.
For other words you might use when you do maths, see **mathematics**
The opposite is subtract

additional *adjective*

OTHER WORDS ARE **extra** **more**

admire *verb*

1 We admired the firemen's skill.
OTHER VERBS YOU MIGHT USE ARE **to praise** **to respect** **to wonder at**

2 I admired the view.
OTHER VERBS ARE **to appreciate** **to enjoy** **to like**

admit *verb*

1 Jo admitted that she was wrong.
OTHER VERBS YOU MIGHT USE ARE **to accept** **to confess** **to own up**

2 They only admit you if you have a ticket.
OTHER VERBS ARE **to allow in** **to let in**

adore *verb*

Jo's dog adores her.
OTHER VERBS YOU MIGHT USE ARE **to idolize** **to love** **to worship**

adult *noun*

ANOTHER WORD IS **grown-up**

advance *verb*
As the army advanced, the enemy ran away.
> OTHER VERBS YOU MIGHT USE ARE **to approach** **to come near** **to move forward** **to progress**
The opposite is retreat

advantage *noun*
It's an advantage to have the wind behind you when you run.
> ANOTHER WORD IS **help**

advertise *verb*
They advertised a new car on TV.
> OTHER VERBS YOU MIGHT USE ARE (*informal*) **to plug** **to promote** **to publicize**

advertisement *noun*
> OTHER WORDS YOU MIGHT USE ARE (*informal*) **ad** or **advert** **commercial** **poster**

advice *noun*
My advice is to save your money.
> OTHER WORDS YOU MIGHT USE ARE **recommendation** **suggestion**

advise *verb*
What did the doctor advise?
> OTHER VERBS YOU MIGHT USE ARE **to recommend** **to suggest**

aeroplane *noun*
For other machines that fly, see **aircraft**

affect *verb*
The weather affects my mood.
> OTHER VERBS YOU MIGHT USE ARE **to alter** **to change** **to influence**

afraid *adjective*
The dog is afraid of thunder.
> OTHER WORDS YOU MIGHT USE ARE **frightened** **scared** **terrified**

aggressive *adjective*
That dog looks rather aggressive.
> OTHER WORDS YOU MIGHT USE ARE **hostile** **rough** **violent**
The opposite is friendly

agree *verb*
1 Mum agreed that I was right.
> OTHER VERBS YOU MIGHT USE ARE **to accept** **to admit**
2 We agreed to go shopping.
> OTHER VERBS ARE **to arrange** **to consent** **to decide**

aim *verb*

1 Aim the gun at the target.
OTHER VERBS YOU MIGHT USE ARE **to direct   to point**
2 We aimed to arrive by teatime.
OTHER VERBS ARE **to intend   to plan   to try   to want**

aircraft *noun*

VARIOUS KINDS OF AIRCRAFT ARE
**aeroplane   airliner   balloon   glider
helicopter   jumbo jet   jet plane**

jumbo jet

glider

helicopter

balloon

alarm *noun*

1 An alarm goes if there is a fire.
OTHER WORDS YOU MIGHT USE ARE **signal   siren   warning**
2 The storm was so bad that the animals were filled with alarm.
OTHER WORDS ARE **dismay   fear   fright   panic   terror**

alarm *verb*

The thunder alarmed the animals.
OTHER VERBS YOU MIGHT USE ARE **to frighten   to scare   to upset**

alert *adjective*

A sentry must be alert.
OTHER WORDS YOU MIGHT USE ARE **attentive   awake   observant   watchful**

allow *verb*

You are allowed to drive when you have passed a test.
OTHER VERBS YOU MIGHT USE ARE **to authorize   to license   to permit**

amaze *verb*
The conjuror's tricks amazed us.
> OTHER VERBS YOU MIGHT USE ARE **to astonish** **to astound** **to surprise**

amazing *adjective*
For other words, see **extraordinary**

ambition *noun*
Sam's ambition is to be a pilot.
> OTHER WORDS YOU MIGHT USE ARE **aim** **goal** **objective** **wish**

ambush *verb*
The soldiers ambushed the enemy.
> OTHER VERBS YOU MIGHT USE ARE **to attack** **to jump out on** **to take by surprise** **to trap**

---

ammunition *noun*
> KINDS OF AMMUNITION ARE
> **bullet** **cannonball** **hand grenade** **missile** **shell**
> For other words, see **weapon**

---

amount *noun*
> OTHER WORDS YOU MIGHT USE ARE **quantity** **total**

amuse *verb*
While we waited for the bus I tried to amuse the others.
> OTHER VERBS YOU MIGHT USE ARE **to cheer up** **to divert** **to entertain**

amusing *adjective*
an amusing joke.
> OTHER WORDS YOU MIGHT USE ARE **comic** **funny** **humorous** **witty**

ancient *adjective*
For other words, see **old**

anger *noun*
He showed his anger by slamming the door.
> OTHER WORDS YOU MIGHT USE ARE **annoyance** **fury** **rage** **temper**

angry *adjective*
Mum was angry when Jo broke the window.
> OTHER WORDS YOU MIGHT USE ARE **annoyed** **cross** **furious** **in a temper** **infuriated** **irate** (*informal*) **mad** **vexed**
The opposite is pleased

animal *noun*, see next page

announce *verb*
1 Jo announced that she was ready.
> OTHER VERBS YOU MIGHT USE ARE **to declare** **to report** **to state**
2 The DJ announced our record.
> ANOTHER VERB IS **to introduce**

announcement *noun*
The head read some announcements.
> OTHER WORDS YOU MIGHT USE ARE **notice** **statement**

a b c d e f g h i j k l m n o p q r s t u v w x y z

animal *noun*

OTHER WORDS YOU MIGHT USE ARE

beast   **creature**

A word you might use for a big animal you don't like is **brute**

DIFFERENT CLASSES OF ANIMAL ARE

amphibian	**bird**	**fish**	**mammal**	**reptile**

ANIMALS THAT FARMERS KEEP ARE

bull	**cow**	**goat**	**horse**	**ox**
pig	**sheep**			

ANIMALS PEOPLE KEEP AS PETS ARE

cat	**dog**	**donkey**	**ferret**	**gerbil**
guinea pig	**hamster**	**horse**	**mouse**	**rabbit**
rat	**tortoise**			

WILD ANIMALS YOU MIGHT SEE IN BRITAIN ARE

badger	**bat**	**deer**	**dormouse**	**fox**
hare	**hedgehog**	**mole**	**otter**	**shrew**
squirrel	**stoat**	**vole**	**weasel**	

OTHER WILD ANIMALS ARE

antelope	**ape**	**baboon**	**bear**	**beaver**
bison	**buffalo**	**camel**	**cheetah**	
chimpanzee	**dromedary**	**elephant**	**elk**	**giraffe**
gorilla	**grizzly bear**	**hippopotamus**		**hyena**
jackal	**jaguar**	**kangaroo**	**koala**	**leopard**
lion	**llama**	**mongoose**	**monkey**	**moose**
panda	**panther**	**platypus**	**polar bear**	**porcupine**
reindeer	**rhinoceros**	**skunk**	**snake**	**tiger**
wallaby	**wolf**	**zebra**		

ANIMALS THAT LIVE IN THE SEA ARE

dolphin	**fish**	**octopus**	**porpoise**	**seal**
sea lion	**turtle**	**walrus**	**whale**	

annoy *verb*
The wasps were annoying me.
> OTHER VERBS YOU MIGHT USE ARE **to bother**   **to irritate**   **to pester**   **to torment**   **to trouble**   **to upset**   **to worry**

answer *noun*
1 an answer to a question.
> OTHER WORDS YOU MIGHT USE ARE **reply**   **response**

2 the answer to a problem.
> OTHER WORDS ARE **explanation**   **solution**

anxious *adjective*
1 Mum gets anxious if I'm late.
> OTHER WORDS YOU MIGHT USE ARE **concerned**   **nervous**   **worried**

2 We were anxious to start.
> OTHER WORDS ARE **eager**   **keen**

apologize *verb*
I apologized for being rude.
> A PHRASE IS **to say sorry**

appeal *verb*
The sick man appealed for help.
> OTHER VERBS YOU MIGHT USE ARE **to ask**   **to beg**   **to plead**

appear *verb*
1 He appeared out of the mist.
> OTHER VERBS YOU MIGHT USE ARE **to arrive**   **to come out**   **to turn up**

2 You appear tired.
> OTHER VERBS ARE **to look**   **to seem**

appetite *noun*
1 an appetite for food.
> OTHER WORDS YOU MIGHT USE ARE **greed**   **hunger**

2 an appetite for adventure.
> OTHER WORDS ARE **desire**   **longing**   **passion**   **wish**

appointment *noun*
The head can't see us this afternoon because she has another appointment.
> OTHER WORDS YOU MIGHT USE ARE **arrangement**   **engagement**   **meeting**

approach *verb*
I got nervous when the big dog approached me.
> A PHRASE IS **to come near**

appropriate *adjective*
£10 was an appropriate price.
> OTHER WORDS YOU MIGHT USE ARE **fitting**   **proper**   **right**   **suitable**

approve *verb*
Did you approve of what I did?
> OTHER VERBS YOU MIGHT USE ARE **to admire**   **to like**   **to praise**

approximately *adverb*
The trip costs approximately £10.
> OTHER WORDS YOU MIGHT USE ARE **about**   **nearly**   **roughly**

a
b
c
d
e
f
g
h
i
j
k
l
m
n
o
p
q
r
s
t
u
v
w
x
y
z

7

area *noun*

1 The playground is a large area.
OTHER WORDS YOU MIGHT USE ARE **expanse** **surface**

2 Uncle Tom lives in a nice area of London.
OTHER WORDS ARE **district** **neighbourhood** **part** **region**

argue *verb*

Jo and Sam are good friends: they don't often argue.
OTHER VERBS YOU MIGHT USE ARE **to disagree** **to quarrel**

argument *noun*

1 We had an argument about who was going to pay.
OTHER WORDS YOU MIGHT USE ARE **disagreement** **dispute** **quarrel**

2 There has been a lot of argument in the paper about a bypass.
OTHER WORDS YOU MIGHT USE ARE **controversy** **debate**

arm *noun*

For other parts of the body, see **body**

arrange *verb*

1 Jo arranged the books on the shelf.
OTHER VERBS YOU MIGHT USE ARE **to set out** **to sort** **to tidy**

2 We arranged a trip to the sea.
OTHER VERBS ARE **to decide on** **to fix** **to organize** **to plan**

arrest *verb*

The police arrested the suspect.
OTHER VERBS YOU MIGHT USE ARE **to capture** **to catch** **to detain**
to take into custody

arrive *verb*

1 When will Granny arrive?
OTHER VERBS YOU MIGHT USE ARE **to appear** **to come** **to turn up**
The opposite is **depart**

2 We arrived home for dinner.
OTHER VERBS ARE **to come** **to get to** **to reach**

art *noun*

KINDS OF ART ARE
collage **drawing** **embroidery** **modelling** **needlework**
painting **photography** **pottery** **sculpture** **sewing** **sketching**
weaving

DIFFERENT ARTISTS ARE
painter **photographer** **potter** **sculptor** **weaver**

artificial *adjective*

1 Sam wore an artificial beard in the play.
OTHER WORDS YOU MIGHT USE ARE **false** **pretend**

2 This dress is made of artificial material.
OTHER WORDS ARE **man-made** **synthetic**
The opposite is **genuine**

ask *verb*

1 What did you ask?
> OTHER VERBS YOU MIGHT USE ARE **to enquire to find out to inquire**

2 The criminal asked to be given another chance.
> OTHER VERBS ARE **to beg to implore to plead to request**

3 My friends asked me to go out.
> ANOTHER VERB IS **to invite**

assistant *noun*

You can't do that job on your own: you need an assistant.
> OTHER WORDS YOU MIGHT USE ARE **helper partner**

Someone who helps a person with an official job is a **deputy**.
Someone who helps a person commit a crime is an **accomplice**.

assorted *adjective*

For other words, see **various**

astonish *verb*

The player's skill astonished us.
> OTHER VERBS YOU MIGHT USE ARE **to amaze to astound to surprise**

athlete *noun*

> OTHER WORDS YOU MIGHT USE ARE **sportsman sportswoman**

For various sports, see **sport**

attach *verb*

> WAYS TO ATTACH THINGS ARE **to bind to connect to fasten to fix to glue to join to link to stick to tie**

attack *verb*

1 The soldiers attacked the enemy.
> DIFFERENT WAYS TO ATTACK ARE **to ambush to assault to bomb to bombard to charge to raid**

2 Two men attacked him in the street.
> OTHER VERBS YOU MIGHT USE ARE **to mug to set on**

The opposite is **defend**

attempt *verb*

Jo attempted to swim ten lengths.
> OTHER VERBS AND PHRASES ARE **to endeavour to exert yourself to make an effort to try**

attend *verb*
1 We attended the school concert.
PHRASES YOU MIGHT USE ARE **to be present at   to go to**
2 Are you attending to me?
OTHER VERBS YOU MIGHT USE ARE **to listen   to pay attention**

attract *verb*
The bright lights attracted us.
OTHER VERBS YOU MIGHT USE ARE **to appeal to   to fascinate   to interest**

attractive *adjective*
1 an attractive person.
OTHER WORDS YOU MIGHT USE ARE **beautiful   charming   glamorous   good-looking   handsome   likeable   pleasant   pretty**
The opposite is **ugly**
2 an attractive idea.
OTHER WORDS ARE **appealing   interesting   pleasing   tempting**
The opposite is **boring**

audience *noun*
The audience enjoyed the play.
OTHER WORDS YOU MIGHT USE ARE **listeners   spectators**

author *noun*
ANOTHER WORD IS **writer**
For other words, see **write**

available *adjective*
Our magazine is now available.
OTHER WORDS YOU MIGHT USE ARE **on sale   ready**

average *adjective*
It was an average kind of day.
OTHER WORDS YOU MIGHT USE ARE **middling   normal   ordinary   typical   usual**
The opposite is **extraordinary**

avoid *verb*
Sam avoided the washing-up.
OTHER VERBS YOU MIGHT USE ARE **to dodge   to escape   to get out of   to shirk**

awake *adjective*
I was awake all night because of the storm.
OTHER WORDS YOU MIGHT USE ARE **alert   conscious**
The opposite is **asleep**

award *noun*
Jo got an award for swimming ten lengths.
OTHER WORDS YOU MIGHT USE ARE **badge   medal   prize   reward   trophy**

aware *adjective*
Jo was aware that Mum would worry if she was late.
ANOTHER WORD IS **conscious**

awful *adjective*
For other words, see **bad**

awkward *adjective*
1 Ducks look awkward when they walk on dry land.
ANOTHER WORD IS **clumsy**
2 Are you trying to be awkward?
OTHER WORDS ARE **difficult** **uncooperative**
3 The visitors came at an awkward time.
ANOTHER WORD IS **inconvenient**

Bb

baby *noun*
ANOTHER WORD IS **infant**
A baby just starting to walk is a **toddler**

back *noun*
I had to wait at the back of the queue
OTHER WORDS ARE **end** **rear** **tail-end**
The opposite is front

back *verb*
Dad backed the car into the gate.
ANOTHER VERB IS **to reverse**

bad *adjective*, see next page

badge *noun*
a school badge.
OTHER WORDS YOU MIGHT USE ARE
crest **emblem** **sign** **symbol**

bad-tempered *adjective*
OTHER WORDS YOU MIGHT USE ARE **angry** **cross** **grumpy** **irritable**
short-tempered
The opposite is cheerful

bag *noun*
For other words, see **container**

bake *verb*
For other ways to cook things, see **cook**

bad *adjective*

THIS WORD HAS MANY USES. HERE ARE SOME OF THE WAYS YOU CAN USE IT, AND SOME OTHER WORDS YOU COULD CHOOSE

1 a bad deed.
criminal   cruel   evil   immoral   sinful   villainous   wicked   wrong

2 a bad child.
disobedient   mischievous   naughty

3 a bad player.
hopeless   incompetent   rotten   useless

4 a bad accident.
appalling   awful   dreadful   frightful   horrible   serious   severe   shocking   terrible

5 a bad piece of work.
careless   incorrect   poor   shoddy   useless   weak   worthless

6 bad food.
decayed   mouldy   rotten   smelly

7 a bad smell.
nasty   objectionable   offensive   revolting   sickening   unpleasant

8 a bad habit.
dangerous   harmful   nasty   unhealthy

9 I feel bad today.
feeble   ill   poorly   sick   unwell
The opposite is good

ball *noun*
THINGS SHAPED LIKE A BALL ARE   **globe   sphere**
For other shapes, see **shape**

ban *verb*
They banned smoking on the buses.
OTHER VERBS YOU MIGHT USE ARE   **to forbid   to make illegal   to prohibit**

band *noun*
1 Robin Hood lived with a band of outlaws.
ANOTHER WORD IS   **gang**
2 Jo plays the guitar in a band.
OTHER WORDS ARE   **group   orchestra**
For more words to do with music, see **music**
3 A wooden barrel has bands of metal round it.
OTHER WORDS ARE   **hoop   loop   ring**

bang *noun*
1 We heard a loud bang.
OTHER WORDS YOU MIGHT USE ARE   **blast   boom   crash   explosion**
For other sounds, see **sound**
2 I got a nasty bang on the head.
OTHER WORDS ARE   **blow   bump   hit   knock**

banish *verb*
The traitor was banished from his country.
OTHER VERBS ARE   **to exile   to expel   to send away**

bank *noun*
We sat on a grassy bank.
OTHER WORDS YOU MIGHT USE ARE   **embankment   slope**

banner *noun*
The people in the procession waved banners.
OTHER WORDS YOU MIGHT USE ARE **flag   standard   streamer**

banquet *noun*
OTHER WORDS ARE **dinner   feast**   (*informal*) **spread**
For other words, see **meal**

bar *noun*
1 a wooden bar.
OTHER WORDS YOU MIGHT USE ARE **beam   rail   rod**
2 an iron bar.
ANOTHER WORD YOU MIGHT USE IS **girder**
3 a bar of chocolate.
ANOTHER WORD IS **block**

bare *adjective*
OTHER WORDS YOU MIGHT USE ARE **naked   nude   unclothed   uncovered
undressed**

barely *adverb*
Sam was so tired that he could barely keep his eyes open.
OTHER WORDS YOU MIGHT USE ARE **hardly   only   just   scarcely**

barren *adjective*
The desert was completely barren.
OTHER WORDS YOU MIGHT USE ARE **bare   lifeless   sterile**

barrier *noun*
They put up a barrier to keep the crowd off the field.
OTHER WORDS ARE **barricade   fence   railings   wall**

base *noun*
1 Dad used cement to make a firm base for the shed.
ANOTHER WORD IS **foundation**
2 Don't sit near the base of the cliff.
OTHER WORDS YOU MIGHT USE ARE **bottom   foot**
3 After a long march, the soldiers returned to their base.
OTHER WORDS ARE **depot   headquarters**

bashful *adjective*
The little boy was too bashful to say 'thank you'.
OTHER WORDS YOU MIGHT USE ARE **modest   shy   timid**

basic *adjective*
I know the basic facts, but I've still got a lot to learn.
OTHER WORDS ARE **chief   essential   important   main   principal**

basin *noun*
OTHER WORDS ARE **bowl   dish**

basket *noun*
For other kinds of container, see **container**

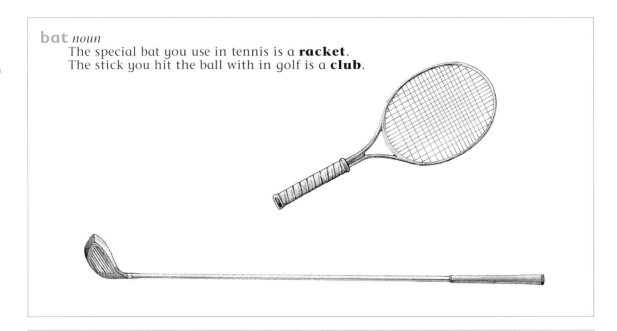

bat *noun*

The special bat you use in tennis is a **racket**.
The stick you hit the ball with in golf is a **club**.

---

bath *noun*

SPECIAL KINDS OF BATH ARE

jacuzzi　　**sauna**　　**shower**

---

battle *noun*

For other words, see **war**

bay *noun*

OTHER WORDS YOU MIGHT USE ARE　**cove**　**estuary**　**gulf**　**inlet**

beach *noun*

Jo and Sam spent a happy day at the beach.

OTHER WORDS YOU MIGHT USE ARE　**sands**　**shore**

For other words, see **seaside**

beam *noun*

1 a beam of wood.

OTHER WORDS YOU MIGHT USE ARE　**bar**　**plank**

2 a beam of light.

OTHER WORDS ARE　**ray**　**shaft**

beam *verb*

He beamed when he heard my voice.

OTHER VERBS YOU MIGHT USE ARE　**to grin**　**to laugh**　**to look happy**　**to smile**

bear *verb*

1 Will this branch bear my weight?

OTHER VERBS YOU MIGHT USE ARE　**to carry**　**to hold**　**to support**

2 She bore the pain bravely.

OTHER VERBS ARE　**to endure**　**to put up with**　**to stand**　**to suffer**

beast *noun*

OTHER WORDS YOU MIGHT USE ARE　**animal**　**creature**

ANIMALS THAT MAKE YOU AFRAID ARE　**brute**　**monster**

a
b
c
d
e
f
g
h
i
j
k
l
m
n
o
p
q
r
s
t
u
v
w
x
y
z

14

beat *verb*

1 We beat our opponents 6–0.
OTHER VERBS YOU MIGHT USE ARE **to conquer** **to defeat** **to outdo** **to overcome** (*informal*) **to thrash**

2 It's cruel to beat animals.
For other verbs, see **hit**

3 Dad beat some eggs to make an omelette.
OTHER VERBS ARE **to mix** **to stir** **to whisk**

4 When I run my heart beats fast.
OTHER VERBS ARE **to knock** **to pound** **to throb**

beautiful *adjective*

1 a beautiful bride.
OTHER WORDS YOU MIGHT USE ARE **attractive** **charming** **elegant** **glamorous** **good-looking** **gorgeous** **handsome** **lovely** **pretty**
The opposite is **ugly**

2 beautiful weather.
OTHER WORDS ARE **enjoyable** **fine** **good** **nice** **pleasant**

beckon *verb*

Sam beckoned to me to join him.
OTHER VERBS YOU MIGHT USE ARE **to make a sign** **to signal**

become *verb*

In time the little shoot will become a big tree.
PHRASES YOU MIGHT USE ARE **to change into** **to grow into** **to turn into**

---

bed *noun*

PARTS OF A BED ARE
base **headboard** **mattress**
A bed with a base and a mattress is a **divan**.
Two beds one above the other are **bunks**.
A bunk on a ship is a **berth**.
An old-fashioned bed with curtains round is a **four-poster**.

THINGS YOU USE TO MAKE A BED ARE
bedclothes or **bedding**

DIFFERENT KINDS OF BEDCLOTHES ARE
bed linen **bedspread** **blanket** **counterpane** **coverlet** **duvet** **eiderdown** **pillow** **pillowcase** **quilt** **sheet**

---

bee *noun*

KINDS OF BEE ARE **bumble-bee** **drone** **queen bee**

begin *verb*

When does the film begin?
OTHER VERBS YOU MIGHT USE ARE **to commence** (*informal*) **to get going** **to start**
The opposite is **end**

behave *verb*

1 Sam behaved strangely today.
ANOTHER VERB IS **to act**

2 Our teacher told us to behave.
A PHRASE IS **to be good**

behaviour *noun*
Our teacher praised our good behaviour.
OTHER WORDS ARE **conduct** **manners**

belief *noun*
1 It's my belief that ghosts don't exist.
OTHER WORDS YOU MIGHT USE ARE **opinion** **view**
2 We had a special service where people with different religious beliefs said prayers together.
OTHER WORDS ARE **creed** **faith** **religion**

believe *verb*
1 You can't believe all he says.
OTHER VERBS YOU MIGHT USE ARE **to accept** **to rely on** **to trust**
2 I believe he cheated.
OTHER VERBS ARE **to consider** **to feel sure** **to think**

bell *noun*
DIFFERENT WAYS BELLS SOUND ARE
chime **clang** **jangle** **jingle** **peal** **ping** **ring** **tinkle** **toll**

belongings *noun*
Be sure to take your belongings when you get off the train.
OTHER WORDS YOU MIGHT USE ARE **possessions** **property** **things**

bench *noun*
1 a bench to sit on.
OTHER WORDS YOU MIGHT USE ARE **form** **seat**
2 a carpenter's bench.
ANOTHER WORD IS **table**

bend *noun*
a bend in the road.
OTHER WORDS YOU MIGHT USE ARE **corner** **curve** **turn** **twist**

bend *verb*
1 The blacksmith bent the metal into fantastic shapes.
OTHER VERBS YOU MIGHT USE ARE **to coil** **to curl** **to curve** **to distort** **to fold** **to twist** **to wind**
2 He was so tall that he had to bend to go through the door.
OTHER VERBS ARE **to bow down** **to crouch** **to duck** **to stoop**

bet *verb*
ANOTHER VERB IS **to gamble**
KINDS OF BETTING ARE **the lottery** **the pools**

16

bewildered *adjective*

We were bewildered by all the different traffic signs.

OTHER WORDS YOU MIGHT USE ARE **confused muddled puzzled**

bewitched *adjective*

I was bewitched by the magical music.

OTHER WORDS ARE **charmed enchanted spellbound**

biased *adjective*

The referee was biased.

OTHER WORDS YOU MIGHT USE ARE **one-sided prejudiced unfair**

big *adjective*

1 a big person. a big thing.

OTHER WORDS YOU MIGHT USE ARE **colossal enormous fat giant gigantic great huge large massive monstrous tall**

2 a big hall.

OTHER WORDS ARE **roomy spacious vast**

3 a big event.

OTHER WORDS ARE **grand impressive spectacular**

4 a big decision.

OTHER WORDS ARE **important serious**

The opposite is small

bill *noun*

Keep the bill to prove how much you paid.

OTHER WORDS YOU MIGHT USE ARE **account receipt**

bind *verb*

They bound the prisoner's hands.

OTHER VERBS YOU MIGHT USE ARE **to secure to tie**

bird *noun*, see next page

bit *noun*

1 I don't want it all, only a bit of it.

OTHER WORDS YOU MIGHT USE ARE **chunk crumb dollop fraction morsel part piece portion section**

2 Mum told Jo to sweep up every bit of the broken mug.

OTHER WORDS ARE **chip fragment speck splinter**

3 I picked up the bits of paper and put them in the rubbish bin.

ANOTHER WORD IS **scrap**

bite *verb*

The dog tried to bite me!

OTHER VERBS YOU MIGHT USE ARE **to nip to snap at**

For other words, see **eat**

bitter *adjective*

1 a bitter taste.

OTHER WORDS YOU MIGHT USE ARE **acid harsh sharp sour**

2 a bitter wind.

OTHER WORDS ARE **biting piercing**

For other words, see **cold**

3 a bitter quarrel.

OTHER WORDS ARE **angry resentful spiteful**

black *adjective*

OTHER WORDS ARE **dark inky pitch-black sooty**

a b c d e f g h i j k l m n o p q r s t u v w x y z

bird *noun*

A male bird is a **cock**.
A female bird is a **hen**.

swan

WORDS FOR A YOUNG BIRD ARE
chick   **fledgling**   **nestling**

SOME BIRDS KEPT AS PETS ARE
budgerigar   **canary**   **cockatoo**   **macaw**
parakeet   **parrot**

BIRDS KEPT ON A FARM ARE
poultry

pheasant

KINDS OF POULTRY ARE
chicken   **duck**   **goose**   **turkey**

COMMON BRITISH GARDEN BIRDS ARE
blackbird   **bullfinch**   **chaffinch**   **goldfinch**
greenfinch   **robin**   **sparrow**   **starling**   **thrush**
tit   **wren**

SOME BIRDS YOU MIGHT SEE OR HEAR IN THE BRITISH COUNTRYSIDE ARE
crow   **cuckoo**   **curlew**   **dove**   **grouse**
jackdaw   **jay**   **lapwing**   **lark**   **linnet**
magpie   **martin**   **nightingale** **partridge**   **peewit**
pheasant   **pigeon**   **raven**   **rook**   **skylark**
swallow   **swift**   **wagtail**   **warbler**
woodpecker   **yellowhammer**

SOME BIRDS OF PREY ARE
buzzard   **eagle**   **falcon**   **hawk**   **kestrel**
kite   **osprey**   **owl**   **sparrowhawk**

BIRDS THAT LIVE NEAR WATER ARE
coot   **duck**   **flamingo**   **goose**   **grebe**
heron   **kingfisher** **moorhen**   **pelican**   **swan**

SOME SEA BIRDS ARE
cormorant   **puffin**   **seagull**   **tern**

OTHER BIRDS ARE
ostrich   **peacock**   **penguin**   **stork**   **vulture**

vulture

owl

parrot

robin

18

blade *noun*
THINGS WITH A SHARP BLADE ARE

axe   dagger   knife   razor   scissors   shears   sword

blame *verb*
When she saw the mess, Mum blamed me!
OTHER VERBS YOU MIGHT USE ARE **to accuse   to criticize   to scold**

blank *adjective*
1 a blank piece of paper.
OTHER WORDS YOU MIGHT USE ARE **clean   unmarked   unused**
2 Fill in the blank spaces.
ANOTHER WORD IS **empty**

blast *noun*
1 a blast of cold air.
For other words, see **wind**
2 the blast of a bomb.
OTHER WORDS ARE **bang   boom   explosion**

blaze *verb*
OTHER VERBS YOU MIGHT USE ARE **to burn   to flame   to flare up**
For other words, see **fire**

bleak *adjective*
a bleak hillside.
OTHER WORDS YOU MIGHT USE ARE **bare   cold   exposed   miserable
windswept   windy**

blend *verb*
Dad blended the ingredients to make a cake.
OTHER VERBS YOU MIGHT USE ARE **to beat   to combine   to mix   to stir together
to whisk**

blessed *adjective*
OTHER WORDS ARE **holy   sacred**

blind *adjective*
OTHER WORDS YOU MIGHT USE ARE **sightless   visually   handicapped**

block *noun*
a block of concrete.
OTHER WORDS ARE **chunk   lump   slab**

block *verb*

1 A flock of sheep blocked the road.
ANOTHER VERB IS **to obstruct**
2 The roads were blocked with traffic.
OTHER VERBS YOU MIGHT USE ARE **to clog**   **to jam**

bloom *verb*

Roses bloom in the summer.
OTHER VERBS YOU MIGHT USE ARE **to blossom**   **to flower**

blossom *noun*

In spring we have masses of blossom on our apple tree.
OTHER WORDS ARE **blooms**   **flowers**

blow *noun*

Sam got a nasty blow on the head.
For other words, see **hit**

blunt *adjective*

The opposite is **sharp**

blurred *adjective*

a blurred photograph.
OTHER WORDS YOU MIGHT USE ARE **cloudy**   **faint**   **fuzzy**   **hazy**   **misty**   **unclear**   **unfocused**
The opposite is **clear**

blush *verb*

She blushed when the teacher praised her work.
OTHER VERBS YOU MIGHT USE ARE **to flush**   **to go red**   **to redden**

boast *verb*

He boasted that he was best at everything.
ANOTHER VERB IS **to brag**

boat *noun*, see opposite page

body *noun*, see next page

bodyguard *noun*

OTHER WORDS YOU MIGHT USE ARE **guard**   (*informal*) **minder**   **protector**

bog *noun*

OTHER WORDS ARE **marsh**   **quicksands**   **swamp**

boil *verb*

1 Is the water boiling?
ANOTHER VERB IS **to bubble**
2 Jo put the potatoes on to boil.
For other ways to cook things, see **cook**

boat *noun*

OTHER WORDS ARE

craft   **ship**   **vessel**

DIFFERENT KINDS OF BOAT ARE

aircraft carrier	**barge**	**battleship**	**canoe**
cruiser	**destroyer**	**dinghy**	**ferry**
galleon	**house boat**	**junk**	**launch**
lifeboat	**liner**	**motor boat**	**oil tanker**
paddle steamer	**punt**	**raft**	**rowing boat**
sailing boat	**speedboat**	**steamer**	**submarine**
tanker	**trawler**	**tug**	**warship**
yacht			

bold *adjective*

1 a bold deed.
For other words, see **brave**
2 bold handwriting.

OTHER WORDS YOU MIGHT USE ARE **big**   **clear**   **large**

bolt *verb*

1 Remember to bolt the back door.

OTHER VERBS YOU MIGHT USE ARE **to bar**   **to fasten**   **to lock**

2 The horse bolted.

OTHER VERBS ARE **to escape**   **to run away**

For other words, see **run**

3 Don't bolt down your food!

OTHER VERBS ARE **to gobble**   **to gulp**

bone *noun*

For other words you might use, see **body**

book *noun*

VARIOUS KINDS OF BOOK ARE

album   **annual**   **atlas**   **diary**   **dictionary**   **directory**
encyclopedia   **hymn book**   **novel**   **paperback**   **story book**
thesaurus

body *noun*

Another word for the body of a dead person is **corpse**.
Another word for the body of a dead animal is **carcass**.
The main part of your body, not including the head, arms, and legs, is the **trunk**.

PARTS OF YOUR TRUNK ARE

abdomen or **tummy**	**back**	**bottom** or **buttocks**
breast	**chest**	**navel** or **tummy button**
nipples	**shoulders**	

THE INNER ORGANS OF YOUR BODY INCLUDE

bladder	**bowels**	**glands**	**heart**	**intestines**
kidneys	**liver**	**lungs**	**ovaries**	**stomach**
womb				

Your **arteries** take blood from the heart to other parts of the body, and your **veins** take blood back to the heart.
Your **muscles** are the parts you use when you move.
The **nerves** take messages to and from the brain.
Your **sexual organs** are your **penis** or **vagina**.

PARTS OF YOUR HEAD ARE

brain	**cheeks**	**chin**	**ears**	**eyes**
forehead	**gums**	**hair**	**jaw**	**lips**
mouth	**nose**	**nostrils**	**scalp**	**teeth**
throat	**tongue**			

Your arms and legs are your **limbs**.

PARTS OF YOUR ARM ARE
elbow   hand   shoulder   wrist

PARTS OF YOUR HAND ARE
fingers   fingernails   knuckles   palm   thumb

PARTS OF YOUR LEG ARE
ankle   calf   foot   knee   shin   thigh

PARTS OF YOUR FOOT ARE
heel   instep   toe   toenails
Your bones are your **skeleton**.

THE MAIN BONES OF YOUR HEAD ARE
jaw   skull

IMPORTANT BONES IN YOUR BODY ARE
backbone or **spine** or **vertebrae**   **pelvis**   **ribs**

THE MAIN JOINTS IN YOUR BODY ARE

ankle	**elbow**	**hip**	**knee**	**knuckle**
neck	**shoulder**	**vertebra**	**wrist**	

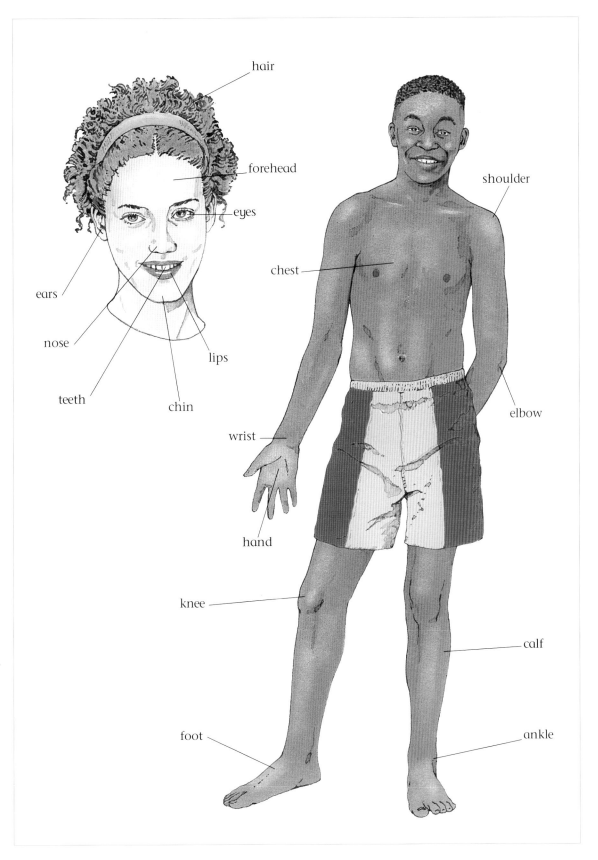

hair

forehead

eyes

ears

nose

lips

teeth

chin

shoulder

chest

elbow

wrist

hand

knee

calf

foot

ankle

boot *noun*
For other things you wear on your feet, see **shoe**

bore *verb*
to bore a hole through something.
OTHER VERBS YOU MIGHT USE ARE **to drill**   **to pierce**

boring *adjective*
a boring television programme.
OTHER WORDS YOU MIGHT USE ARE **dreary   dry   dull   monotonous   tedious   tiresome   uninteresting   wearisome**
The opposite is **interesting**

borrow *verb*
If someone lets you use something for a time, you borrow it.
If you give something to someone to use, you lend it.

boss *noun*
For other words, see **chief**

bother *verb*
Is the loud music bothering you?
OTHER VERBS YOU MIGHT USE ARE **to annoy   to disturb   to irritate   to pester   to trouble   to upset   to worry**

bottle *noun*
For other kinds of container, see **container**

bottom *noun*
1 the bottom of a wall.
OTHER WORDS YOU MIGHT USE ARE **base   foot   foundation**
The opposite is **top**
2 the bottom of the sea.
ANOTHER WORD IS **bed**
The opposite is **surface**
3 the bottom that you sit on.
OTHER WORDS ARE **backside   behind   buttocks**

boulder *noun*
There were some huge boulders on the beach.
OTHER WORDS ARE **rock   stone**

bounce *verb*
The ball bounced off the wall.
ANOTHER VERB IS **to rebound**

bound *verb*
The dog bounded over the gate.
OTHER VERBS YOU MIGHT USE ARE **to jump   to leap   to spring**

bound *adjective*
bound to It's bound to rain if we go out.
PHRASES ARE **certain to   sure to**
bound for The rocket is bound for the moon.
PHRASES YOU MIGHT USE ARE **aimed at   going towards**

boundary *noun*
OTHER WORDS YOU MIGHT USE ARE **border   edge   frontier   limit**

bouquet *noun*

a bouquet of flowers.

OTHER WORDS YOU MIGHT USE ARE

bunch **posy** **spray**

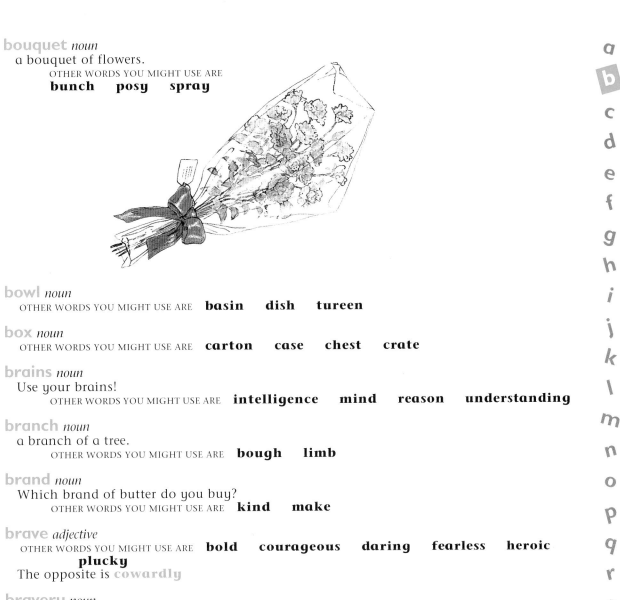

bowl *noun*

OTHER WORDS YOU MIGHT USE ARE **basin** **dish** **tureen**

box *noun*

OTHER WORDS YOU MIGHT USE ARE **carton** **case** **chest** **crate**

brains *noun*

Use your brains!

OTHER WORDS YOU MIGHT USE ARE **intelligence** **mind** **reason** **understanding**

branch *noun*

a branch of a tree.

OTHER WORDS YOU MIGHT USE ARE **bough** **limb**

brand *noun*

Which brand of butter do you buy?

OTHER WORDS YOU MIGHT USE ARE **kind** **make**

brave *adjective*

OTHER WORDS YOU MIGHT USE ARE **bold** **courageous** **daring** **fearless** **heroic**
plucky

The opposite is cowardly

bravery *noun*

OTHER WORDS YOU MIGHT USE ARE **courage** **daring** **heroism** **valour**

---

bread *noun*

DIFFERENT FORMS IN WHICH YOU BUY BREAD ARE

baguette **French stick** **loaf** **roll** **sliced bread**

For different kinds of bread, see **food**

---

break *noun*

1 a break in a pipe. a break in the fence.

OTHER WORDS YOU MIGHT USE ARE **crack** **cut** **gap** **hole** **leak** **opening**
slit **split** **tear**

2 a break in a game.

OTHER WORDS ARE **half time** **interval** **lull** **pause** **rest**

a
b
c
d
e
f
g
h
i
j
k
l
m
n
o
p
q
r
s
t
u
v
w
x
y
z

break *verb*

DIFFERENT WAYS THINGS BREAK ARE

to chip	to collapse	to crack	to crumble	to decay
to fall apart	to fracture	to shatter	to snap	to splinter
to split				

DIFFERENT WAYS YOU CAN BREAK THINGS ARE

to crush	to demolish	to destroy	to drop	to smash
to squash	to wreck			

breed *noun*

What breed of dog is that?

OTHER WORDS YOU MIGHT USE ARE **kind   species   variety**

breed *verb*

Most birds breed in the spring.

OTHER VERBS YOU MIGHT USE ARE **to produce young ones   to reproduce**

bridge *noun*

KINDS OF BRIDGE ARE **flyover   viaduct**

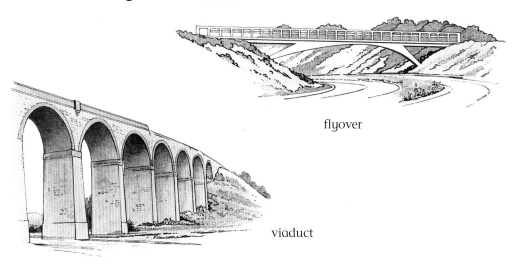

flyover

viaduct

brief *adjective*

OTHER WORDS YOU MIGHT USE ARE **concise   little   short**
The opposite is long

bright *adjective*

1 bright lights.

OTHER WORDS YOU MIGHT USE ARE **brilliant   colourful   dazzling   flashing   gleaming   glittering   shining   shiny   sparkling**

2 a bright boy.

OTHER WORDS ARE **brainy   clever   intelligent   quick   smart**

3 a bright smile.

OTHER WORDS ARE **cheerful   happy   radiant**
The opposite is dull

brilliant *adjective*

For other words, see **bright**

brim *noun*
My cup was full to the brim.
OTHER WORDS YOU MIGHT USE ARE **brink** **edge** **rim** **top**

bring *verb*
1 I helped to bring the shopping home.
OTHER VERBS YOU MIGHT USE ARE **to carry** **to fetch** **to take**
2 The captain brought her team onto the field.
OTHER VERBS ARE **to guide** **to lead**

brisk *adjective*
We set off at a brisk walk.
OTHER WORDS YOU MIGHT USE ARE **fast** **lively** **quick** **rapid**

brittle *adjective*
The shell of an egg is brittle.
OTHER WORDS YOU MIGHT USE ARE **fragile** **weak**
The opposite is strong

broad *adjective*
a broad area of sand.
OTHER WORDS YOU MIGHT USE ARE **extensive** **large** **wide**
The opposite is narrow

brook *noun*
ANOTHER WORD IS **stream**

brother *noun*
For other members of a family, see **family**

brush *noun*
A brush with a long handle is a **broom**

bubbles *noun*
OTHER WORDS YOU MIGHT USE ARE **foam** **froth** **lather** **suds**

bubbly *adjective*
OTHER WORDS YOU MIGHT USE ARE **boiling** **effervescent** **fizzy** **foaming**
sparkling

build *verb*
OTHER VERBS YOU MIGHT USE ARE **to construct** **to erect** **to put up**

building *noun*, see next page

bully *verb*
I was angry with the big girl who bullied the small ones.
OTHER VERBS YOU MIGHT USE ARE **to frighten** **to persecute** **to threaten**
to torment

bump *noun*
Jo has a nasty bump on the head.
OTHER WORDS YOU MIGHT USE ARE **bulge** **hump** **lump** **swelling**

bump *verb*
For other words, see **hit**

a
b
c
d
e
f
g
h
i
j
k
l
m
n
o
p
q
r
s
t
u
v
w
x
y
z

27

building *noun*

VARIOUS BUILDINGS ARE

abbey	barn	bungalow	cabin
castle	cathedral	chapel	church
cinema	cottage	factory	farmhouse
flats	garage	hotel	house
inn	lighthouse	mansion	monastery
mosque	museum	pagoda	palace
police station	post office	power station	prison
pub	restaurant	shop	skyscraper
stable	synagogue	temple	theatre
tower	warehouse	windmill	

PARTS OF BUILDINGS ARE

balcony	doors	floors	foyer
lobby	passage	porch	rooms
staircase	veranda	walls	windows

TOP PARTS OF A BUILDING ARE

ceilings	chimney	dome	eaves
gable	gutters	rafters	roof
spire	steeple	tower	turret

UNDERGROUND PARTS OF A BUILDING ARE

basement	cellar	crypt	foundations

For various rooms in a house, see **home**

church

lighthouse

windmill

pagoda

noun

a bunch of carrots.

OTHER WORDS YOU MIGHT USE ARE **clump** **cluster**

a bunch of flowers.

OTHER WORDS ARE **bouquet** **posy** **spray**

a bunch of friends.

OTHER WORDS ARE **crowd** **gathering** **group** **set**

noun

a bundle of papers.

OTHER WORDS YOU MIGHT USE ARE **pack** **package** **parcel** **sheaf**

noun

a heavy burden.

OTHER WORDS YOU MIGHT USE ARE **load** **weight**

noun

OTHER WORDS YOU MIGHT USE ARE **intruder** **robber** **thief**

For other words, see **steal**

verb

OTHER VERBS YOU MIGHT USE ARE **blaze** **flame** **flare** **smoulder**

WAYS YOU CAN DAMAGE THINGS BY HEAT ARE **to char** **to scald** **to scorch** **to singe**

To burn a dead person's body is **to cremate** it.

For other useful words, see **fire**

noun

Rabbits live in a burrow.

OTHER WORDS YOU MIGHT USE ARE **hole** **tunnel**

A place where rabbits make a lot of burrows is a **warren**.

verb

He burst open the door.

OTHER VERBS YOU MIGHT USE ARE **to break** **to force open**

The balloon burst.

OTHER VERBS ARE **to explode** **to pop**

noun

ANOTHER WORD IS **shrub**

noun

Dad's business is selling cars.

OTHER WORDS YOU MIGHT USE ARE **job** **occupation** **trade** **work**

I work for a computer business.

OTHER WORDS ARE **company** **firm** **industry** **organization** **shop**

Don't be nosey—it's none of your business!

OTHER WORDS ARE **affair** **concern**

adjective

Our teacher is always busy.

OTHER WORDS YOU MIGHT USE ARE **active** **doing things** **occupied**

(*informal*) **on the go**

The opposite is

The shops are busy during the sales.

OTHER WORDS ARE **bustling** **lively**

verb

I bought my bike for £30.

OTHER VERBS YOU MIGHT USE ARE **to get** **to obtain** **to purchase**

a
b
c
d
e
f
g
h
i
j
k
l
m
n
o
p
q
r
s
t
u
v
w
x
y
z

a
b
c
d
e
f
g
h
i
j
k
l
m
n
o
p
q
r
s
t
u
v
w
x
y
z

cable *noun*

1 electric cables.
   OTHER WORDS YOU MIGHT USE ARE **flex** **lead** **wire**

2 cables for tying up a ship.
   OTHER WORDS ARE **cord** **line** **rope**

---

café *noun*

We went into a café for a snack.

OTHER PLACES WHERE YOU MIGHT GET THINGS TO EAT ARE

| **bar** | **bistro** | **buffet** | **cafeteria** | **canteen** |
| **fish and chip shop** | | **restaurant** | **snack bar** | **takeaway** |

---

cage *noun*

OTHER WORDS FOR PLACES TO KEEP ANIMALS IN ARE

an **aviary** for birds
a **coop** for chickens
an **enclosure** for zoo animals
a **hutch** for rabbits
a **kennel** for a dog
a **pen** for sheep

---

cake *noun*

For kinds of cake, see **food**

call *verb*

1 I heard someone call.
   OTHER VERBS YOU MIGHT USE ARE **to cry out** **to exclaim** **to shout** **to yell**

2 They called the baby Robert.
   ANOTHER VERB IS **to name**

3 Mum called us in for dinner.
   OTHER VERBS ARE **to send for** **to summon**

4 I didn't call because the phone wasn't working.
   OTHER VERBS ARE **to phone** **to ring** **to telephone**

calm *adjective*

1 a calm sea.
   OTHER WORDS YOU MIGHT USE ARE **even** **flat** **peaceful** **smooth** **still**
The opposite is **stormy**

2 Don't panic—keep calm!
   OTHER WORDS ARE **cool** **patient** **quiet** **sensible**

camera *noun*, see opposite page

cancel *verb*

They cancelled the game because of the snow.
   OTHER VERBS YOU MIGHT USE ARE **to abandon** **to give up** **to postpone**

cap *noun*

For things you wear on your head, see **hat**

camera *noun*

DIFFERENT KINDS OF CAMERA ARE

camcorder   cine-camera   Polaroid

PARTS OF A CAMERA ARE

**flash   focus   lens   light meter
shutter   viewfinder   zoom lens**

capacity *noun*

What is the capacity of this kettle?

OTHER WORDS YOU MIGHT USE ARE   **size   volume**

captain *noun*

the captain of a team.
For words for people in charge, see **chief**

captive *noun*

The captives were locked in a dungeon.

OTHER WORDS YOU MIGHT USE ARE   **hostage   prisoner**

capture *verb*

Did they capture the thief?

OTHER VERBS YOU MIGHT USE ARE   **to arrest   to catch   to seize**

car *noun*

VARIOUS KINDS OF CAR ARE

estate   hatchback   racing car   saloon   taxi
For other things you ride in, see **travel**

card *noun*

1 CARDS YOU CAN SEND TO PEOPLE ARE

**birthday card   Christmas card   get-well card   invitation
postcard   Valentine**

2 IN CARD GAMES, THE SUITS ARE

**clubs   diamonds
hearts   spades**

THE CARDS WITH PICTURES ON ARE

**Jack   Joker
King   Queen**

care *noun*

1 He hasn't a care in the world!

OTHER WORDS YOU MIGHT USE ARE **trouble**   **worry**

2 Mum drives with great care.

OTHER WORDS ARE **attention**   **caution**

to take care Take care when you cross the road.

VERBS YOU MIGHT USE ARE **to be careful**   **to look out**

to take care of I took care of Jo's money while she went swimming.

PHRASES YOU MIGHT USE ARE **to keep something safe**   **to look after something**

care *verb*

He doesn't care who wins.

ANOTHER VERB IS **to mind**

to care for

1 We care for our pets.

OTHER VERBS ARE **to look after**   **to protect**   **to take care of**

2 You send a Valentine card to show that you care for someone.

For other words, see **love**

careful *adjective*

1 Mum is a careful driver.

OTHER WORDS YOU MIGHT USE ARE **alert**   **attentive**   **cautious**

2 Jo's work is always careful.

OTHER WORDS ARE **neat**   **orderly**   **organized**   **thorough**

The opposite is careless

careless *adjective*

1 careless driving.

OTHER WORDS YOU MIGHT USE ARE **negligent**   **reckless**   **thoughtless**

2 careless work.

OTHER WORDS ARE **disorganized**   **hasty**   **messy**   **untidy**

The opposite is careful

cargo *noun*

The ship unloaded its cargo at the docks.

OTHER WORDS YOU MIGHT USE ARE **freight**   **goods**

carnival *noun*

OTHER WORDS YOU MIGHT USE ARE **fair**   **festival**   **fête**   **gala**   **show**

carry *verb*

1 Sam carried the food into the dining room.

OTHER VERBS YOU MIGHT USE ARE **to bring**   **to lift**   **to move**   **to take**   **to transfer**

2 Trains can carry a lot of passengers.

OTHER VERBS ARE **to convey**   **to transport**

cart *noun*

OTHER WORDS YOU MIGHT USE ARE **barrow**   **wagon**   **wheelbarrow**

carve *verb*

For ways to cut things, see **cut**

castle *noun*

OTHER WORDS YOU MIGHT USE ARE
fort   **fortress**

PARTS OF A CASTLE ARE
battlements   **courtyard**   **drawbridge**   **dungeon**   **keep**
moat   **parapet**   **portcullis**   **tower**   **turret**

cat *noun*, see next page

catalogue *noun*
a shopping catalogue.
ANOTHER WORD IS **brochure**
a catalogue of books in the library.
OTHER WORDS FOR A LIST OF NAMES OR THINGS YOU MIGHT WANT TO LOOK UP ARE   **directory**
index   **register**

catch *verb*
to catch a ball.
OTHER VERBS YOU MIGHT USE ARE   **to grasp**   **to hold**   **to seize**
to take hold of
The opposite is **miss**
to catch a thief.
OTHER VERBS ARE   **to arrest**   **to capture**   **to stop**
to catch fish.
OTHER VERBS ARE   **to hook**   **to net**
to catch an animal.
OTHER VERBS ARE   **to snare**   **to trap**
to catch a bus.
ANOTHER VERB IS **to get**

catching *adjective*
I hope your cold isn't catching.
ANOTHER WORD IS **infectious**

cat *noun*

INFORMAL WORDS ARE

moggy   pussy   pussy cat
A young cat is a **kitten**.
A male cat is a **tomcat**.

KINDS OF CAT ARE

Manx	**marmalade cat**	
Persian	**Siamese**	**tabby**

For other pets, see **pet**

'BIG CATS' OR WILD ANIMALS RELATED TO CATS ARE

cheetah	**jaguar**	**leopard**
lion	**lynx**	**panther**
puma	**tiger**	**wildcat**

Siamese

lynx

Persian

cattle *noun*

ANIMALS THAT FARMERS KEEP AS CATTLE ARE

bull   bullock   cow   ox
Young cattle are called **calves**.

cause *verb*
The storm caused terrible floods.
PHRASES YOU MIGHT USE ARE **to bring about   to lead to   to result in**

cautious *adjective*
For other words, see **careful**

cave *noun*
OTHER WORDS YOU MIGHT USE ARE **cavern   grotto   pothole**

cease *verb*
Cease work!
OTHER VERBS YOU MIGHT USE ARE **to break off   to end   to finish   to stop**

cellar *noun*
OTHER UNDERGROUND PARTS OF BUILDINGS ARE **basement   crypt   vault**

cemetery *noun*
ANOTHER WORD IS **graveyard**
A graveyard round a church is a **churchyard**.

centre *noun*

the centre of the earth.

OTHER WORDS YOU MIGHT USE ARE **core   heart   middle**

The centre of a wheel is the **hub**.

---

cereal *noun*

OTHER WORDS ARE

corn   grain

1 KINDS OF CEREAL FARMERS GROW ARE

barley   maize or **sweet corn   oats   rice   rye   wheat**

2 KINDS OF BREAKFAST CEREAL ARE

bran   cornflakes   muesli   porridge

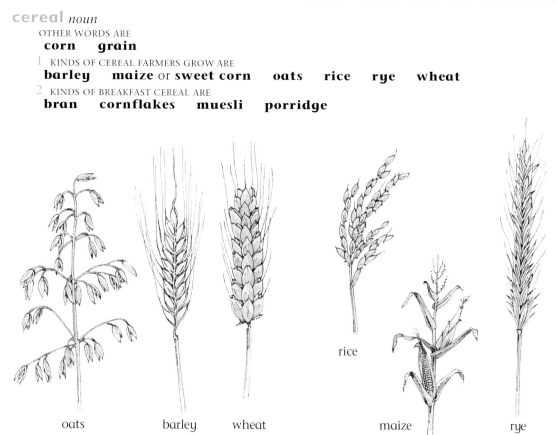

oats   barley   wheat   rice   maize   rye

---

certain *adjective*

Are you certain it will rain?

OTHER WORDS YOU MIGHT USE ARE **confident   definite   positive   sure**

chair *noun*

For things to sit on, see **seat**

champion *noun*

OTHER WORDS YOU MIGHT USE ARE **hero   winner   victor**

chance *noun*

1 This is your last chance.

ANOTHER WORD IS **opportunity**

2 I met him by chance.

OTHER WORDS ARE **accident   coincidence**

3 There's a chance of rain.

OTHER WORDS ARE **danger   possibility   risk**

change *noun*

I need some change to pay for the bus.

OTHER WORDS YOU MIGHT USE ARE **cash   coins**

change *verb*

1 I changed the end of my story.

OTHER VERBS YOU MIGHT USE ARE **to adjust** **to alter** **to make different** **to revise** **to transform**

2 I want to change this apple for an orange.

OTHER VERBS YOU MIGHT USE ARE **to exchange** **to substitute** **to switch** (*informal*) **to swap**

3 Tadpoles change into frogs.

OTHER VERBS YOU MIGHT USE ARE **to become** **to develop into** **to turn into**

channel *noun*

1 a channel to take water away.

OTHER WORDS YOU MIGHT USE ARE **canal** **ditch** **gutter**

2 a TV channel.

ANOTHER WORD IS **station**

chaos *noun*

There was chaos when the lights went out.

OTHER WORDS YOU MIGHT USE ARE **confusion** **a mix-up**

character *noun*

1 My favourite character in the pantomime was Cinderella.

OTHER WORDS YOU MIGHT USE ARE **part** **role**

2 Granny has a kind character.

OTHER WORDS ARE **manner** **nature** **personality**

3 Who is that character at the bus stop?

OTHER WORDS ARE **individual** **person**

charge *verb*

1 They charge £1 for an ice cream.

PHRASES YOU MIGHT USE ARE **to ask** **to make you pay**

2 The soldiers charged the enemy.

OTHER VERBS ARE **to attack** **to rush at**

charm *verb*

He charmed us with his music.

OTHER VERBS ARE **to bewitch** **to enchant** **to fascinate**

charming *adjective*

OTHER WORDS YOU MIGHT USE ARE **attractive** **pretty**

For other words, see **beautiful**

chart *noun*

OTHER WORDS YOU MIGHT USE ARE **diagram** **graph** **map** **plan**

36

chase *verb*

The dog chased the hare for miles.

OTHER VERBS YOU MIGHT USE ARE **to follow   to hunt   to pursue   to tail   to track   to trail**

chat, chatter *verbs*

For other verbs, see **talk**

cheap *adjective*

Jo bought a cheap coat in a sale.

OTHER WORDS YOU MIGHT USE ARE **cut-price   inexpensive   reasonable**

The opposite is expensive

cheat *verb*

He cheated us by keeping all the money for himself.

OTHER VERBS YOU MIGHT USE ARE **to deceive   to fool   to swindle   to trick**

check *verb*

Mum always checks the car before we go on a journey.

OTHER VERBS YOU MIGHT USE ARE **to examine   to look over   to test**

A traffic jam checked our progress.

OTHER VERBS YOU MIGHT USE ARE **to halt   to hold up   to prevent   to slow down   to stop**

cheeky *adjective*

My teacher hates cheeky behaviour.

OTHER WORDS YOU MIGHT USE ARE **bold   impertinent   impolite   impudent   insolent   rude**

The opposite is polite

cheer *verb*

The audience cheered.

ANOTHER VERB IS **to applaud**

to cheer someone up

OTHER VERBS YOU MIGHT USE ARE **to comfort   to encourage**

cheerful *adjective*

OTHER WORDS YOU MIGHT USE ARE **bright   happy   jolly   laughing   light-hearted   lively   merry   pleased**

The opposite is gloomy

chest *noun*

a chest full of treasure.

OTHER WORDS YOU MIGHT USE ARE **box   case   crate**

For other words, see **container**

chew *verb*

For other verbs, see **eat**

chief *adjective*

We learned the chief spelling rules.

OTHER WORDS YOU MIGHT USE ARE
basic   essential   important   main   major   principal

chief *noun*

WORDS FOR PEOPLE IN CHARGE OF VARIOUS THINGS ARE
**boss   captain   commander   director   employer   governor
head   leader   manager   president   principal   ruler**

child *noun*

OTHER WORDS ARE **baby   boy   girl   infant**   (*informal*) **kid**   (*informal*) **toddler**
(*informal*) **youngster**

china *noun*

When you wash up, make sure you don't chip the china.

OTHER WORDS YOU MIGHT USE ARE
**crockery   porcelain   pots
pottery**

THINGS MADE OF CHINA ARE
**bowl   cup   dish
jug   plate   saucer
teapot**

chip *noun*

OTHER WORDS FOR A SMALL PIECE BROKEN OFF SOMETHING ARE   **flake   fragment   splinter**

choke *verb*

This collar is choking me.

OTHER VERBS YOU MIGHT USE ARE   **to stifle   to strangle   to suffocate**

choose *verb*

We chose Jo as captain.

OTHER VERBS YOU MIGHT USE ARE   **to decide on   to elect   to name   to pick
to select   to settle on   to vote for**

chunk *noun*

a chunk of cheese.

OTHER WORDS YOU MIGHT USE ARE   **block   hunk   lump   piece   slab**

church *noun*

For places where people worship, see **religion**

cinema *noun*

OTHER WORDS ARE   **the pictures   the movies**

circle *noun*

OTHER WORDS YOU MIGHT USE ARE   **disc   hoop   ring**
For other shapes, see **shape**

circus *noun*

PEOPLE WHO PERFORM IN A CIRCUS ARE
**acrobat   clown   juggler   lion-tamer
ringmaster   trapeze   artist**

citizen *noun*

the citizens of a town.
OTHER WORDS YOU MIGHT USE ARE **inhabitant   resident**

claim *verb*

Jo claimed her lost property.
OTHER VERBS YOU MIGHT USE ARE **to ask for   to demand   to request**

clap *verb*

We clapped at the end of the play.
ANOTHER VERB IS **to applaud**

class *noun*

Which class are you in?
OTHER WORDS YOU MIGHT USE ARE **form   group   set**

clean *adjective*

1 clean clothes.
ANOTHER WORD IS **spotless**
2 clean water.
OTHER WORDS YOU MIGHT USE ARE **clear   fresh   pure**
3 a clean sheet of paper.
OTHER WORDS ARE **blank   unmarked   unused**
The opposite is **dirty**

---

clean *verb*

Sam cleaned the floor while Jo was cleaning the car.

WAYS TO CLEAN THINGS ARE

to brush	**to dust**	**to hoover**	**to mop up**
to rinse	**to scrub**	**to shampoo**	**to sponge down**
to sweep out	**to swill**	**to vacuum**	**to wash**
to wipe			

---

clear *adjective*

THIS WORD HAS MANY USES. HERE ARE SOME OF THE WAYS YOU CAN USE IT, AND SOME OTHER WORDS YOU COULD CHOOSE

1 clear water.
clean   colourless   pure
2 a clear sky.
blue   bright   cloudless   starlit   sunny
3 clear plastic.
transparent
4 a clear photograph.
focused   sharp   well defined
5 a clear voice.
audible   distinct
6 a clear space.
empty   free   open
7 a clear case of cheating.
obvious
8 a clear explanation.
plain   simple   understandable

clear *verb*

1 We cleared a space to play in.
OTHER VERBS YOU MIGHT USE ARE **to empty**   **to free**

2 Please clear the dishes.
OTHER VERBS ARE **to carry away**   **to move**   **to remove**   **to take away**

3 The fog cleared.
OTHER VERBS ARE **to disappear**   **to melt away**   **to vanish**

clever *adjective*

1 a clever pupil.
OTHER WORDS YOU MIGHT USE ARE (*informal*) **brainy**   **bright**   **brilliant**   **intelligent**   **quick**   **sharp**   **talented**   **wise**

2 clever with your hands.
OTHER WORDS ARE **expert**   **handy**   **skilful**

3 a clever trick.
OTHER WORDS ARE **crafty**   **cunning**

The opposite is stupid

cliff *noun*
ANOTHER WORD IS **precipice**

climb *verb*
Take care when you climb the ladder.
OTHER VERBS YOU MIGHT USE ARE **to ascend**   **to go up**   **to mount**

cling *verb*

1 The ivy clings to the wall.
ANOTHER VERB IS **to stick**

2 The baby clung to her mother.
OTHER VERBS YOU MIGHT USE ARE **to hold on on**   **to grasp**   **to hug**

clock *noun*
THINGS WHICH TELL THE TIME ARE
alarm clock   **digital clock**   **grandfather clock**   **hourglass**   **sundial**   **watch**

clog *verb*
The leaves clogged up the drain.
OTHER VERBS YOU MIGHT USE ARE **to block**   (*informal*) **to bung up**

(rhymes with *dose*) *adjective*

Our house is close to the park.
> ANOTHER WORD IS **near**

Mum took a close look at the cut on Jo's hand.
> OTHER WORDS YOU MIGHT USE ARE **careful** **thorough**

(rhymes with *doze*) *verb*

Please close the door.
> OTHER VERBS YOU MIGHT USE ARE **to fasten** **to lock** **to shut**

We closed the concert with some songs.
> OTHER VERBS ARE **to conclude** **to end** **to finish**

The opposite is

noun
> OTHER WORDS YOU MIGHT USE ARE
> **fabric** **material** **textiles**

DIFFERENT KINDS OF CLOTH ARE

canvas	**corduroy**	**cotton**	**denim**	**felt**	**flannel**
lace	**linen**	**muslin**	**nylon**	**polyester**	**satin**
silk	**tartan**	**tweed**	**velvet**	**viscose**	**wool**

noun, see next page

adjective

a cloudy sky.
> OTHER WORDS YOU MIGHT USE ARE **dull** **grey** **overcast**

cloudy water.
> OTHER WORDS ARE **milky** **murky**

a cloudy atmosphere.
> OTHER WORDS ARE **misty** **steamy**

The opposite is

noun

a football club. a chess club.
> OTHER WORDS YOU MIGHT USE ARE **association** **group** **league** **organization**
> **society**

The intruder tried to hit me with a club.
> OTHER WORDS ARE **baton** **cudgel** **stick** **truncheon**

noun

Give me a clue about what we are having for dinner.
> OTHER WORDS YOU MIGHT USE ARE **hint** **indication** **sign** **suggestion**

adjective

She's clumsy and keeps dropping things.
> OTHER WORDS YOU MIGHT USE ARE **awkward** **blundering**

verb

I clutched the rope to stop myself from falling.
> OTHER VERBS YOU MIGHT USE ARE **to cling to** **to grab** **to grasp** **to grip**
> **to hold on to** **to seize** **to snatch**

clothes, clothing *nouns*

OTHER WORDS YOU MIGHT USE ARE

costume	**dress**	**garments**

DIFFERENT THINGS YOU WEAR ARE

belt	**blazer**	**blouse**	**braces**	**cardigan**
coat	**dress**	**frock**	**jacket**	**jeans**
jersey	**jumper**	**kilt**	**leotard**	**miniskirt**
pullover	**rompers**	**sari**	**shawl**	**shorts**
skirt	**socks** ·	**stockings**	**suit**	**sweater**
sweatshirt	**tie**	**trousers**	**t-shirt**	**tunic**
waistcoat				

THINGS YOU WEAR TO KEEP CLEAN ARE

apron	**bib**	**dungarees**	**overalls**	**pinafore**

CLOTHES YOU WEAR WHEN YOU GO OUT ARE

anorak	**cagoule**	**cloak**	**duffle coat**	**gloves**
(*informal*) **mac** or **mack**	**mackintosh**	**mittens**	**muffler**
overcoat	**raincoat**	**scarf**		

CLOTHES YOU USE AT NIGHT ARE

dressing gown	**nightdress**	**nightie**	**pyjamas**

UNDERCLOTHES ARE

bra	**knickers**	**panties**	**pants**	**petticoat**
slip	**tights**	**underpants**	**vest**	

THINGS YOU WEAR WHEN YOU GO SWIMMING ARE

bikini	**swimming costume**	**swimsuit**	**trunks**

For things you wear on your head, see **hat**
For things you wear on your feet, see **shoe**

42

coach *noun*

1 We went to the seaside by coach.
For other things you travel in, see **travel**
2 Our team has got a new coach.
ANOTHER WORD IS **trainer**

coarse *adjective*

The coarse cloth tickled my skin.
OTHER WORDS YOU MIGHT USE ARE **hairy rough scratchy**
The opposite is smooth

coat *noun*

For things we wear, see **clothes**

coil *verb*

The snake coiled round a branch.
OTHER VERBS YOU MIGHT USE ARE **to curl to entwine to loop to twist to wind**

cold *adjective*

1 cold weather.
OTHER WORDS YOU MIGHT USE ARE **Arctic bitter chilly cool freezing fresh frosty icy** (*informal*) **nippy wintry**
2 I feel cold.
OTHER WORDS ARE **chilled frozen shivery**
The opposite is hot

collapse *verb*

1 The shed collapsed in the storm.
PHRASES YOU MIGHT USE ARE (*informal*) **to cave in to fall down to tumble down**
2 People collapsed because it was so hot.
ANOTHER VERB IS **to faint**

collect *verb*

1 A crowd collected to watch the fire.
OTHER VERBS YOU MIGHT USE ARE **to assemble to gather**
2 We collected all the litter.
OTHER VERBS ARE **to accumulate to gather together to heap up to pile up**
3 Mum collected Jo from school.
OTHER VERBS ARE **to bring to fetch to pick up**

collection *noun*

Jo has a collection of toys.
OTHER WORDS YOU MIGHT USE ARE **assortment gathering hoard pile set stack**
For other words, see **group**

collide *verb*

The car collided with a van.
OTHER PHRASES YOU MIGHT USE ARE **to bump into to crash into to run into**
For other words, see **hit**

collision *noun*

OTHER WORDS YOU MIGHT USE ARE **accident bump crash smash**

a b c d e f g h i j k l m n o p q r s t u v w x y z

colour *noun*
We admired the lovely colours of the sunset.

OTHER WORDS YOU MIGHT USE ARE
hue   **shade**   **tint**

DIFFERENT COLOURS ARE
amber	**black**	**blue**	**bronze**	**brown**
cream	**crimson**	**fawn**	**gold**	**green**
grey	**ivory**	**jet-black**	**khaki**	**maroon**
mauve	**navy blue**	**orange**	**pink**	**purple**
red	**rosy**	**scarlet**	**tan**	**turquoise**
vermilion	**violet**	**white**	**yellow**	

colour *verb*
OTHER VERBS YOU MIGHT USE ARE
to dye   **to paint**   **to stain**   **to tinge**   **to tint**

colourful *adjective*
1 colourful flowers.
OTHER WORDS YOU MIGHT USE ARE **bright**   **brilliant**   **flashy**   **gaudy**   **showy**
2 a colourful description.
OTHER WORDS ARE **lively**   **interesting**   **vivid**
The opposite is dull

column *noun*

The palace had stone columns in front of the door.
OTHER WORDS YOU MIGHT USE ARE **pillar** **pole**
post **shaft** **support**

column

combine *verb*

Our class combined with Jo's class to put on a play.
OTHER VERBS YOU MIGHT USE ARE **to come together** **to join** **to merge** **to unite**
I combined the cake ingredients in a big bowl.
OTHER VERBS ARE **to add together** **to blend** **to mix** **to put together**

come *verb*

Some dark clouds are coming.
OTHER VERBS YOU MIGHT USE ARE **to advance** **to approach** **to draw near**
Our visitors have come.
OTHER VERBS ARE **to appear** **to arrive** **to turn up**
The opposite is go

comfort *verb*

Jo comforts the baby when he cries.
OTHER VERBS YOU MIGHT USE ARE **to calm** **to reassure** **to soothe**

comfortable *adjective*

a comfortable chair.
OTHER WORDS YOU MIGHT USE ARE **cosy** **luxurious** **relaxing** **snug** **soft**

comic *adjective*

We laughed at his comic remarks.
OTHER WORDS YOU MIGHT USE ARE **amusing** **comical** **funny** **humorous**
laughable **witty**
The opposite is serious

command *verb*

The general commanded that the fighting must stop.
OTHER VERBS YOU MIGHT USE ARE **to instruct** **to order**
The captain commands the ship.
OTHER VERBS ARE **to be in charge of** **to control** **to govern** **to manage**
to supervise **to take over**

comment *noun*

The teacher asked for our comments.
OTHER WORDS YOU MIGHT USE ARE **opinion** **remark**

commit *verb*

to commit a crime.
OTHER VERBS YOU MIGHT USE ARE **to be guilty of** **to carry out**

a
b
c
d
e
f
g
h
i
j
k
l
m
n
o
p
q
r
s
t
u
v
w
x
y
z

common *adjective*

1 It's common for people to go to the seaside for a holiday.
  OTHER WORDS YOU MIGHT USE ARE **customary normal ordinary usual**
2 Colds are common in winter.
  OTHER WORDS ARE **frequent widespread**
3 'Too many cooks spoil the broth' is a common saying.
  ANOTHER WORD IS **well known**
The opposite is **rare**

---

communications *noun*
    DIFFERENT WAYS TO COMMUNICATE ARE
    **computer network letter newspaper magazine radar radio
    satellite telephone television**

---

compact *adjective*

1 a compact set of instructions.
  OTHER WORDS YOU MIGHT USE ARE **brief concise short**
2 a compact typewriter.
  OTHER WORDS ARE **neat portable small**

company *noun*

We enjoy the company of other people.
  OTHER WORDS YOU MIGHT USE ARE **companionship friendship**
For other words, see **crowd**

compare *verb*

Compare your answers with your neighbour's.
  OTHER VERBS YOU MIGHT USE ARE **to check to contrast**

compartment *noun*

The box has separate compartments for knives, forks, and spoons.
  OTHER WORDS YOU MIGHT USE ARE **division section space**

compel *verb*

You can't compel me to go swimming in this weather!
  OTHER VERBS YOU MIGHT USE ARE **to force to order**

competition *noun*

1 a sports competition.
  OTHER WORDS YOU MIGHT USE ARE **championship contest game match
        tournament**
2 There was fierce competition between the two teams.
  ANOTHER WORD IS **rivalry**

complain *verb*

We complained about the bad food.
  OTHER VERBS YOU MIGHT USE ARE **to grumble to object to protest**

complete *adjective*

1 Did he tell you the complete story?
  OTHER WORDS YOU MIGHT USE ARE **entire full whole**
2 He was talking complete rubbish.
  OTHER WORDS ARE **absolute pure total utter**

complete *verb*

Can I go out when I've completed my homework?
  OTHER VERBS YOU MIGHT USE ARE **to carry out to end to finish**

a b c d e f g h i j k l m n o p q r s t u v w x y z

complicated *adjective*
The instructions were too complicated for me to understand.
OTHER WORDS YOU MIGHT USE ARE **complex** **difficult** **involved**
The opposite is simple

computer *noun*, see next page

conceal *verb*
1 The bird concealed its nest.
OTHER VERBS YOU MIGHT USE ARE **to camouflage** **to disguise** **to hide**
2 He tried to conceal the truth.
PHRASES ARE **to cover up** **to keep quiet about**
The opposite is show

conceited *adjective*
There's no need to be conceited just because you got a prize.
OTHER WORDS YOU MIGHT USE ARE **boastful** (*informal*) **cocky** **proud**
The opposite is modest

concentrate *verb*
Concentrate on your work.
PHRASES YOU MIGHT USE ARE **to attend to** **to think about**

concern *verb*
Road safety concerns all of us.
OTHER VERBS YOU MIGHT USE ARE **to affect** **to be important to** **to involve**
to matter to

concerned *adjective*
Dad is concerned about Jo's cough.
OTHER WORDS YOU MIGHT USE ARE **anxious** **bothered** **worried**

conclude *verb*
1 We concluded the concert with a song.
OTHER VERBS YOU MIGHT USE ARE **to close** **to end** **to finish** **to round off**
2 After waiting 15 minutes, I concluded that I'd missed the bus.
OTHER VERBS ARE **to decide** **to reach a conclusion**

condemn *verb*
1 The head condemned the vandals who broke the window.
OTHER VERBS YOU MIGHT USE ARE **to blame** **to criticize**
2 The judge condemned the thief to spend a year in prison.
OTHER VERBS ARE **to convict** **to punish** **to sentence**

condition *noun*
1 Is your bike in good condition?
ANOTHER WORD IS **order**
2 Is your dog in good condition?
ANOTHER WORD IS **health**

confess *verb*
Jo confessed that she had lost her gloves.
OTHER VERBS YOU MIGHT USE ARE **to admit** **to own up**

a
b
c
d
e
f
g
h
i
j
k
l
m
n
o
p
q
r
s
t
u
v
w
x
y
z

computer *noun*

WORDS TO DO WITH COMPUTING ARE

cursor data disk drive floppy disk hard disk hardware interface joystick keyboard microchip microcomputer microprocessor monitor mouse PC printer printout program screen software terminal VDU word processor

monitor

screen

floppy disks

mouse

joystick

keyboard

confident *adjective*

1 Sam is a confident swimmer.

OTHER WORDS YOU MIGHT USE ARE **bold fearless**

The opposite is nervous

2 Jo was confident that she knew the answer.

OTHER WORDS ARE **certain definite positive sure**

The opposite is doubtful

48

confuse *verb*

Complicated sums confuse me.
OTHER VERBS YOU MIGHT USE ARE **to bewilder** **to puzzle**

I always confuse the names of the twins.
OTHER VERBS ARE **to mix up** **to muddle**

congratulate *verb*

We congratulated Sam when he won.
OTHER VERBS YOU MIGHT USE ARE **to compliment** **to praise**

connect *verb*

Dad connected a loudspeaker to the TV set.
OTHER VERBS YOU MIGHT USE ARE **to attach** **to join** **to link**

conquer *verb*

We easily conquered the opposition.
OTHER VERBS YOU MIGHT USE ARE **to beat** **to defeat** **to overcome**
(*informal*) **to thrash** **to win against**

conscious *adjective*

In spite of the knock on the head, he remained conscious.
OTHER WORDS YOU MIGHT USE ARE **alert** **awake**
The opposite is **unconscious**

consent *verb*

We can go on the trip if Mum and Dad consent.
OTHER VERBS YOU MIGHT USE ARE **to agree** **to allow it** **to approve** **to permit it**

consider *verb*

We considered the problem.
OTHER VERBS YOU MIGHT USE ARE **to study** **to think about**

considerate *adjective*

It was considerate of you to lend me your umbrella.
OTHER WORDS YOU MIGHT USE ARE **friendly** **helpful** **kind** **thoughtful**
unselfish
The opposite is **selfish**

construct *verb*

We constructed a model aeroplane.
OTHER VERBS YOU MIGHT USE ARE **to assemble** **to build** **to make**
to put together

contain *verb*

What does this box contain?
ANOTHER VERB IS **to hold**

What does this stew contain?
A PHRASE IS **to consist of**

container *noun*, see next page

contented *adjective*

The cat looks very contented.
OTHER WORDS YOU MIGHT USE ARE **happy** **relaxed** **satisfied**

contest *noun*

For other words, see **competition** or **fight**

container *noun*

THINGS THAT CONTAIN WATER OR LIQUID ARE

**barrel basin bath bin bottle bucket can cask
casserole cauldron churn cup dish flask glass goblet
jar jug kettle mug pail pan pot saucepan tank
teapot tub tumbler vase watering can**

CONTAINERS FOR OTHER THINGS ARE

**bag basket box carton case casket chest dustbin
envelope handbag haversack holdall knapsack money box
pouch purse rucksack sack satchel suitcase tin trunk
wallet**

continent *noun*

THE SEVEN CONTINENTS ARE

**Africa Antarctica Asia Oceania Europe North America
South America**

continual *adjective*

Continual chatter annoys the teacher.

OTHER WORDS YOU MIGHT USE ARE **ceaseless constant continuous endless
everlasting incessant non-stop persistent repeated
unending**

continue *verb*

1 How long will this rain continue?

OTHER VERBS YOU MIGHT USE ARE **to go on to keep on to last to persist**

2 Please continue with your work.

OTHER VERBS ARE **to carry on to keep going to persevere**

continuous *adjective*

For other words, see **continual**

contribute *verb*

I contributed £1 to the collection.

OTHER VERBS YOU MIGHT USE ARE **to donate to give**

control *verb*

She couldn't control the horse.

OTHER VERBS YOU MIGHT USE ARE **to command to deal with to handle
to manage to restrain**

convenient *adjective*

1 There's a convenient shop just round the corner.

OTHER WORDS YOU MIGHT USE ARE **handy useful**

2 It isn't convenient for Granny to visit us today.

OTHER WORDS ARE **appropriate easy suitable**

The opposite is **inconvenient**

conversation *noun*

Jo and Sam had a long conversation about their holiday.

OTHER WORDS ARE *(informal)* **chat discussion talk**

cook *noun*

The chief cook in a big restaurant or hotel is the **chef**.

cook *verb*
WAYS TO COOK THINGS ARE
to bake   to barbecue   to boil   to fry   to grill   to poach   to roast to steam   to stew   to toast

cool *adjective*
1 a cool wind.
OTHER WORDS YOU MIGHT USE ARE   **chilly   cold**
The opposite is **warm**
2 Don't panic–keep cool!
ANOTHER WORD IS   **calm**

copy *noun*
The painting was not genuine: it was a copy.
OTHER WORDS YOU MIGHT USE ARE   **counterfeit   fake   forgery**

copy *verb*
1 The budgie copies Jo's voice.
OTHER VERBS YOU MIGHT USE ARE   **to imitate   to impersonate**
2 Our teacher copied our poems so that everyone could read them.
OTHER VERBS ARE   **to duplicate   to photocopy   to reproduce**

corn *noun*
ANOTHER WORD IS   **cereal**
KINDS OF CORN ARE   **barley   maize** or **sweet corn   oats   rye   wheat**

corner *noun*
1 a corner between two walls.
ANOTHER WORD IS   **angle**
2 the corner of the road.
OTHER WORDS ARE   **bend   crossroads   junction**

correct *adjective*
Is that the correct time?
OTHER WORDS YOU MIGHT USE ARE   **accurate   exact   precise   right   true**
The opposite is **wrong**

corridor *noun*
ANOTHER WORD IS   **passage**

costly *adjective*
costly jewels.
OTHER WORDS YOU MIGHT USE ARE   **expensive   precious   valuable**
The opposite is **cheap**

costume *noun*
costumes for a play.
OTHER WORDS YOU MIGHT USE ARE   **clothes   clothing   disguise   fancy dress**

cosy *adjective*
For other words, see **comfortable**

council *noun*
GROUPS OF PEOPLE WHO DISCUSS THINGS AND MAKE DECISIONS ARE
assembly   committee   conference   parliament

a b **c** d e f g h i j k l m n o p q r s t u v w x y z

51

count *verb*

Jo counted her pocket money.

OTHER VERBS YOU MIGHT USE ARE   **to add up   to calculate   to total   to work out**

country *noun*

1 I like to visit other countries.

OTHER WORDS YOU MIGHT USE ARE   **land   nation   state**

2 There's some lovely country near here.

OTHER WORDS ARE   **countryside   landscape   scenery**

courage *noun*

The firemen showed great courage.

OTHER WORDS ARE   **bravery   daring   heroism**

---

cover *noun*

DIFFERENT KINDS OF COVER ARE

cap   coat   covering   envelope   folder   hat   lid   roof   top   wrapper

---

cover *verb*

DIFFERENT WAYS TO COVER THINGS ARE

to bury   to camouflage   to clothe   to conceal   to hide   to mask   to screen

---

crack *noun*

a crack in the wall.

OTHER WORDS YOU MIGHT USE ARE   **break   crevice   gap   opening   split**

crafty *adjective*

People say that the fox is a crafty animal.

OTHER WORDS YOU MIGHT USE ARE   **clever   cunning   sly   wily**

crash *noun*

1 a crash on the motorway.

OTHER WORDS YOU MIGHT USE ARE   **accident   collision**

For other words, see **hit**

2 There was a loud crash when Sam dropped the plates.

For other words, see **sound**

crazy *adjective*

1 The poor dog went crazy when she was stung by a wasp.

OTHER WORDS YOU MIGHT USE ARE   **berserk   frantic   wild**

2 It was a crazy idea to go for a walk in the rain.

OTHER WORDS ARE   **absurd   mad   ridiculous   silly   stupid**

The opposite is sensible

crease *verb*

Don't crease the paper.

OTHER VERBS YOU MIGHT USE ARE   **to crumple   to fold   to wrinkle**

create *verb*

Mum created a new kind of cake.

OTHER VERBS YOU MIGHT USE ARE   **to invent   to make   to produce   to think up**

For other words, see **make**

noun

ANOTHER WORD IS **maker**
The creator of a new way to do something is an **inventor**.
The creator of a book is an **author** or **poet** or **writer**.
The creator of a piece of music is a **composer**.
The creator of a painting or a statue is an **artist**.

noun
For names of different creatures, see **animal** and **bird**

verb
For other ways to move, see **move**

noun
OTHER WORDS YOU MIGHT USE ARE
dishonesty   offence   wrongdoing

SOME CRIMES ARE
**arson   blackmail   burglary   forgery   hijacking   joyriding
kidnapping   manslaughter   murder   poaching   robbery
shoplifting   smuggling   stealing**

noun
OTHER WORDS YOU MIGHT USE ARE
(*informal*) **crook   culprit   delinquent   offender   wrongdoer**

DIFFERENT KINDS OF CRIMINAL ARE
**blackmailer   burglar   gangster   hijacker   kidnapper   mugger
murderer   poacher   robber   shoplifter   smuggler   terrorist
vandal**

adjective
She has been crippled since her road accident.
OTHER WORDS YOU MIGHT USE ARE **disabled   handicapped   lame**

adjective
I like biscuits if they are crisp.
OTHER WORDS TO DESCRIBE THINGS WHICH BREAK EASILY ARE **brittle   crackly   fragile**
The opposite is

adjective
a crooked path.
OTHER WORDS YOU MIGHT USE ARE **bent   twisting   winding   zigzag**
The opposite is

adjective
For other words, see **angry**

verb
Take care when you cross the road.
A PHRASE YOU MIGHT USE IS **to go across**

OTHER VERBS ARE **to cancel   to delete   to erase**

crossroads *noun*
OTHER WORDS ARE **intersection   junction**

crouch *verb*
We had to crouch to go through the small opening.
OTHER VERBS YOU MIGHT USE ARE **to bend   to stoop**

crowd *noun*
a crowd of people.
OTHER WORDS YOU MIGHT USE ARE **company   group   horde**
A noisy, violent crowd is a **mob**.
Another word for the crowd at a football match is **spectators**.
For other words, see **group**

cruel *adjective*
I think it's cruel to hunt foxes.
OTHER WORDS YOU MIGHT USE ARE **bloodthirsty   brutal   cold-hearted   heartless   merciless   pitiless   ruthless   unkind   vicious**
The opposite is **kind**

crumb *noun*
a crumb of bread.
OTHER WORDS YOU MIGHT USE ARE **bit   fragment   scrap**

crumple *verb*
Don't crumple the clothes I've just ironed!
OTHER VERBS YOU MIGHT USE ARE **to crease   to crush   to fold   to wrinkle**

crush *verb*
I crushed my finger in the door.
OTHER VERBS YOU MIGHT USE ARE **to smash   to squash   to squeeze**

cry *verb*
The baby cries when she's tired.
OTHER VERBS YOU MIGHT USE ARE **to grizzle   to shed tears   to sob   to wail   to weep**
to cry out
OTHER VERBS ARE **to call   to shout   to yell**

cuddle *verb*
Sam loves to cuddle the baby.
OTHER VERBS YOU MIGHT USE ARE **to embrace   to hug**

cunning *adjective*
We had a cunning plan to trick our friends.
OTHER WORDS YOU MIGHT USE ARE **clever   crafty   ingenious   skilful   sly   wily**

cup *noun*
THINGS YOU CAN DRINK FROM ARE
beaker   glass   goblet   mug   tumbler

cure *noun*
Have you got a cure for a cold?
OTHER WORDS YOU MIGHT USE ARE **medicine   remedy   treatment**

cure *verb*
Will this medicine cure me?
ANOTHER VERB IS **to heal**

curious *adjective*

1 Jo is curious about what she will get for Christmas.
  OTHER WORDS YOU MIGHT USE ARE **inquisitive   interested**
2 Sam thought there was a curious smell in the pantry.
  OTHER WORDS ARE **funny   odd   peculiar   queer   strange   unusual**

curl *verb*

I curl my hair round my fingers.
  OTHER VERBS YOU MIGHT USE ARE **to bend   to coil   to loop   to twist   to wind**

curse *verb*

He cursed when he hit his finger with the hammer.
  ANOTHER VERB IS **to swear**

curtain *noun*

OTHER WORDS YOU MIGHT USE ARE **blind   drape   screen**

---

curve *noun*

The driver slowed down as she approached the curve in the road.

OTHER WORDS YOU MIGHT USE ARE
bend   turn   twist

THINGS THAT MAKE THE SHAPE OF A CURVE ARE
arch   bow   curl   hook   horseshoe   loop   rainbow   semicircle   wave

---

curved *adjective*

OTHER WORDS YOU MIGHT USE ARE
arched   bent   bowed   concave   convex   crescent-shaped   curled   rounded   twisted

---

custom *noun*

It's a custom to give presents on a person's birthday.
  OTHER WORDS YOU MIGHT USE ARE **convention   habit   tradition**

cut *noun*, see next page

---

cutlery *noun*

ITEMS OF CUTLERY ARE
breadknife   carving knife   dessertspoon   fork   knife   spoon   tablespoon   teaspoon

cut *noun*

a cut on your finger.

OTHER WORDS ARE

gash **injury** **nick** **wound**

cut *verb*

There are a lot of verbs which mean 'to cut'.
You **carve** meat, or an artist can **carve** a statue.
You can **chisel** wood.
You **chop** things with an axe.
You **clip** the hedge with shears.
You **mince** meat into tiny pieces.
You **mow** the lawn.
You can **prune** branches off a tree.
You **saw** wood.
You **shave** with a razor.
You **slice** bread with a breadknife.
You can **slit** open an envelope.
You **snip** things with scissors.
You **stab** with a dagger.
You **trim** your hair to make it tidy.
To **cut** prices is to lower or reduce them.

cycle *noun*

A cycle with two wheels is a **bicycle** or **bike**.
A cycle with three wheels is a **tricycle**.
A cycle with an engine is a **moped** or **motorbike**.

Dd

damage *noun*

The storm caused a lot of damage.
OTHER WORDS YOU MIGHT USE ARE **destruction** **havoc**

damage *verb*

OTHER VERBS YOU MIGHT USE ARE **to harm**   **to hurt**   **to injure**   **to spoil**

WAYS YOU CAN DAMAGE THINGS ARE **to break**   **to chip**   **to dent**   **to scratch**   **to smash**   **to wound**

damp *adjective*

Don't sit on the damp grass.

OTHER WORDS YOU MIGHT USE ARE **moist**   **rather wet**

The opposite is **dry**

dance *noun*

Sam and Jo went to a dance on St Valentine's Day.

A very formal dance is a **ball**.

A dance where music is played on records is a **disco**.

A dance you see in a theatre or on TV which tells a story is a **ballet**.

dance *verb*

OTHER VERBS YOU MIGHT USE ARE **to jump about**   **to leap about**   **to prance**   **to skip**

danger *noun*

The rocks are a danger to ships.

ANOTHER WORD IS **peril**

In summer there's a danger of getting sunburnt.

OTHER WORDS YOU MIGHT USE ARE **chance**   **possibility**   **risk**   **threat**

dangerous *adjective*

a dangerous adventure.

OTHER WORDS YOU MIGHT USE ARE **hazardous**   **perilous**   **risky**   **unsafe**

a dangerous criminal.

OTHER WORDS ARE **desperate**   **treacherous**   **violent**

a dangerous poison.

OTHER WORDS ARE **deadly**   **harmful**   **lethal**

The opposite is **safe**

daring *adjective*

Sam thought Jo was very daring to climb up the big rock.

OTHER WORDS YOU MIGHT USE ARE **adventurous**   **bold**   **brave**   **fearless**

The opposite is **cowardly**

dark *adjective*

a dark night.

OTHER WORDS YOU MIGHT USE ARE **black**   **starless**

a dark place.

OTHER WORDS YOU MIGHT USE ARE **gloomy**   **shadowy**   **shady**   **sunless**   **unlit**

The opposite is **bright**

darling *noun*

OTHER WORDS YOU MIGHT USE ARE **beloved**   **dear**   **love**   **sweetheart**

dawdle *verb*

Don't dawdle: we're late!

OTHER VERBS YOU MIGHT USE ARE **to be slow**   **to hang about**   **to linger**

The opposite is **hurry**

a
b
c
d
e
f
g
h
i
j
k
l
m
n
o
p
q
r
s
t
u
v
w
x
y
z

day *noun*

THE DAYS OF THE WEEK ARE

Monday   Tuesday   Wednesday   Thursday   Friday   Saturday Sunday

For times of the day and special days of the year, see **time**

dead *adjective*

OTHER WORDS YOU MIGHT USE ARE **deceased   killed   lifeless**
The opposite is alive

deal *verb*

I dealt the cards.

OTHER VERBS YOU MIGHT USE ARE **to distribute   to give out   to share out**
to deal with
Jo can deal with the problem.

OTHER VERBS ARE **to attend to   to handle   to manage   to sort out**

dear *adjective*

1 a dear friend.

OTHER WORDS YOU MIGHT USE ARE **beloved   loved   precious**
2 Mum didn't buy any shoes because they were too dear.

OTHER WORDS ARE **costly   expensive   (*informal*) pricey**

decay *verb*

Meat smells nasty when it decays.

OTHER VERBS YOU MIGHT USE ARE **to decompose   to go bad   to rot**

deceitful *adjective*

We knew he was often deceitful, so we didn't believe him.

OTHER WORDS YOU MIGHT USE ARE **dishonest   insincere   lying   untrustworthy**
The opposite is honest

deceive *verb*

He tried to deceive us, but we discovered the truth.

OTHER VERBS YOU MIGHT USE ARE **to cheat   to mislead   to swindle   to trick**

decorate *verb*

1 I decorated the room with flowers.

ANOTHER VERB YOU MIGHT USE IS **to adorn**
2 Dad decorated Sam's bedroom.

OTHER VERBS ARE **to paint   to paper**

decrease *verb*

1 They decreased my pocket money!

OTHER VERBS YOU MIGHT USE ARE **to cut   to reduce**
2 The number of children in Jo's class decreased this term.

OTHER VERBS ARE **to get smaller   to go down   to lessen**
The opposite is increase

deep *adjective*

deep water. a deep hole.
The opposite is shallow

defeat *verb*

Our team defeated them 8–0.

OTHER VERBS YOU MIGHT USE ARE **to beat   to conquer   (*informal*) to thrash**

defend *verb*
The mother bird defended her babies.
>OTHER VERBS YOU MIGHT USE ARE **to guard   to keep safe   to protect**
The opposite is **attack**

definite *adjective*
1 Is it definite that I can go?
>OTHER WORDS YOU MIGHT USE ARE **certain   positive   settled**
2 He gave a definite signal.
>OTHER WORDS ARE **clear   noticeable   obvious   sure**
The opposite is **vague**

delay *verb*
1 A traffic jam delayed us.
>OTHER VERBS YOU MIGHT USE ARE **to hinder   to hold up   to slow down**
2 They had to delay the start of the match.
>OTHER VERBS ARE **to postpone   to put off**
3 Don't delay—do it now!
>OTHER VERBS ARE **to hang about   to hesitate   to wait**

deliberate *adjective*
a deliberate mistake.
>OTHER WORDS YOU MIGHT USE ARE **intentional   planned**
The opposite is **accidental**

delicate *adjective*
1 delicate material.
>OTHER WORDS YOU MIGHT USE ARE **dainty   fine   flimsy   fragile   soft**
2 a delicate child.
>OTHER WORDS ARE **sickly   unhealthy   weak**
The opposite is **strong**

delicious *adjective*
a delicious dinner.
>OTHER WORDS YOU MIGHT USE ARE **appetizing   tasty**
For other words, see **taste**

delighted *adjective*
I was delighted with your gift.
>ANOTHER WORD IS **pleased**
For other words, see **happy**

deliver *verb*
The postman delivers letters.
>PHRASES YOU MIGHT USE ARE **to hand over   to take round**

demand *verb*
When the new TV didn't work, Mum demanded to have her money back.
>OTHER VERBS YOU MIGHT USE ARE **to ask   to beg   to request**

demolish *verb*
They had to demolish some houses when they built the new road.
>OTHER VERBS YOU MIGHT USE ARE **to destroy   to dismantle   to knock down**

demonstration *noun*
1 We gave a PE demonstration.
>OTHER WORDS YOU MIGHT USE ARE **display   exhibition   show**
2 There was a big demonstration against the new motorway.
>OTHER WORDS YOU MIGHT USE ARE *(informal)* **demo   march   protest**

a
b
c
d
e
f
g
h
i
j
k
l
m
n
o
p
q
r
s
t
u
v
w
x
y
z

59

dense *adjective*

dense fog. a dense crowd.

ANOTHER WORD IS **thick**

a dense pupil.

For other words, see **stupid**

deny *verb*

He denied that he had cheated.

PHRASES YOU MIGHT USE ARE **to refuse** **to agree** **to reject the idea**

depart *verb*

She departed without saying where she was going.

OTHER VERBS YOU MIGHT USE ARE **to go away** **to go out** **to leave** **to set off** **to set out**

depend *verb*

We can depend on Jo to do her best.

OTHER VERBS YOU MIGHT USE ARE **to count on** **to rely on** **to trust**

depress *verb*

His dog's death depressed him.

OTHER VERBS YOU MIGHT USE ARE **to sadden** **to upset**

depressed, **depressing** *adjectives*, see **sad**

describe *verb*

Can you describe what happened?

OTHER VERBS YOU MIGHT USE ARE **to explain** **to tell**

deserted *adjective*

a deserted house.

OTHER WORDS YOU MIGHT USE ARE **abandoned** **empty** **forsaken**

design *verb*

When we moved into our new house, we helped Mum design the garden.

OTHER VERBS YOU MIGHT USE ARE **to draw** **to plan** **to sketch**

desire *verb*

The fairy promised he could have what he desired.

OTHER VERBS YOU MIGHT USE ARE **to fancy** **to long for** **to want** **to wish for**

desperate *adjective*

The situation was desperate.

OTHER WORDS YOU MIGHT USE ARE **hopeless** **serious**

destroy *verb*

1 The explosion destroyed the building.

OTHER VERBS YOU MIGHT USE ARE **to demolish** **to knock down** **to ruin** **to wreck**

2 Dad used a special powder to destroy the ants in the garden.

OTHER VERBS YOU MIGHT USE ARE **to exterminate** (*informal*) **to finish off** **to kill** **to wipe out**

detest *verb*

Jo detests the smell of onions.

OTHER VERBS YOU MIGHT USE ARE **to dislike** **to hate** **to loathe**

The opposite is **love**

develop *verb*

1 Jo's swimming is developing.
OTHER VERBS YOU MIGHT USE ARE **to get better**   **to improve**   **to progress**

2 You must water plants if you want them to develop.
OTHER VERBS YOU MIGHT USE ARE **to get bigger**   **to grow**

device *noun*

Our new tin-opener is a clever device.
OTHER WORDS YOU MIGHT USE ARE **contraption**   **gadget**   **implement**   **instrument**   **tool**

diagram *noun*

We drew a diagram to show how the machine worked.
OTHER WORDS YOU MIGHT USE ARE **chart**   **graph**   **plan**   **sketch**

die *verb*

OTHER VERBS YOU MIGHT USE ARE **to pass away**   **to perish**

difference *noun*

1 Will it make any difference to our plans if it rains?
OTHER WORDS YOU MIGHT USE ARE **alteration**   **change**

2 Can you see any difference between these two colours?
OTHER WORDS YOU MIGHT USE ARE **contrast**   **distinction**

different *adjective*

1 The sweets are different flavours.
OTHER WORDS YOU MIGHT USE ARE **assorted**   **mixed**   **various**

2 Jo and Sam often have different ideas about things.
OTHER WORDS YOU MIGHT USE ARE **contradictory**   **contrasting**   **dissimilar**   **opposite**
The opposite is the same

difficult *adjective*

a difficult problem.
OTHER WORDS YOU MIGHT USE ARE **complex**   **complicated**   **hard**   **tough**   (*informal*) **tricky**
The opposite is easy

difficulty *noun*

The explorers met many difficulties before they reached home.
OTHER WORDS YOU MIGHT USE ARE **complication**   **hardship**   **obstacle**   **problem**   **snag**   **trouble**

dig *verb*

OTHER VERBS ARE **to burrow**   **to excavate**   **to hollow out**   **to scoop**   **to tunnel**

dignified *adjective*

Please behave in a dignified way.
OTHER WORDS YOU MIGHT USE ARE **calm**   **formal**   **proper**   **serious**   **sober**   **solemn**   **stately**

dilute *verb*

You dilute squash with water.
PHRASES YOU MIGHT USE ARE **to make weaker**   **to water down**

dim *adjective*

We saw a dim outline in the mist.
OTHER WORDS YOU MIGHT USE ARE **dark**   **faint**   **gloomy**   **indistinct**   **shadowy**
The opposite is clear

a
b
c
d
e
f
g
h
i
j
k
l
m
n
o
p
q
r
s
t
u
v
w
x
y
z

din *noun*

OTHER WORDS YOU MIGHT USE ARE **noise** (*informal*) **racket** (*informal*) **row** **uproar**

For other words, see **sound**

direct *verb*

1 Please direct me to the bus stop.

OTHER VERBS YOU MIGHT USE ARE **to guide** **to point** **to show**

2 The officer directed the soldiers to stand in a line.

OTHER VERBS YOU MIGHT USE ARE **to command** **to instruct** **to order** **to tell**

dirt *noun*

OTHER WORDS YOU MIGHT USE ARE **dust** **filth** **grime** **muck** **mud** **pollution**

dirty *adjective*

OTHER WORDS YOU MIGHT USE ARE **dusty** **filthy** **foul** **grimy** **grubby** **mucky** **muddy** **polluted** **soiled** **stained**

The opposite is **clean**

disagree *verb*

OTHER VERBS YOU MIGHT USE ARE **to argue** **to differ** **to quarrel**

The opposite is **agree**

disappear *verb*

OTHER VERBS YOU MIGHT USE ARE **to fade** **to melt away** **to vanish**

The opposite is **appear**

disapprove *verb*

We disapprove of cruelty to pets.

OTHER VERBS YOU MIGHT USE ARE **to condemn** **to criticize** **to dislike**

disaster *noun*

Many people died in the disaster.

OTHER WORDS YOU MIGHT USE ARE **accident** **calamity** **catastrophe**

discipline *noun*

Our teacher likes to have discipline in the classroom.

OTHER WORDS YOU MIGHT USE ARE **control** **obedience** **order**

discover *verb*

1 I discovered a lot about dinosaurs in the library.

OTHER VERBS YOU MIGHT USE ARE **to find** **to learn** **to research** **to track down**

2 Dad discovered an old coin in the garden.

OTHER VERBS YOU MIGHT USE ARE **to come across** **to uncover** **to unearth**

The opposite is **hide**

discuss *verb*

Let's discuss the problem.

OTHER VERBS YOU MIGHT USE ARE **to argue about** **to consider** **to talk about**

disease *noun*

OTHER WORDS YOU MIGHT USE ARE **ailment** **illness** **sickness**

For other words, see **health**

disguise *verb*

1 Dad disguised himself as Father Christmas.

PHRASES ARE **to dress up as** **to pretend to be**

2 We disguised our hiding place.

OTHER VERBS ARE **to camouflage** **to conceal** **to cover up** **to hide**

disgust *verb*
The dirty kitchen disgusted us.
OTHER VERBS YOU MIGHT USE ARE **to offend** **to revolt** **to sicken**
disgusting *adjective*, see **nasty**

dishonest *adjective*
1 It is dishonest to tell lies.
OTHER WORDS YOU MIGHT USE ARE **deceitful** **insincere**
2 It is dishonest to steal.
OTHER WORDS YOU MIGHT USE ARE **cheating** **criminal** **unfair**
The opposite is **honest**

dislike *verb*
OTHER VERBS YOU MIGHT USE ARE **to detest** **to loathe** **to hate**
The opposite is **like**

dismiss *verb*
1 The teacher dismissed the class.
OTHER VERBS YOU MIGHT USE ARE **to let go** **to release** **to send away**
2 The boss dismissed her from her job.
OTHER VERBS ARE **to fire** **to sack**

disorder *noun*
Jo and Sam cleared up the disorder after the party.
OTHER WORDS YOU MIGHT USE ARE **chaos** **confusion** **muddle**

display *noun*
We put up a display of our work.
OTHER WORDS YOU MIGHT USE ARE **exhibition** **presentation** **show**

display *verb*
We display our work when parents come to school.
OTHER VERBS YOU MIGHT USE ARE **to exhibit** **to present** **to show**

distance *noun*
What's the distance between the goal posts?
OTHER WORDS YOU MIGHT USE ARE **gap** **space**
For more words, see **measurement**

distant *adjective*
distant places.
OTHER WORDS YOU MIGHT USE ARE **faraway** **remote**
The opposite is **near**

distinct *adjective*
1 I heard a distinct echo.
OTHER WORDS YOU MIGHT USE ARE **audible** **clear**
2 The footprints in the mud were quite distinct.
OTHER WORDS ARE **definite** **obvious** **plain** **visible**
3 The twins wear distinct colours.
OTHER WORDS ARE **contrasting** **different**

distressed *adjective*
The mother blackbird was very distressed when she saw the cat.
OTHER WORDS YOU MIGHT USE ARE **anxious** **frightened** **upset** **worried**

distribute *verb*
Jo distributed the pencils and paper.
OTHER VERBS YOU MIGHT USE ARE **to deal out** **to give out** **to hand out**
to share out

a
b
c
d
e
f
g
h
i
j
k
l
m
n
o
p
q
r
s
t
u
v
w
x
y
z

district *noun*

We live in a hilly district.

OTHER WORDS YOU MIGHT USE ARE **area   locality   region   zone**

disturb *verb*

1 Don't disturb me while I'm working.

OTHER VERBS YOU MIGHT USE ARE **to bother   to interrupt   to trouble   to worry**

2 A fox disturbed the chickens.

OTHER VERBS ARE **to alarm   to excite   to frighten   to upset**

dive *verb*

We watched the sea birds diving into the water.

OTHER VERBS YOU MIGHT USE ARE **to drop   to plunge   to swoop**

divide *verb*

1 Divide the sweets between you.

OTHER VERBS YOU MIGHT USE ARE **to deal out   to distribute   to share**

2 At the next junction the road divides.

OTHER VERBS YOU MIGHT USE ARE **to branch   to fork   to separate   to split**

dizzy *adjective*

I feel dizzy if I stand up quickly.

OTHER WORDS YOU MIGHT USE ARE **faint   giddy   unsteady**

---

do *verb*

THIS VERB HAS MANY USES. HERE ARE SOME OF THE WAYS YOU CAN USE IT, AND SOME OTHER VERBS YOU COULD CHOOSE.

1 I have done my work.

to carry out   to complete   to finish   to perform

2 Sam is going to do the dinner.

**to attend to   to deal with   to handle   to make   to manage
to prepare**

3 Will four big potatoes do?

to be enough   to be sufficient   to be suitable

---

doctor *noun*

For other people who look after our health, see **health**

dog *noun*, see opposite page

dot *noun*

OTHER WORDS YOU MIGHT USE ARE **mark   point   speck   spot**

doubt *noun*

There's some doubt about whether Sam is well enough to play.

OTHER WORDS YOU MIGHT USE ARE **anxiety   hesitation   question   uncertainty
worry**

doubtful *adjective*

The rain made us doubtful about our picnic.

OTHER WORDS YOU MIGHT USE ARE **uncertain   unsure   worried**

The opposite is certain

drag *verb*

The tractor was dragging a load of logs.

OTHER VERBS YOU MIGHT USE ARE **to draw   to haul   to pull   to tow   to tug**

dog *noun*

A female dog is a **bitch**.
A young dog is a **pup** or **puppy**.
VARIOUS BREEDS OF DOG ARE

Alsatian	**bloodhound**	**bulldog**	**collie**	
dachshund	**Dalmatian**	**greyhound**	**Labrador**	**Pekinese**
poodle	**retriever**	**Rottweiler**	**sheepdog**	**spaniel**
terrier	**whippet**			

A dog of mixed breed is a **mongrel**.

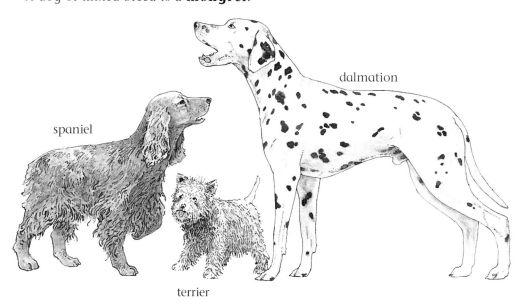

dalmation

spaniel

terrier

drama *noun*

1 Drama is one of Sam's favourite lessons.
OTHER WORDS YOU MIGHT USE ARE **acting   improvisation   plays**
2 We had some drama today when the fire engines came.
ANOTHER WORD IS **excitement**

draw *verb*

1 Jo drew a picture with a pencil.
ANOTHER VERB IS **to sketch**
2 The pony was drawing a cart.
OTHER VERBS YOU MIGHT USE ARE **to haul   to pull   to tow**
3 The match drew a large crowd.
OTHER VERBS ARE **to attract   to bring in   to pull in**
4 We drew 1–1 on Saturday.
OTHER VERBS ARE **to be equal   to tie**

dreadful *adjective*

a dreadful storm.
OTHER WORDS YOU MIGHT USE ARE **alarming   awful   fearful   frightening   horrifying   terrible**
The opposite is wonderful

a
b
c
d
e
f
g
h
i
j
k
l
m
n
o
p
q
r
s
t
u
v
w
x
y
z

dream *noun*

A nasty dream is a **nightmare**.
SOMETHING LIKE A DREAM WHICH YOU HAVE WHILE YOU ARE AWAKE IS A
daydream   fantasy   illusion   vision

dream *verb*
OTHER VERBS YOU MIGHT USE ARE   **to fancy   to imagine**

dress *noun*
A DRESS FOR A SPECIAL OCCASION IS   **evening dress   gown   party dress**
For things you wear, see **clothes**

dribble *verb*
When I cut my knee, blood dribbled down my leg.
OTHER VERBS YOU MIGHT USE ARE   **to drip   to flow   to ooze   to run   to trickle**

drink *verb*

To drink greedily is **to gulp** or **to guzzle** or to **swig**.
To drink a tiny bit at a time is **to sip**.
To drink with your tongue like a cat is **to lap**.

DIFFERENT COLD DRINKS ARE
**juice   lemonade   milk   mineral water   orangeade   squash
water**

SOME ALCOHOLIC DRINKS ARE
beer   champagne   cider   lager   whisky   wine

SOME HOT DRINKS ARE
cocoa   coffee   tea

drip *verb*
Don't let paint drip on to the carpet!
OTHER VERBS YOU MIGHT USE ARE   **to dribble   to drop   to leak   to trickle**

drive *verb*
1 Is it easy to drive a car?
OTHER VERBS YOU MIGHT USE ARE   **to control   to steer**
2 I drove the cow into the field.
OTHER VERBS ARE   **to force   to push   to urge**

droop *verb*
The weather was so dry that the flowers began to droop.
OTHER VERBS YOU MIGHT USE ARE   **to flop   to go limp   to sag   to wilt**

drop *noun*
drops of water.
OTHER WORDS YOU MIGHT USE ARE   **bead   drip   tear**

drop *verb*
1 A lorry dropped its load on the motorway.
    OTHER VERBS YOU MIGHT USE ARE **to dump**   **to shed**
2 The waterfall drops from a high cliff.
    OTHER VERBS ARE **to cascade**   **to fall**   **to plunge**
3 The temperature drops at night.
    OTHER VERBS ARE **to decrease**   **to fall**   **to go down**

dry *adjective*
1 Is the washing dry?
The opposite is wet
2 I feel dry: can I have a drink?
    OTHER WORDS YOU MIGHT USE ARE **parched**   **thirsty**

duck *noun*
A male duck is a **drake**.
A young duck is a **duckling**.

dull *adjective*
1 dull colours.
    OTHER WORDS YOU MIGHT USE ARE **dingy**   **drab**   **gloomy**
2 a dull day.
    OTHER WORDS ARE **cloudy**   **grey**   **overcast**
3 a dull pupil.
    OTHER WORDS ARE **dim**   **slow**   **stupid**
The opposite is bright
4 a dull film.
    OTHER WORDS ARE **boring**   **uninteresting**
The opposite is interesting

dumb *adjective*
She was dumb with amazement.
    OTHER WORDS YOU MIGHT USE ARE **mute**   **silent**   **speechless**

dump *verb*
1 I hate people who dump rubbish by the side of the road.
    OTHER VERBS YOU MIGHT USE ARE **to abandon**   **to discard**   **to throw away**
2 I dumped my things on the table.
    OTHER VERBS ARE **to drop**   **to leave**   **to unload**

duty *noun*
1 If you see a crime, it's your duty to tell the police.
    ANOTHER WORD IS **responsibility**
2 We can go to play when we've finished our duties.
    OTHER WORDS ARE **job**   **task**

Ee

eager *adjective*
We were eager to start the game.
<small>OTHER WORDS YOU MIGHT USE ARE</small> **enthusiastic   impatient   keen**

earn *verb*
How much does Sam earn when he washes the car?
<small>OTHER VERBS YOU MIGHT USE ARE</small> **to deserve   to get   to make**

earth *noun*
1 We live on the planet Earth.
<small>OTHER WORDS YOU MIGHT USE ARE</small> **the globe   the world**
2 Plants grow in the earth.
<small>OTHER WORDS ARE</small> **ground   land   soil**

easy *adjective*
1 Jo finished her work quickly because the sums were easy.
<small>OTHER WORDS YOU MIGHT USE ARE</small> **simple   straightforward   uncomplicated**
The opposite is **difficult**
2 The cat has an easy life.
<small>OTHER WORDS ARE</small> **carefree   comfortable   relaxing   restful**

---

eat *verb*
The dog ate our dinner!
<small>OTHER VERBS YOU MIGHT USE ARE</small>
to consume   to feed on   to swallow   to tuck into

<small>DIFFERENT WAYS TO EAT THINGS ARE</small>
to bite   to chew   to munch

<small>IF YOU EAT FOOD GREEDILY, OTHER VERBS ARE</small>
to bolt   to devour   to gobble   to gulp   to guzzle

If you eat a tiny bit at a time, you **nibble**.
A cow **grazes** on grass.
A chicken **pecks** at its food.
A dog will **gnaw** at a bone.

---

edge *noun*
<small>THIS WORD HAS MANY USES. HERE ARE SOME OF THE WAYS YOU CAN USE IT, AND SOME OTHER WORDS YOU CAN CHOOSE</small>
1 The edge of a picture.
border   frame
2 The edge of a cricket field.
boundary   perimeter
3 The edge of the road.
side   verge
4 The edge of a curtain.
frill   fringe   hem
5 The edge of a cup.
brim   rim
6 The edge of a circle.
circumference

The space down the edge of a piece of paper you have written on is the **margin**.

educate *verb*

Our parents and teachers educate us.

OTHER VERBS YOU MIGHT USE ARE

to bring up   to instruct   to teach   to train

PLACES WHERE PEOPLE GO TO BE EDUCATED ARE

college   playgroup   school   university

DIFFERENT KINDS OF SCHOOL ARE

**boarding school   comprehensive school   infant school
junior school   kindergarten   nursery school
playgroup   primary school   secondary school**

effort *noun*

1 You deserve a rest after all that effort.
OTHER WORDS YOU MIGHT USE ARE **labour   toil   trouble   work**

2 I made an effort to be good.
OTHER WORDS ARE **attempt   try**

elect *verb*

We elected Jo as captain of the rounders team.
OTHER VERBS YOU MIGHT USE ARE **to choose   to pick   to select   to vote for**

election *noun*

We had an election to choose the captain of the team.
OTHER WORDS YOU MIGHT USE ARE **ballot   vote**

embarrassed *adjective*

1 Jo was embarrassed when she forgot her words in the play.
OTHER WORDS YOU MIGHT USE ARE **ashamed   upset**

2 He was too embarrassed to ask for a second helping.
ANOTHER WORD IS **shy**

emergency *noun*

We knew there was an emergency when we heard the fire engine.
ANOTHER WORD IS **crisis**

empty *adjective*

1 an empty cup.
ANOTHER WORD IS **unfilled**
The opposite is full

2 an empty space.
ANOTHER WORD IS **hollow**
The opposite is solid

3 an empty house.
OTHER WORDS YOU MIGHT USE ARE **deserted   uninhabited   unoccupied   vacant**
The opposite is occupied

encourage *verb*

We shouted to encourage our team.
OTHER VERBS YOU MIGHT USE ARE **to support   to urge on**

a
b
c
d
e
f
g
h
i
j
k
l
m
n
o
p
q
r
s
t
u
v
w
x
y
z

end *noun*

1 We didn't stay for the end of the film.
OTHER WORDS YOU MIGHT USE ARE **conclusion   ending   finish**

2 We walked to the end of the train.
OTHER WORDS ARE **back   rear   tail**

3 He poked me with the end of a stick.
OTHER WORDS ARE **point   tip**

end *verb*

1 We waited for the storm to end.
OTHER VERBS YOU MIGHT USE ARE **to cease   to finish   to stop**
The opposite is begin

2 It would be wonderful if we could end all wars.
ANOTHER VERB IS **to abolish**

enemy *noun*
OTHER WORDS YOU MIGHT USE ARE **attacker   foe   opponent**
Opposites are ally, friend

energetic *adjective*
Mum says that we are so energetic that she can't keep up with us.
OTHER WORDS YOU MIGHT USE ARE **active   enthusiastic   lively   vigorous**
The opposite is lazy

energy *noun*
You use up a lot of energy playing rounders.
OTHER WORDS YOU MIGHT USE ARE **power   strength**

---

engine *noun*
Cars, ships, and aeroplanes have engines to keep them going.

DIFFERENT KINDS OF ENGINE ARE
**diesel engine   electric motor   jet engine   petrol engine
steam engine**
A railway engine is a **locomotive**.

---

enjoy *verb*
The things Jo enjoys most are ice-skating and reading.
OTHER VERBS YOU MIGHT USE ARE **to appreciate   to like   to love**
The opposite is dislike

enough *adjective*
Have you had enough food?
OTHER WORDS YOU MIGHT USE ARE **adequate   sufficient**

enter *verb*
Don't enter the classroom until the teacher tells you to.
PHRASES YOU MIGHT USE ARE **to come in   to go in**

entertain *verb*
A conjuror entertained us at Jo's party.
ANOTHER VERB IS **to amuse**

entertainment *noun*

OTHER WORDS YOU MIGHT USE ARE

amusement   enjoyment   fun

ENTERTAINMENTS YOU GO OUT TO ENJOY INCLUDE

**ballet   cinema   circus   concert   dance   disco   drama   fair
opera   pantomime   play   waxworks   zoo**

ENTERTAINMENTS YOU ENJOY AT HOME INCLUDE

computer games   music   radio   television   video

PEOPLE WHO ENTERTAIN US IN THE THEATRE OR ON RADIO AND TV ARE

**actor   actress   broadcaster   comedian   comic   conjuror
dancer   DJ   magician   musician   singer   ventriloquist**

PEOPLE WHO ENTERTAIN US IN A CIRCUS ARE

acrobat   clown   juggler   lion tamer   trapeze artist

enthusiastic *adjective*

Sam is an enthusiastic member of the football team.

OTHER WORDS YOU MIGHT USE ARE **eager   interested   keen**

entrance *noun*

Pay your money at the entrance.

OTHER WORDS YOU MIGHT USE ARE **door   entry   way in**

The opposite is exit

envious *adjective*

Jo was a bit envious when she saw what Sam got for his birthday.

ANOTHER WORD IS **jealous**

equal *adjective*

At half time the scores were equal.

OTHER WORDS YOU MIGHT USE ARE **even   identical   level   the same**

The opposite is different

equipment *noun*

We keep the games equipment in a shed in the playground.

OTHER WORDS YOU MIGHT USE ARE **apparatus**   (*informal*) **gear   tackle**

error *noun*

Our teacher corrects the errors in our work.

OTHER WORDS YOU MIGHT USE ARE **fault   mistake**   (*informal*) **slip**

escape *verb*

The cat chased the mouse, but it escaped.

PHRASES YOU MIGHT USE ARE **to get away   to run away**

essential *adjective*

It's essential to start early if you want to avoid traffic jams.

OTHER WORDS YOU MIGHT USE ARE **important   necessary   vital**

The opposite is unnecessary

estimate *verb*

Jo estimated how many sandwiches everyone would eat at her party.

OTHER VERBS YOU MIGHT USE ARE **to calculate   to guess   to work out**

even *adjective*

1 You need an even field for playing rounders.
OTHER WORDS ARE **flat   level   smooth**
The opposite is bumpy

2 At half time the scores were even.
OTHER WORDS YOU MIGHT USE ARE **equal   level   the same**
The opposite is different

3 Even numbers are numbers you can divide by two, such as 2, 8, 20.
The opposite is odd

evening *noun*
VARIOUS TIMES OF THE EVENING ARE **dusk   sunset   twilight**

event *noun*
The fathers' sack race was the funniest event on sports day.
OTHER WORDS YOU MIGHT USE ARE **happening   incident   occasion**

evidence *noun*
The police had evidence that he was guilty.
OTHER WORDS YOU MIGHT USE ARE **information   proof**

evil *adjective*
Murder is an evil thing.
OTHER WORDS YOU MIGHT USE ARE **hateful   immoral   sinful   wicked   wrong**
The opposite is good

exact *adjective*
Have you got the exact time?
OTHER WORDS YOU MIGHT USE ARE **accurate   correct   precise   right   true**

examination *noun*

1 Sam had a music examination at the end of term.
OTHER WORDS YOU MIGHT USE ARE (*informal*) **exam   test**

2 When I was ill, I went to the doctor's for an examination.
ANOTHER WORD IS (*informal*) **check-up**

examine *verb*

1 We examined the strange insect carefully.
OTHER VERBS YOU MIGHT USE ARE **to inspect   to study**

2 The police examined the suspect.
OTHER VERBS ARE **to interrogate   to question**

example *noun*
When the parents come to school, we display examples of our work.
OTHER WORDS YOU MIGHT USE ARE **sample   specimen**

excellent *adjective*
OTHER WORDS YOU MIGHT USE ARE (*informal*) **brilliant**   (*informal*) **fantastic   marvellous   outstanding**   (*informal*) **tremendous   wonderful**
For other words, see **good**

exchange *verb*
Sam exchanged his old bike for some roller skates.
OTHER VERBS YOU MIGHT USE ARE **to substitute**   (*informal*) **to swop   to trade in**

excite *verb*
The amazing goal excited the crowd.
OTHER VERBS YOU MIGHT USE ARE **to arouse   to provoke   to rouse   to stimulate   to stir up   to thrill**

excited *adjective*
We were excited on the morning before we had the party.
OTHER WORDS YOU MIGHT USE ARE **boisterous** **lively** **worked up**

excitement *noun*
The game was full of excitement.
OTHER WORDS YOU MIGHT USE ARE **action** **drama** **suspense** **thrills**

exclaim *verb*
OTHER VERBS YOU MIGHT USE ARE **to call out** **to shout** **to yell**

excuse *verb*
1 Please excuse our dog's bad behaviour.
OTHER VERBS YOU MIGHT USE ARE **to forgive** **to overlook** **to pardon**
2 I was excused from swimming because I had a cold.
A PHRASE IS **to let off**

exhausted *adjective*
I was exhausted after my long walk.
OTHER WORDS YOU MIGHT USE ARE **tired** **weary** **worn out**

exhibition *noun*
We had an exhibition of our work.
OTHER WORDS YOU MIGHT USE ARE **display** **show**

exist *verb*
Plants can't exist without water.
OTHER VERBS YOU MIGHT USE ARE **to keep going** **to live** **to survive**

exit *noun*
OTHER WORDS YOU MIGHT USE ARE **door** **way out**
The opposite is entrance

expect *verb*
I expect it will rain later.
ANOTHER VERB IS **to forecast**

expedition *noun*
On Saturday, Mum and Jo went on an expedition to the shops.
OTHER WORDS YOU MIGHT USE ARE **journey** **outing** **trip**

expel *verb*
The dog was expelled from the shop because he was a nuisance.
OTHER VERBS YOU MIGHT USE ARE *(informal)* **to kick out** **to throw out**
TO EXPEL SOMEONE FROM A COUNTRY **to banish** **to deport** **to exile**
TO EXPEL SOMEONE FROM THEIR HOME **to evict**

expensive *adjective*
Mum didn't buy me any new jeans because they were too expensive.
OTHER WORDS YOU MIGHT USE ARE **costly** **dear** *(informal)* **pricey**
The opposite is cheap

explain *verb*
Mum explained how computers work.
OTHER VERBS YOU MIGHT USE ARE **to make clear** **to show**

explode *verb*
The firework exploded.
OTHER VERBS YOU MIGHT USE ARE **to blow up** **to burst** **to go off**

a
b
c
d
e
f
g
h
i
j
k
l
m
n
o
p
q
r
s
t
u
v
w
x
y
z

explore *verb*
Sam went off with his friends to explore the caves.
OTHER VERBS YOU MIGHT USE ARE **to investigate   to look round**

expression *noun*
I noticed Jo's unhappy expression.

OTHER WORDS YOU MIGHT USE ARE
face   look

DIFFERENT EXPRESSIONS YOU SEE ON PEOPLE'S FACES ARE
frown   glare   grin   laugh   scowl   smile   sneer   yawn

extra *adjective*
Do you want some extra milk in your tea?
OTHER WORDS YOU MIGHT USE ARE **additional   more**

extraordinary *adjective*
I didn't believe his extraordinary story about a space ship.
OTHER WORDS YOU MIGHT USE ARE **amazing   incredible   odd   peculiar   queer   remarkable   strange   unbelievable   uncommon   unusual**
The opposite is **ordinary**

extravagant *adjective*
Mum says it's extravagant to cook more food than you can eat.
OTHER WORDS YOU MIGHT USE ARE **expensive   wasteful**

extreme *adjective*
1 extreme cold.
OTHER WORDS YOU MIGHT USE ARE **exceptional   great   intense   severe**
2 the extreme corner of the playground.
OTHER WORDS ARE **farthest   furthest**

Ff

face *noun*
1 He made a funny face.
For other words, see **expression**
2 Each face of a dice has a different number of dots.
OTHER WORDS YOU MIGHT USE ARE **side   surface**

facts *noun*
You find lots of facts in an encyclopedia.
OTHER WORDS YOU MIGHT USE ARE **data   evidence   information**

fade *verb*
1 The sun faded the curtains.
OTHER VERBS YOU MIGHT USE ARE **to bleach   to discolour   to whiten**
2 In the evening, the light fades and the stars begin to shine.
OTHER VERBS ARE **to disappear   to dwindle   to melt away**

fail *verb*

1 He failed to stop at the red light.
>OTHER VERBS YOU MIGHT USE ARE **to neglect   to omit**

2 He failed his driving test.
>A PHRASE IS **to be unsuccessful**

The opposite is pass

faint *adjective*

1 I saw a faint shape in the mist.
>OTHER WORDS YOU MIGHT USE ARE **blurred   dim   hazy   misty   pale   unclear**

The opposite is clear

2 We heard faint cries for help.
>OTHER WORDS ARE **distant   low   muffled   weak**

The opposite is loud

3 Sam felt faint because he stood up too quickly.
>OTHER WORDS ARE **dizzy   giddy   unsteady**

faint *verb*

It was so hot that he fainted.
>OTHER VERBS ARE **to become unconscious   to collapse**

fair *adjective*

1 fair hair.
>OTHER WORDS YOU MIGHT USE ARE **blond   light   pale**

The opposite is dark

2 It's not fair if she gets more than me.
>OTHER WORDS ARE **just   proper   right**

The opposite is unfair

3 Was the referee fair?
>OTHER WORDS YOU MIGHT USE ARE **honest   unbiased**

The opposite is biased

4 I had a fair chance of winning.
>OTHER WORDS ARE **moderate   reasonable**

faithful *adjective*

The dog is his faithful companion.
>OTHER WORDS YOU MIGHT USE ARE **devoted   loyal   reliable   trustworthy**

The opposite is treacherous

fall *verb*

1 The dog was so excited that he fell in the river.
>OTHER VERBS YOU MIGHT USE ARE **to drop   to plunge   to slip   to topple   to tumble**

2 The burning tower fell to the ground.
>OTHER VERBS YOU MIGHT USE ARE **to collapse   to crash**

3 The temperature falls at night.
>OTHER VERBS ARE **to decrease   to go down**

The opposite is rise

false *adjective*

1 He gave us false information.
>OTHER WORDS YOU MIGHT USE ARE **inaccurate   incorrect   made-up   misleading   wrong**

The opposite is correct

2 Father Christmas wore a false beard.
>OTHER WORDS ARE **artificial   fake   imitation**

The opposite is real

a b c d e **f** g h i j k l m n o p q r s t u v w x y z

familiar *adjective*
I like to be back in my familiar surroundings after a holiday.
> OTHER WORDS YOU MIGHT USE ARE **normal** **regular** **usual** **well-known**

The opposite is strange

---

family *noun*

The members of your family are your **relations** or **relatives**.

MEMBERS OF YOUR IMMEDIATE FAMILY ARE
brother **daughter** **father** **husband** **mother** **sister** **son** **stepfather** **stepmother** **wife**

OTHER RELATIONS YOU MIGHT HAVE ARE
aunt **cousins** **grandfather** **grandmother** **nephew** **niece** **uncle**

Members of your family who lived in the past are your **ancestors**.

---

famous *adjective*
a famous TV actor.
> ANOTHER WORD IS **well-known**

fan *noun*
Sam is a fan of our football team.
> OTHER WORDS YOU MIGHT USE ARE **admirer** **follower** **supporter**

fancy *verb*
1 What do you fancy to eat?
> OTHER VERBS YOU MIGHT USE ARE **to feel like** **to long for** **to want** **to wish for**

2 I fancied I saw a ghost.
> OTHER VERBS ARE **to dream** **to imagine** **to think**

fantastic *adjective*
1 We heard a fantastic story about dragons and wizards.
> OTHER WORDS YOU MIGHT USE ARE **amazing** **extraordinary** **incredible** **strange** **weird**

2 (*informal*) We had a fantastic time at the party.
For other words, see **good**

farm *noun*, see next page

fashion *noun*
Sam knows about the latest fashion in music.
> OTHER WORDS YOU MIGHT USE ARE **craze** **style** **trend**

fast *adjective*
1 We started off at a fast pace.
> OTHER WORDS YOU MIGHT USE ARE **brisk** **hurried** **quick** **rapid** **smart** **speedy** **swift**

2 Granny caught a fast train to London.
> OTHER WORDS ARE **express** **high-speed**

The opposite is slow

fat *adjective*

1 a fat person.
OTHER WORDS YOU MIGHT USE ARE **chubby** **overweight** **plump** (*informal*) **podgy** **stout** (*informal*) **tubby**
2 a fat book.
ANOTHER WORD IS **thick**
The opposite is thin

---

fat *noun*

KINDS OF FAT YOU MIGHT EAT OR USE IN COOKING ARE
butter **cooking oil** **dripping** **lard** **margarine** **suet**

---

fault *noun*

The teacher pointed out the faults in my work.
OTHER WORDS YOU MIGHT USE ARE **error** **flaw** **mistake** (*informal*) **slip** **weakness**

favour *noun*

She did me a favour and lent me her umbrella.
OTHER WORDS YOU MIGHT USE ARE **good deed** **kindness**

fear *noun*

Fear spread through the town when the earthquake started.
OTHER WORDS YOU MIGHT USE ARE **alarm** **dread** **fright** **horror** **panic** **terror**

feeble *adjective*

I felt feeble after I was ill.
OTHER WORDS YOU MIGHT USE ARE **delicate** **frail** **weak**
The opposite is strong

feel *verb*

1 Feel the cat's soft fur.
OTHER VERBS YOU MIGHT USE ARE **to finger** **to stroke** **to touch**
2 Granny feels the cold more than I do.
OTHER VERBS YOU MIGHT USE ARE **to notice** **to suffer from**

feeling *noun*

My feeling is that it will be fine tomorrow.
OTHER WORDS YOU MIGHT USE ARE **guess** **instinct** **intuition** **opinion**
feelings
1 When you are very sad, it's hard not to show your feelings.
ANOTHER WORD IS **emotions**
2 Vegetarians often have strong feelings about killing animals.
OTHER WORDS ARE **beliefs** **opinions**

---

female *noun*

THERE ARE SPECIAL WORDS FOR MALE AND FEMALE HUMAN BEINGS AND SOME ANIMALS.
A female human being is a **girl** or **woman**.
A female dog is a **bitch.**
A female deer or rabbit is a **doe.**
A female sheep is a **ewe**.
A female bird is a **hen**.
A female lion is a **lioness**.
A female horse is a **mare.**
A female goat is a **nanny goat**.
A female pig is a **sow**.
A female fox is a **vixen**.

farm *noun*

Another word for a small farm is **smallholding**.
A word for a small farm in Scotland is a **croft**.
A word for a cattle farm in North America is a **ranch**.

BUILDINGS YOU SEE ON A FARM ARE

barn	**cowshed**	**farmhouse**
granary	**pigsty**	**stable**

MACHINES AND EQUIPMENT YOU SEE ON A FARM ARE

combine harvester	**cultivator**	**drill**
harrow	**milking machine**	**mower**
plough	**tractor**	**wagon**

OTHER THINGS YOU MIGHT SEE ON A FARM ARE

battery	**cages**	**farmyard**
hayrick or **haystack**	**silo**	

Farmers grow various crops.

KINDS OF CORN OR CEREALS ARE

barley	**maize** or **sweetcorn**	**oats**
rye	**wheat**	

OTHER CROPS ARE

potatoes	**sugar beet**	**vegetables**

ANIMALS THAT FARMERS KEEP ARE

bull	**calf**	**cow**
goat	**horse**	**lamb**
pig	**sheep**	

Bulls and cows are called **cattle**.

BIRDS THAT YOU SEE ON A FARM ARE

chicken	**duck**	**goose**
hen	**turkey**	

These birds are called **poultry**.

chicken

horse

goose

barn

tractor

cow

goat

pig

sugar beet

cabbage

fence *noun*

OTHER THINGS USED TO MARK THE EDGE OF A PIECE OF LAND ARE **barrier   hedge   railings   wall**

fetch *verb*

Jo's dog fetched the newspaper.

OTHER VERBS YOU MIGHT USE ARE **to bring   to carry   to collect   to get**

fidget *verb*

Please don't fidget!

OTHER VERBS YOU MIGHT USE ARE **to be restless   to fiddle**

field *noun*

OTHER WORDS YOU MIGHT USE ARE

a field of grass: **meadow   pasture**

a small field for horses: **paddock**

fierce *adjective*

a fierce dog.

OTHER WORDS YOU MIGHT USE ARE **ferocious   savage   vicious**

The opposite is **gentle**

---

fight *noun*

OTHER WORDS YOU MIGHT USE ARE

combat   conflict   contest   quarrel   (*informal*) **row**

WORDS FOR DIFFERENT KINDS OF FIGHTING ARE

a fight between armies
battle   war
a fight between two people
duel
a fight between two families or gangs
feud
a fight in the street
brawl   riot   scuffle
a fight to entertain people
bout   boxing match   wrestling match
a fight between knights in old times
joust
a friendly or unimportant fight
(*informal*) **scrap   squabble   tussle**

WORDS FOR FIGHTER ARE
soldier   warrior
An archer used to fight with a **bow** and **arrow**.
A boxer fights with **fists**.
A gladiator used to fight to **entertain** people.
A gunman fights with **guns**.
Knights used to fight on **horses**.
A wrestler fights with **hands** and **arms**.
For other words, see **soldier**

---

figure *noun*

1 Jo added up the figures.

OTHER WORDS YOU MIGHT USE ARE **digit   number**

2 Sam has a slim figure.

ANOTHER WORD IS **shape**

80

file *noun*

We lined up in a single file.
> OTHER WORDS YOU MIGHT USE ARE **column**   **line**   **queue**   **row**

fill *verb*

I filled the box with sweets.
> OTHER VERBS YOU MIGHT USE ARE **to cram**   **to load**   **to pack**

---

film *noun*

I watched a good film on TV.
> ANOTHER WORD IS
> **movie**

> DIFFERENT KINDS OF FILM ARE
> **adventure**   **cartoon**   **comedy**   **documentary**   **horror**
> **science fiction**   **western**

---

filthy *adjective*

Put those filthy jeans in the washing machine!
> OTHER WORDS YOU MIGHT USE ARE **dirty**   **foul**   (*informal*) **grubby**   **messy**
>   (*informal*) **mucky**   **muddy**

The opposite is clean

final *adjective*

They scored in the final moments of the game.
> OTHER WORDS YOU MIGHT USE ARE **closing**   **concluding**   **last**

The opposite is first

find *verb*

1 Did you find the money you lost?
> OTHER VERBS YOU MIGHT USE ARE **to come across**   **to discover**   **to get back**
>   **to recover**

The opposite is lose

2 Did the police find the thief?
> OTHER VERBS ARE **to trace**   **to track down**

3 I found the information I need.
> ANOTHER VERB IS **to discover**

fine *adjective*

1 fine thread.
> OTHER WORDS YOU MIGHT USE ARE **slender**   **thin**

The opposite is thick

2 fine sand.
> ANOTHER WORD IS **powdery**

The opposite is coarse

3 fine weather.
> OTHER WORDS ARE **bright**   **dry**   **sunny**

The opposite is wet

4 a fine piece of work.
> OTHER WORDS ARE **good**   **great**   **excellent**

The opposite is bad

finish *verb*

1 Finish your work now.
OTHER VERBS YOU MIGHT USE ARE **to complete**   **to round off**   **to stop**
2 The film finished with an exciting car chase.
OTHER VERBS ARE **to conclude**   **to end**
3 Did you finish those sweets?
OTHER WORDS ARE **to consume**   **to use up**
The opposite is start

---

fire *noun*

We watched the firemen put out the fire.

OTHER WORDS YOU MIGHT USE ARE
blaze   **flames**   **inferno**

FIRES USED FOR HEAT OR COOKING ARE
barbecue   **boiler**   **camp fire**   **central heating**   **coal fire**
electric fire   **furnace**   **gas fire**   **gas ring**   **grill**   **hot plate**
immersion heater   **oven**   **stove**

FIRES WHICH BURN THINGS WE DON'T WANT ARE
bonfire   **incinerator**

---

fire *verb*

to fire a gun.
OTHER VERBS YOU MIGHT USE ARE **to let off**   **to shoot**

firm *adjective*

1 Make sure the rock is firm before you step on it.
OTHER WORDS YOU MIGHT USE ARE **fixed**   **secure**   **steady**
2 Mum whisked the cream until it was firm.
OTHER WORDS ARE **set**   **solid**   **stiff**

first *adjective*

1 Jo was the first to arrive at the party.
OTHER WORDS YOU MIGHT USE ARE **earliest**   **soonest**
2 Who was the first man in space?
ANOTHER WORD IS **original**
The opposite is last

fish *noun,* see opposite page

fisherman *noun*

A person who fishes with a rod is an **angler**.
A person who goes to sea in a boat to catch fish is a **trawlerman**.

fit *adjective*

1 You have to be fit to play football.
OTHER WORDS YOU MIGHT USE ARE **healthy**   **strong**   **well**
2 Is the old house fit to live in?
ANOTHER WORD IS **suitable**

fit *verb*

Jo helped Sam fit the pieces of his model aeroplane together.
OTHER VERBS YOU MIGHT USE ARE **to assemble**   **to put together**

fish *noun*

SOME DIFFERENT KINDS OF FISH ARE

carp	**cod**	**eel**	**goldfish**	**haddock**
herring	**mackerel**	**minnow**	**perch**	**pike**
pilchard	**plaice**	**salmon**	**sardine**	**shark**
sole	**stickleback**	**trout**		

ANIMALS WHICH LIVE IN WATER BUT ARE NOT REAL FISH ARE

dolphin　　**jellyfish**　　**octopus**　　**porpoise**　　**whale**

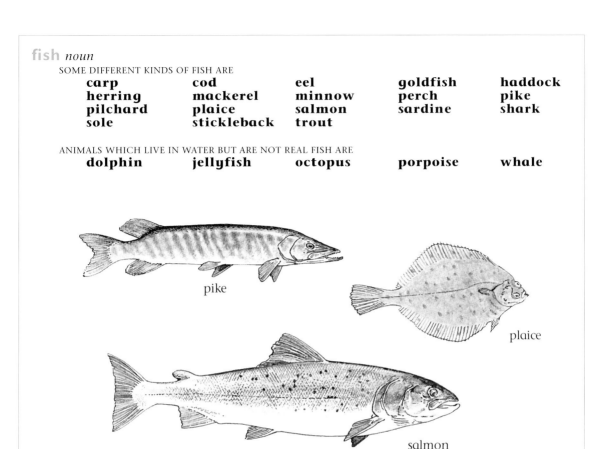

pike

plaice

salmon

fix *verb*
Dad fixed a shelf to the wall.
OTHER VERBS YOU MIGHT USE ARE **to attach**　**to secure**
For other verbs, see **fasten**

fizzy *adjective*
fizzy drinks.
OTHER WORDS YOU MIGHT USE ARE **bubbly**　**effervescent**　**sparkling**

flap *verb*
The flags flapped in the wind.
OTHER VERBS YOU MIGHT USE ARE **to flutter**　**to wave**

flat *adjective*
A games field must be flat.
OTHER WORDS YOU MIGHT USE ARE **even**　**level**　**smooth**

flavour *noun*
I like the flavour of this drink.
ANOTHER WORD IS **taste**

fling *verb*
I flung a pebble into the water.
OTHER VERBS YOU MIGHT USE ARE *(informal)* **to chuck**　**to throw**　**to toss**

float *verb*

1 Will this toy boat float?
A PHRASE IS **to stay up**
The opposite is **sink**

2 The smoke from the bonfire floated in the air.
OTHER VERBS YOU MIGHT USE ARE **to drift   to hover**

flock *noun*

For other words, see **group**

flow *verb*

Water flowed from the broken pipe.
OTHER VERBS YOU MIGHT USE ARE

to flow fast   **to gush   to pour   to run   to spurt   to squirt   to stream**
to flow slowly   **to dribble   to drip   to leak   to ooze   to trickle**
to flow over the edge   **to overflow   to spill**

---

flower *noun*

OTHER WORDS YOU MIGHT USE ARE
bloom   blossom

WORDS FOR A BUNCH OF FLOWERS ARE
arrangement   bouquet   posy

FLOWERS YOU SEE IN GARDENS ARE
carnation   chrysanthemum   crocus   daffodil
daisy   forget-me-not   geranium   hollyhock
hyacinth   lily   marigold   pansy   rose
snowdrop   sunflower   tulip   wallflower   lupin

FLOWERS THAT OFTEN GROW WILD ARE
bluebell   buttercup
dandelion   foxglove
poppy   primrose
violet

daisy   tulip   sunflower   rose

---

fluffy *adjective*

OTHER WORDS YOU MIGHT USE ARE **feathery   furry   soft   woolly**

fly *verb*

Birds, bats, and aeroplanes fly.
OTHER VERBS YOU MIGHT USE ARE **to glide   to hover   to rise   to soar   to swoop**

fog *noun*

I couldn't see because of the fog.
OTHER WORDS YOU MIGHT USE ARE **haze   mist**

fold *verb*
The paper will go in the envelope if you fold it.
OTHER VERBS YOU MIGHT USE ARE **to bend over**   **to crease**   **to double over**

follow *verb*
1 A dog followed me.
OTHER VERBS YOU MIGHT USE ARE **to chase**   **to come after**   **to pursue**   **to tail**
  to track
2 Follow this road.
OTHER VERBS ARE **to go along**   **to take**
3 Did you follow what she said?
ANOTHER VERB IS **to understand**

food *noun*, see next page

foolish *adjective*
It's foolish to run across the main road.
OTHER WORDS YOU MIGHT USE ARE (*informal*) **daft**   **idiotic**   **mad**   **silly**
  stupid   **unwise**
The opposite is sensible

foot *noun*
An animal's foot is a **hoof** or **paw**.
A bird has **toes** or **claws**.
For other parts of the body, see **body**

forbid *verb*
The head forbids eating in class.
OTHER VERBS YOU MIGHT USE ARE **to ban**   **to prohibit**
The opposite is allow

force *noun*
We had to use force to open the door.
OTHER WORDS YOU MIGHT USE ARE **might**   **power**   **strength**   **violence**

force *verb*
They can't force me to play.
OTHER VERBS YOU MIGHT USE ARE **to compel**   **to make**   **to order**

forest *noun*
Don't get lost in the forest!
OTHER WORDS YOU MIGHT USE ARE **jungle**   **wood**

forgery *noun*
The shopkeeper checked to see if the £10 note was a forgery.
OTHER WORDS YOU MIGHT USE ARE **copy**   **fake**   **imitation**

forget *verb*
I forgot my money.
OTHER VERBS YOU MIGHT USE ARE **to leave behind**   **to overlook**
The opposite is remember

forgetful *adjective*
He was so forgetful that he left his money behind.
OTHER WORDS YOU MIGHT USE ARE **absent-minded**   **careless**   **scatterbrained**
  thoughtless

forgive *verb*
Sam forgave Jo for forgetting his birthday.
OTHER VERBS YOU MIGHT USE ARE **to excuse**   **to pardon**

a
b
c
d
e
f
g
h
i
j
k
l
m
n
o
p
q
r
s
t
u
v
w
x
y
z

food *noun*

OTHER WORDS YOU MIGHT USE ARE

diet   nourishment   provisions   refreshments
Food for farm animals is **fodder**.

BASIC INGREDIENTS OF FOOD ARE

carbohydrate   fat   fibre   protein   starch   vitamins

CEREALS ARE

barley   maize or **sweetcorn   oats   rice   rye   wheat**

FOOD MADE FROM CEREALS:

bran   cornflakes   cornflour   flour   muesli   oatmeal   porridge

KINDS OF BREAD:

**bagel   brown bread   chapatti   crusty bread   French bread   nan
rye bread   white bread   wholemeal bread**

OTHER FOODS MADE FROM FLOUR:

biscuits   cake   dumplings   noodles   pasta   pastry   pizza

SOME KINDS OF CAKE ARE

bun   doughnut or **donut   flan   fruit cake   gingerbread
meringue   muffin   scone   shortbread   sponge cake   tart**

KINDS OF PASTA:

lasagne   macaroni   spaghetti

THINGS MADE WITH PASTRY:

pasty   pie   mince pies   quiche   sausage rolls

FOOD MADE WITH MILK:

**blancmange   butter   cheese   cream   custard   milk pudding
yogurt**

KINDS OF MEAT ARE

**bacon   beef   chicken   ham   lamb   pork   turkey   veal
venison**

FOOD USUALLY MADE WITH MEAT:

**burgers   chop suey   curry   fritters   goulash   hash   hotpot
meat pie   mince   paté   rissole   sausage   stew**
Food which doesn't contain any meat is **vegetarian** food.

FOOD MADE WITH EGGS:
omelette   pancakes   soufflé

FISH WHICH PEOPLE EAT ARE
**cod   haddock   herring   kipper   mackerel   pilchard   plaice
salmon   sardine   scampi   shellfish   sole   trout   tuna**
A mixture of fish and shellfish is **seafood**.
Caviare is a very expensive food from a fish called **sturgeon**.

FRUIT WHICH YOU CAN EAT ARE
**apple   apricot   banana   blackberry   blackcurrant   cherry
coconut   damson   date   fig   gooseberry   grape   grapefruit
kiwi fruit   lemon   lime   melon   orange   peach   pear
pineapple   plum   raspberry   strawberry   tangerine   tomato**

VEGETABLES PEOPLE EAT INCLUDE
**asparagus   beans   Brussels sprouts   cabbage   carrot
cauliflower   greens   leek   marrow   nuts   onion   parsnip   pea
potato   pumpkin   spinach   swede   turnip**

VEGETABLES WE EAT IN SALAD ARE
**beetroot   celery   cress   cucumber   lettuce   mustard & cress
onion   potato   radish   tomato   watercress**

SOME SWEET FOODS:
**honey   ice cream   icing   jam   jelly   marmalade   mousse
pudding   syrup   tart   treacle   trifle**

THINGS USED TO ADD FLAVOUR TO FOOD
**chutney   dressing   garlic   gravy   herbs   ketchup   mayonnaise
mustard   pepper   pickle   salt   sauce   seasoning   spice   sugar
vanilla   vinegar**

a
b
c
d
e
f
g
h
i
j
k
l
m
n
o
p
q
r
s
t
u
v
w
x
y
z

form *noun*
The wizard could change his form.
OTHER WORDS YOU MIGHT USE ARE **appearance   shape**

fortunate *adjective*
It's fortunate that it didn't rain.
ANOTHER WORD IS **lucky**
The opposite is unlucky

foul *adjective*
foul slime. foul weather.
OTHER WORDS YOU MIGHT USE ARE **dirty   disgusting   filthy   horrible   nasty   revolting**
The opposite is nice

fragile *adjective*
Take care with the best china because it is fragile.
OTHER WORDS YOU MIGHT USE ARE **brittle   delicate   thin**
The opposite is strong

fragment *noun*
When Jo broke the teapot, Mum made her sweep up the fragments.
OTHER WORDS YOU MIGHT USE ARE **bit   chip   piece   scrap**

frail *adjective*
I felt frail after my illness.
OTHER WORDS YOU MIGHT USE ARE **delicate   feeble   weak**
The opposite is strong

free *adjective*
1 The cat is free to wander about.
A PHRASE YOU MIGHT USE IS **at liberty**
2 Is the bathroom free?
OTHER WORDS ARE **available   unoccupied   vacant**

free *verb*
The prisoner asked the guards when they were going to free him.
OTHER VERBS YOU MIGHT USE ARE **to let out   to liberate   to release**
The opposite is capture

frequent *adjective*
Our picnic was spoiled by frequent showers.
OTHER WORDS YOU MIGHT USE ARE **many   numerous   repeated**

fresh *adjective*
1 fresh bread.
ANOTHER WORD IS **new**
The opposite is stale
2 fresh air.
OTHER WORDS YOU MIGHT USE ARE **clean   cool   pure**
3 fresh after a rest.
OTHER WORDS ARE **lively   rested**
4 a fresh page.
OTHER WORDS ARE **different   new   unused**

friend *noun*
An informal word is **mate**.
A friend who fights on your side is an **ally**
A friend who works with you is a **partner**.
Someone you don't know very well is an **acquaintance**.
The opposite is enemy

friendly *adjective*
a friendly smile.
OTHER WORDS YOU MIGHT USE ARE **affectionate   kind   loving**
The opposite is unfriendly

frighten *verb*
Don't frighten the animals.
OTHER VERBS YOU MIGHT USE ARE **to alarm   to scare   to startle   to terrify**
frightened *adjective*, see **afraid**
frightening *adjective*, see **terrible**

froth *noun*
The soap leaves froth in the bowl.
OTHER WORDS YOU MIGHT USE ARE **bubbles   foam   lather   scum**

frown *verb*
Dad frowns when he is angry.
OTHER VERBS YOU MIGHT USE ARE **to look stern   to scowl**

fruit *noun*
For fruit you can eat, see **food**

---

fuel *noun*
THINGS WE USE AS FUEL ARE
coal   electricity   gas   oil   petrol   wood

---

full *adjective*
1 The bus was full.
OTHER WORDS YOU MIGHT USE ARE **crowded   jammed   packed**
2 My cup is full.
ANOTHER WORD IS **overflowing**
The opposite is empty

fun *noun*
We had lots of fun at Jo's party.
OTHER WORDS YOU MIGHT USE ARE **amusement   enjoyment   games   jokes   laughing   pleasure**

funeral *noun*
KINDS OF FUNERAL ARE **burial   cremation**

funny *adjective*
1 funny jokes.
OTHER WORDS YOU MIGHT USE ARE **amusing   comic   comical   humorous   laughable   ridiculous   witty**
The opposite is serious
2 The ice cream has a funny taste.
For other words, see **peculiar**

furious *adjective*
For other words, see **angry**

furniture *noun*

KINDS OF FURNITURE YOU PUT THINGS IN OR ON ARE
**bookcase   bureau   cabinet   chest of drawers   coffee table
cupboard   desk   dresser   sideboard   table   wardrobe**

KINDS OF FURNITURE YOU SIT ON ARE
armchair   chair   pouffe   rocking chair   settee   sofa   stool

KINDS OF FURNITURE YOU CAN SLEEP ON ARE
bed   cot   couch   divan

furry *adjective*
furry animals.
OTHER WORDS YOU MIGHT USE ARE   **fluffy   hairy   woolly**

fuss *noun*
There was a lot of fuss when a lion escaped from the zoo.
OTHER WORDS YOU MIGHT USE ARE   **bother   commotion   excitement   trouble
uproar**

90

fussy *adjective*

Our cat is fussy about her food.

    OTHER WORDS YOU MIGHT USE ARE   **choosy**   **particular**

Gg

gain *verb*

Sam gained first prize for swimming.

    OTHER VERBS YOU MIGHT USE ARE   **to earn**   **to get**   **to obtain**   **to receive**
    to win

game *noun*

1 What's your favourite game?

OTHER WORDS YOU MIGHT USE ARE

amusement   **entertainment**   **pastime**   **sport**

2 Let's have a game of chess.

OTHER WORDS ARE

competition   **match**   **tournament**

VARIOUS GAMES ARE

bingo   **cards**   **charades**   **chess**   **darts**   **dominoes**   **draughts**
hide-and-seek   **hopscotch**   **ludo**   **marbles**   **skittles**   **snooker**
table tennis   **tiddlywinks**

For other games, see **sport**

91

gang *noun*
For other words, see **group**

gaol *noun*
Some people spell this word as 'jail'
OTHER WORDS ARE **dungeon   prison**

gap *noun*
1 a gap in the fence.
OTHER WORDS YOU MIGHT USE ARE **break   hole   space**
2 a gap between lessons.
OTHER WORDS ARE **break   interval   pause   rest**

garden *noun*, see opposite page

garment *noun*
For other words, see **clothes**

gasp *verb*
The smoke made us gasp.
OTHER VERBS YOU MIGHT USE ARE **to choke   to pant   to puff   to wheeze**

gather *verb*
1 People gathered to watch the fire.
OTHER VERBS YOU MIGHT USE ARE **to assemble   to crowd round   to meet**
2 We gathered information for our project.
OTHER VERBS ARE **to collect   to put together**

general *adjective*
1 The general opinion is that our team is the best.
OTHER WORDS YOU MIGHT USE ARE **common   usual   widespread**
2 He only gave us a general idea of what he wanted.
OTHER WORDS ARE **broad   vague**

generous *adjective*
1 It was generous of Jo to share her sweets.
OTHER WORDS YOU MIGHT USE ARE **kind   unselfish**
The opposite is mean
2 Mum gave us generous helpings of pudding.
OTHER WORDS ARE **big   large   sizeable**
The opposite is small

gentle *adjective*
1 a gentle kiss.
OTHER WORDS YOU MIGHT USE ARE **kind   soft-hearted   tender**
2 a gentle breeze.
OTHER WORDS ARE **pleasant   slight**
The opposite is rough
3 gentle music.
OTHER WORDS ARE **quiet   relaxing   restful   soft**
The opposite is noisy

genuine *adjective*
genuine gold.
ANOTHER WORD IS **real**
The opposite is false

garden *noun*

THINGS YOU GROW IN A GARDEN ARE

flowers   fruit   shrubs   trees   vegetables

PARTS OF A GARDEN ARE

**border   compost heap   flower bed   greenhouse   hedge   lawn
orchard   path   patio   pond   rockery   shed   shrubbery**

TOOLS YOU USE IN THE GARDEN ARE

**broom   fork   hoe   lawnmower   rake   shears   spade   trowel
watering can**

OTHER THINGS YOU USE IN THE GARDEN ARE

compost   fertilizer   manure   peat   weedkiller

shed

watering can

spade

trowel

vegetables

border

rake

weed

get *verb*

THIS WORD HAS MANY USES. HERE ARE SOME OF THE WAYS YOU CAN USE IT, AND SOME OTHER WORDS YOU COULD CHOOSE

1 What did you get at the shop?
to buy   to obtain   to purchase

2 Sam got a nice present from Jo.
to be given   to receive

3 Jo got first prize for swimming.
to earn   to win

4 Did the thief get anything valuable?
to steal   to take

5 Tell the dog to get the ball.
to bring   to fetch   to retrieve

6 I got cold waiting for the bus.
to become   to grow   to turn

ghost *noun*

Sam doesn't believe in ghosts.

OTHER WORDS YOU MIGHT USE ARE **phantom   spectre   spirit**   (*informal*) **spook**

gift *noun*

1 a birthday gift.

ANOTHER WORD IS **present**

2 a gift to charity.

OTHER WORDS YOU MIGHT USE ARE **contribution   donation   offering**

give *verb*

1 I gave some sweets to Sam.

OTHER VERBS YOU MIGHT USE ARE **to hand over   to offer   to pass   to present**

2 Dad gives money to charity.

OTHER VERBS ARE **to contribute   to donate**

3 Our teacher gave us pencils to write with.

OTHER VERBS ARE **to provide with   to supply with**

4 Jo gave out the books.

OTHER VERBS ARE **to deal out   to distribute   to hand out**

glass *noun*

A sheet of glass in a window is a **pane**.
A glass you drink out of is a **tumbler**.
Glasses you wear to help you see better are **spectacles**.
GLASSES YOU LOOK THROUGH TO MAKE DISTANT OBJECTS SEEM NEARER ARE
binoculars   field glasses

gloomy *adjective*

1 a gloomy room.

OTHER WORDS YOU MIGHT USE ARE **cheerless   dark   depressing   dismal**

2 a gloomy face.

OTHER WORDS ARE **depressed   glum   miserable   sad   unhappy**

The opposite is cheerful

glow *verb*

The ashes of the bonfire glowed in the dark.

OTHER VERBS YOU MIGHT USE ARE **to gleam   to shine**

glue *noun*
OTHER SUBSTANCES YOU STICK THINGS WITH ARE **adhesive   cement   gum   paste**

go *verb*
1 Jo has gone to the shops.
OTHER VERBS YOU MIGHT USE ARE **to travel   to walk**
For more verbs, see **move**
2 What time does the train go?
OTHER VERBS ARE **to depart   to leave   to set out   to start**
3 This road goes into the town.
OTHER VERBS ARE **to continue   to lead**
4 My watch doesn't go.
OTHER VERBS ARE **to function   to operate   to work**
5 She went quiet when she heard the bad news.
OTHER VERBS ARE **to become   to grow   to turn**

---

good *adjective*
SOME WORDS WHICH MEAN GOOD IN A GENERAL WAY ARE
lovely   marvellous   nice   wonderful

SOME INFORMAL WORDS ARE
brilliant   fabulous   great

THESE ARE SOME PARTICULAR WAYS WE USE THE WORD, AND SOME OF THE OTHER WORDS YOU MIGHT USE
1 good work.
correct   faultless   perfect   thorough
2 a good friend.
**caring   considerate   faithful   generous   helpful   honest   kind
loving   loyal   reliable   thoughtful   true**
3 a good dog.
obedient   well-behaved
4 a good footballer.
clever   skilful   skilled   talented
5 a good film.
entertaining   exciting   interesting
The opposite is bad

---

govern *verb*
At election time, we choose people to govern the country.
OTHER VERBS YOU MIGHT USE ARE **to be in charge of   to control   to look after
to manage   to rule   to run**

---

government *noun*
The person in charge of the government is the **prime minister**.
The people who help the prime minister run the government are the **cabinet**.
Decisions about how to govern the country are discussed in **parliament**.

---

grab *verb*
For other verbs, see **seize**

graceful *adjective*
graceful movements.
OTHER WORDS YOU MIGHT USE ARE **attractive   elegant   flowing**
The opposite is clumsy

gradual *adjective*
There was a gradual improvement in the weather.
OTHER WORDS YOU MIGHT USE ARE **slow   steady**
The opposite is sudden

grand *adjective*
The wedding was a grand occasion.
For other words, see **great**

grant *verb*
The fairy granted Cinderella what she wanted.
OTHER VERBS YOU MIGHT USE ARE **to allow   to give**

---

grass *noun*
An area of grass in a garden is a **lawn**.
An area of grass on a farm is a **field** or **meadow** or **pasture.**
An area of grass in a village is a **green**.
A large area of grass in North America is a **prairie**.
A large area of grass in South Africa is **veld** or **veldt**.

---

grateful *adjective*
I was grateful for her help.
OTHER WORDS YOU MIGHT USE ARE **appreciative   thankful**
The opposite is ungrateful

grave *adjective*
Mum looked grave when she heard the bad news.
OTHER WORDS YOU MIGHT USE ARE **gloomy   serious   solemn   thoughtful**
The opposite is cheerful

greasy *adjective*
I don't like greasy chips.
OTHER WORDS YOU MIGHT USE ARE **fatty   oily**

great *adjective*
1 a great storm.
OTHER WORDS YOU MIGHT USE ARE **huge   tremendous**
For more words, see **big**
2 a great occasion.
OTHER WORDS ARE **grand   important   impressive   magnificent   spectacular   splendid**
3 a great piece of music.
OTHER WORDS ARE **classic   famous   well-known**
4 We had a great time.
OTHER WORDS ARE **excellent   marvellous   wonderful**
For more words, see **good**

greedy *adjective*
It was greedy to eat all the cake.
OTHER WORDS YOU MIGHT USE ARE (*informal*) **piggish   selfish**

greet *verb*
I greeted our guests at the door.
ANOTHER VERB IS **to welcome**

grief *noun*
I sympathized with Jo's grief when the dog died.
OTHER WORDS YOU MIGHT USE ARE **misery   sadness   sorrow   unhappiness**

grim *adjective*
a grim look on someone's face.
OTHER WORDS YOU MIGHT USE ARE **bad-tempered   gloomy   serious   severe   stern   unfriendly**
The opposite is happy

groan *verb*
The injured man groaned because of the pain.
OTHER VERBS YOU MIGHT USE ARE **to moan   to wail**

grope *verb*
I groped about to find the light switch.
OTHER VERBS YOU MIGHT USE ARE **to feel   to fumble**

---

ground *noun*

1 Potatoes grow in the ground.
OTHER WORDS YOU MIGHT USE ARE
earth   soil

2 We play football on a piece of ground behind the school.
ANOTHER WORD IS
land

PLACES WHERE YOU CAN PLAY GAMES ARE
playground   playing field   pitch   recreation ground   stadium

Ground where you build something is a **plot** or **site**.
A big area of ground owned by one person or used for a special purpose is an **estate**.
The grounds of a big school or college are called a **campus**.

---

group *noun*, see next page

grow *verb*
1 Jo grows flowers in the garden.
OTHER VERBS YOU MIGHT USE ARE **to cultivate   to plant   to raise**
2 The seeds only grow when the weather is warm.
OTHER VERBS ARE **to germinate   to spring up   to sprout**
3 Jo looks to see how much her vegetables have grown.
OTHER VERBS ARE **to develop   to fill out   to get bigger   to get taller   to increase**

grown-up *adjective*
OTHER WORDS YOU MIGHT USE ARE **adult   mature**

gruesome *adjective*
I didn't like the gruesome picture of the accident.
OTHER WORDS YOU MIGHT USE ARE **disgusting   gory   horrible   nasty   sickening**

gruff *adjective*
a gruff voice.
OTHER WORDS YOU MIGHT USE ARE **deep   harsh   hoarse   rough**

grumble *verb*
Mum doesn't like it when Sam grumbles about the food.
OTHER VERBS YOU MIGHT USE ARE **to complain**   (*informal*) **to moan**

a b c d e f **g** h i j k l m n o p q r s t u v w x y z

group *noun*

OTHER WORDS YOU MIGHT USE ARE

a group of things:
assortment   collection   set

a group of people:
assembly   company   crowd   gang   gathering   mob   throng

an organized group of people:
alliance   army   association   club   force   society   team

a group of musicians:
band   choir   chorus   orchestra

OTHER GROUPS ARE:

An **army** of ants.

A **brood** of chicks.

A **bunch** of flowers.

A **class** of children.

A **clump** of trees.

A **clutch** of eggs.

A **colony** of ants.

A **congregation** in church.

A **constellation** or **galaxy** of stars.

A **convoy** or **fleet** of ships.

A **covey** of partridges.

A **crew** of sailors.

A **flock** of birds.

A **flock** of sheep.

A **gaggle** of geese.

A **gang** of robbers.

A **herd** of cows.

A **herd** of elephants.

A **leap** of leopards.

A **litter** of puppies.

A **pack** of wolves.

A **pride** of lions.

A **school** of whales.

A **shoal** of fish.

A **swarm** of bees.

A **troop** of soldiers.

guard *verb*

The farmer's dog guards the sheep.

OTHER VERBS YOU MIGHT USE ARE **to care for   to defend   to look after   to protect   to shield   to tend   to watch over**

guess *verb*

1 I guess you are hungry.

OTHER VERBS YOU MIGHT USE ARE **to assume   to suppose**

2 Jo tried to guess how many sweets there were in the jar.

ANOTHER VERB IS **to estimate**

guide *verb*

I wish someone would guide us out of this maze!

OTHER VERBS YOU MIGHT USE ARE **to direct   to escort   to lead   to steer**

guilty *adjective*

He was guilty of stealing.

The opposite is **innocent**

gun *noun*

KINDS OF GUN ARE

airgun   cannon   machine-gun   pistol   revolver   rifle   shotgun

Hh

habit *noun*

1 It's our habit to send people a card when they have a birthday.

OTHER WORDS YOU MIGHT USE ARE   **custom   practice   tradition**

2 Smoking is a bad habit.

ANOTHER WORD IS   **addiction**

hair *noun*

DIFFERENT WAYS PEOPLE DO THEIR HAIR ARE

**in curls   with a fringe   permed   in a pigtail   in plaits
in a ponytail**

WORDS TO DESCRIBE THE COLOUR OF PEOPLE'S HAIR ARE

**auburn   black   blond   brown   fair   ginger   grey   red
silver   white**

WORDS FOR HAIR ON AN ANIMAL ARE

bristles   fur

hairy *adjective*

OTHER WORDS YOU MIGHT USE ARE   **bristly   furry   fuzzy   shaggy   woolly**

halt *verb*

You must halt if the light is red.

OTHER VERBS YOU MIGHT USE ARE   **to draw up   to pull up   to stop**

hand *noun*

For other parts of the body, see **body**

handicap *noun*

When you run for the bus, it's a handicap to have lots of shopping.

OTHER WORDS YOU MIGHT USE ARE

disadvantage   drawback   hindrance   inconvenience

handicapped *adjective*

It's hard for you to do some things if you are handicapped.

WAYS YOU CAN BE HANDICAPPED ARE

blind   deaf   disabled   dumb   lame   limbless   paralysed

a
b
c
d
e
f
g
h
i
j
k
l
m
n
o
p
q
r
s
t
u
v
w
x
y
z

handle *verb*
1 Handle the kittens carefully.
OTHER VERBS YOU MIGHT USE ARE **to feel   to stroke   to touch**
2 The rider handled the frightened horse well.
OTHER VERBS ARE **to control   to deal with   to look after   to manage**

handsome *adjective*
a handsome man.
OTHER WORDS YOU MIGHT USE ARE **attractive   good-looking**
The opposite is ugly

hang *verb*
to hang on to something Hang on to the rope!
OTHER VERBS YOU MIGHT USE ARE **to cling on to   to grasp   to hold   to seize**
to hang about Don't hang about after school.
OTHER VERBS ARE **to be slow   to dawdle   to delay   to loiter**

happen *verb*
Did anything interesting happen?
OTHER VERBS YOU MIGHT USE ARE **to occur   to take place**

happy *adjective*
Jo is happy when the sun shines.
OTHER WORDS YOU MIGHT USE ARE **cheerful   contented   delighted   glad   good-humoured   joyful   light-hearted   merry   pleased**
The opposite is sad

---

harbour *noun*
PLACES WHERE SHIPS UNLOAD GOODS ARE
docks   port
A place where you see lots of **pleasure boats** is a **marina**.

PLACES WHERE SHIPS TIE UP ARE
jetty   landing stage   mooring   pier   quay   wharf

---

hard *adjective*
1 hard concrete.
OTHER WORDS YOU MIGHT USE ARE **firm   rigid   solid**
The opposite is soft
2 hard work.
OTHER WORDS ARE **exhausting   tiring   tough**
The opposite is easy
3 a hard problem.
OTHER WORDS ARE **complex   complicated   difficult   puzzling**
The opposite is simple
4 a hard punishment.
OTHER WORDS ARE **cruel   harsh   merciless   severe**
The opposite is merciful

hardly *adverb*
I'm so tired I can hardly walk.
OTHER WORDS YOU MIGHT USE ARE **barely   only just   scarcely**

harm *verb*
1 Jo would never harm an animal.
OTHER VERBS YOU MIGHT USE ARE **to hurt   to injure   to wound**
2 Did the accident harm the car?
OTHER VERBS ARE **to damage   to spoil**

harmful *adjective*
It can be harmful to take too much medicine.
> OTHER WORDS YOU MIGHT USE ARE **bad   damaging   dangerous**

harsh *adjective*
1 The teacher's harsh voice showed that she was angry.
> OTHER WORDS YOU MIGHT USE ARE **grating   rough   shrill**
2 We blinked in the harsh light.
> OTHER WORDS ARE **brilliant   dazzling   glaring**
3 We thought the decision to send the player off was harsh.
> OTHER WORDS ARE **cruel   hard   merciless   severe**
The opposite is gentle

hasty *adjective*
The teacher said we were too hasty doing our work.
> OTHER WORDS YOU MIGHT USE ARE **careless   hurried   impetuous   quick**
> (*informal*) **slapdash   thoughtless**

hat *noun*
> DIFFERENT THINGS PEOPLE WEAR ON THEIR HEADS ARE
> **beret   bonnet   cap   crash helmet   crown   helmet   hood
> turban**

hate *verb*
Sam can't understand why some people hate cabbage.
> OTHER VERBS YOU MIGHT USE ARE **to detest   to dislike   to loathe**
The opposite is like

haul *verb*

We hauled our sledge to the top of the hill.

OTHER VERBS YOU MIGHT USE ARE **to drag**   **to draw**   **to pull**   **to tow**   **to tug**

---

have *verb*

THIS VERB HAS MANY USES. HERE ARE SOME OF THE WAYS YOU CAN USE IT, AND SOME OTHER VERBS YOU COULD CHOOSE.

1 Jo has a new kitten.
to own   **to possess**

2 Jo's class has thirty pupils.
to consist of   **to contain**   **to include**

3 I was having a good time, but Sam had a cold.
to enjoy   **to experience**   **to suffer**

4 I had some nice presents on my birthday.
to be given   **to get**   **to obtain**   **to receive**

---

hazy *adjective*

The view from the top of the hill was hazy.

OTHER WORDS YOU MIGHT USE ARE **blurred**   **foggy**   **misty**

The opposite is **clear**

head *noun*

For other parts of your body, see **body**

heal *verb*

The ointment helps to heal spots.

OTHER VERBS YOU MIGHT USE ARE **to cure**   **to make better**   **to remedy**

health *noun*, see opposite page

healthy *adjective*

We all want to be healthy.

OTHER WORDS YOU MIGHT USE ARE **fit**   **sound**   **strong**   **well**

The opposite is **ill**

heap *noun*

Sam left his clothes in a heap.

OTHER WORDS ARE **mound**   **pile**   **stack**

hear *verb*

Did you hear the weather forecast?

ANOTHER VERB IS **to listen to**

heart *noun*

The explorers were lost in the heart of the jungle.

OTHER WORDS YOU MIGHT USE ARE **centre**   **core**   **middle**

heat *noun*

The cat loves the heat from the fire.

OTHER WORDS YOU MIGHT USE ARE **glow**   **warmth**

heat *verb*

VARIOUS WAYS TO HEAT THINGS ARE **to boil**   **to burn**   **to melt**   **to scald**   **to scorch**

For other verbs, see **cook**

health *noun*

We all want to have good health.

OTHER WORDS YOU MIGHT USE ARE
fitness   strength

PEOPLE WHO LOOK AFTER OUR HEALTH ARE
doctor   health visitor   nurse
A **paediatrician** is a specialist in children's health.
A **midwife** helps to deliver babies.
A **surgeon** does operations.
A **dentist** looks after your teeth.
An **optician** looks at your eyes.
A **physiotherapist** helps people recover from injuries.
A **pharmacist** makes up medicines.
A person who looks after the health of animals is a **vet** or **veterinary surgeon**.

PLACES WHERE WE CAN GET HELP WITH OUR HEALTH ARE
clinic   health centre   hospital   nursing home   surgery
We can get medicines at a **chemist's** or a **pharmacy**.

OTHER WORDS FOR MEDICINE ARE
cure   remedy   treatment
Medicine you get with a note from the doctor is a **prescription**.

SOME MEDICINES YOU MIGHT TAKE ARE
**antibiotic   aspirin   capsule   drug   gargle   linctus   lotion
ointment   pill   tablet   tonic**

ILLNESSES PEOPLE CAN HAVE ARE

allergy	**appendicitis**	**arthritis**	**asthma**
bilious attack	**bronchitis**	**cancer**	**catarrh**
chickenpox	**chill**	**cholera**	**cold**
constipation	**cough**	**diabetes**	**diarrhoea**
diphtheria	**dysentery**	**earache**	**epilepsy**
fever	**flu**	**hay fever**	**headache**
indigestion	**influenza**	**jaundice**	**leprosy**
leukaemia	**malaria**	**measles**	**migraine**
mumps	**paralysis**	**plague**	**pneumonia**
polio	**rabies**	**rheumatism**	**scarlet fever**
seasickness	**smallpox**	**spina bifida**	**stroke**
sunstroke	**tonsillitis**	**toothache**	**tuberculosis**
typhoid	**typhus**	**whooping cough**	

COMPLAINTS YOU CAN GET ON YOUR SKIN ARE

abscess	**blister**	**boil**	**chilblains**
corns	**dermatitis**	**sty**	**ulcer**
verruca	**wart**		

heater *noun*

VARIOUS KINDS OF HEATER ARE
**central heating   coal fire   convector   electric fire   gas fire
immersion heater   radiator   stove**

heavy *adjective*

a heavy load.
ANOTHER WORD IS **weighty**
The opposite is light

a
b
c
d
e
f
g
h
i
j
k
l
m
n
o
p
q
r
s
t
u
v
w
x
y
z

help *noun*

The policeman radioed for help.
OTHER WORDS YOU MIGHT USE ARE **assistance   backing   back-up   support**

help *verb*

1 I help Dad with the washing up.
OTHER VERBS YOU MIGHT USE ARE **to assist   to support**
2 I couldn't help laughing.
ANOTHER VERB IS **to stop**

helpful *adjective*

1 Our neighbours are very helpful.
OTHER WORDS YOU MIGHT USE ARE **considerate   kind   willing**
2 She gave me some helpful advice.
OTHER WORDS ARE **useful   valuable**

helping *noun*

I had a big helping of pudding.
OTHER WORDS YOU MIGHT USE ARE **portion   serving**

hesitate *verb*

Jo hesitated before diving in.
OTHER VERBS YOU MIGHT USE ARE **to delay   to pause   to wait   to waver**

hide *verb*

He hid his money under the carpet.
OTHER VERBS YOU MIGHT USE ARE **to conceal   to cover   to put away**

high *adjective*

1 a high building.
OTHER WORDS YOU MIGHT USE ARE **lofty   tall**
2 high prices.
ANOTHER WORD IS **expensive**
The opposite is low

hill *noun*

1 We climbed a hill to see the view.
OTHER WORDS YOU MIGHT USE ARE **mountain   peak**
2 It's hard cycling up that hill.
OTHER WORDS ARE **incline   rise   slope**

hinder *verb*

The firemen were angry because the people watching the fire hindered them.
OTHER VERBS YOU MIGHT USE ARE **to check   to delay   to get in the way of
to hamper**

hint *noun*

1 I can't guess the answer—give me a hint.
ANOTHER WORD IS **clue**
2 The expert gave us some hints on playing chess.
OTHER WORDS ARE **suggestion   tip**

hit verb

VARIOUS WAYS TO HIT THINGS ARE

to bang (informal) **to bash**   **to batter**   **to beat**   **to bump into**
to collide with   **to hammer**   **to knock**   **to rap**   **to smash**   **to strike**
to tap   **to thump**   (informal) **to wallop**   (informal) **to whack**   **to whip**

A goat may **butt** you with horns.
Teachers used to **cane** pupils as a punishment.
You can **flog** someone with a whip.
You **jog** someone with your elbow.
You **kick** with your foot.
You **lash** or **thrash** someone with a whip.
You **poke** or **prod** with a stick.
You **punch** with your fist.
You can **ram** a vehicle into something.
You **slap** or **smack** or **spank** someone with your hand.
You **stub** your toe on something.
You **swat** a fly.

hoarse adjective

Dad's voice was hoarse because he had a cold.

OTHER WORDS YOU MIGHT USE ARE   **croaking**   **deep**   **husky**   **rough**

hobby noun

My hobbies are skating and chess.

OTHER WORDS YOU MIGHT USE ARE   **interest**   **pastime**

hold verb

1 I held the ladder while Dad climbed up.
   OTHER VERBS YOU MIGHT USE ARE   **to grasp**   **to grip**   **to hang on to**   **to seize**
   to support
2 Sam held the baby carefully.
   OTHER VERBS ARE   **to carry**   **to embrace**   **to hug**
3 The box holds all Jo's toys.
   ANOTHER VERB IS   **to contain**

hole noun

1 a hole in the ground.
   OTHER WORDS YOU MIGHT USE ARE   **burrow**   **cave**   **crater**   **pit**   **pothole**
   tunnel
2 a hole in the fence.
   OTHER WORDS ARE   **break**   **chink**   **crack**   **gap**   **opening**
3 a hole in your jacket.
   OTHER WORDS ARE   **slit**   **split**   **tear**
4 a hole in a tyre.
   OTHER WORDS ARE   **leak**   **puncture**

holiday noun

VARIOUS KINDS OF HOLIDAY ARE

adventure holiday   **activity holiday**   **camping holiday**   **cruise**
honeymoon   **package holiday**   **safari**   **seaside holiday**
touring holiday

PLACES PEOPLE STAY ON HOLIDAY ARE

bed and breakfast   **camp site**   **guest house**   **hotel**   **motel**
self-catering accommodation   **youth hostel**

hollow *noun*
a hollow in the ground.
OTHER WORDS YOU MIGHT USE ARE **depression   dip   hole   valley**

holy *adjective*
The temple is a holy place.
OTHER WORDS YOU MIGHT USE ARE **religious   sacred**

home *noun*, see opposite page

honest *adjective*
Mum believed Sam because he is always honest.
OTHER WORDS YOU MIGHT USE ARE **sincere   trustworthy   truthful**
The opposite is **dishonest**

hop *verb*
Dad hopped up and down when he dropped the hammer on his foot.
OTHER VERBS YOU MIGHT USE ARE **to jump   to leap   to spring**

hopeful *adjective*
I'm hopeful that my cold will be better tomorrow.
OTHER WORDS YOU MIGHT USE ARE **confident   optimistic**

hopeless *adjective*
Sam's friend is hopeless at games.
OTHER WORDS YOU MIGHT USE ARE **no good   useless**

horizontal *adjective*
A snooker table must be perfectly horizontal.
OTHER WORDS YOU MIGHT USE ARE **flat   level**
The opposite is **vertical**

horrible *adjective*
1 a horrible taste.
OTHER WORDS YOU MIGHT USE ARE **horrid   nasty   unpleasant**
2 a horrible shock.
OTHER WORDS ARE **dreadful   frightening   terrible**

horror *noun*
We were filled with horror when the huge beast ran towards us.
OTHER WORDS YOU MIGHT USE ARE **dread   fear   terror**

horse *noun*
VARIOUS WORDS FOR HORSE ARE
**carthorse   nag   piebald   pony
racehorse   shire-horse   steed**
A female horse is a **mare**.
A male horse is a **stallion**.
A young horse is a **colt** or **foal**.

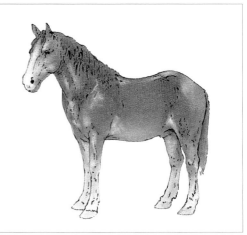

home *noun*

PLACES WHERE PEOPLE LIVE ARE

apartment bungalow caravan chalet cottage council house detached house farmhouse flat maisonette manor house mansion mobile home semi-detached house terrace house thatched cottage

DIFFERENT ROOMS IN A HOME ARE

attic bathroom bedroom cellar cloakroom conservatory dining room drawing room hall kitchen landing larder lavatory living room loft lounge pantry parlour passage porch scullery sitting room study toilet WC

cottage

manor house

terrace house

bungalow

hospital *noun*
For other places where you can go if you are ill, see **health**

hostile *adjective*
I didn't like the opposing team's hostile comments.
OTHER WORDS YOU MIGHT USE ARE **aggressive threatening unfriendly**
The opposite is friendly

hot *adjective*
1 a hot fire.
OTHER WORDS YOU MIGHT USE ARE **blazing glowing red-hot roasting scorching sizzling**
2 hot weather.
ANOTHER WORD IS **sweltering**
3 hot water.
OTHER WORDS ARE **boiling scalding**
For other words, see **warm**
The opposite is cold
4 hot-tasting food.
OTHER WORDS ARE **peppery spicy**

hotel *noun*
For other places where people stay, see **holiday**

house *noun*
For places where people live, see **home**

hug *verb*
Granny hugged us and said goodbye.
OTHER VERBS YOU MIGHT USE ARE **to cuddle to embrace to hold**

huge *adjective*
For other words, see **big**

human *noun*
For other words, see **person**

humble *adjective*
Sam was humble about winning a prize.
ANOTHER WORD IS **modest**
The opposite is proud

humorous *adjective*
We laughed at her humorous remark.
OTHER WORDS YOU MIGHT USE ARE **amusing comic funny witty**
The opposite is serious

hump *noun*
They put humps in the road to make cars go slower.
OTHER WORDS YOU MIGHT USE ARE **bulge bump lump**

hunger *noun*
1 Will a sandwich satisfy your hunger?
ANOTHER WORD IS **appetite**
2 In some countries many people die of hunger.
OTHER WORDS ARE **famine starvation**

hungry *adjective*
I was hungry after my long walk.
> OTHER WORDS YOU MIGHT USE ARE **famished** (*informal*) **peckish** **ravenous** **starved** **starving**

If you eat more food than you need you are **greedy**.

hunt *verb*
1 I think it's cruel to hunt foxes.
> OTHER VERBS YOU MIGHT USE ARE **to chase** **to pursue** **to stalk** **to track down**

2 We hunted for Mum's lost purse.
> OTHER VERBS ARE **to look for** **to search for** **to seek**

hurry *verb*
I hurried home from school.
> OTHER VERBS YOU MIGHT USE ARE **to dash** **to hasten** **to hurtle** **to race** **to run** **to rush** **to speed**

The opposite is **dawdle**

hurt *verb*
1 The cut on my hand hurts.
> OTHER VERBS YOU MIGHT USE ARE **to ache** **to be painful** **to smart** **to sting** **to throb**

2 Don't hurt the kittens!
> OTHER VERBS ARE **to damage** **to harm** **to injure** **to torment** **to wound**

Ii

ice *noun*
A river of ice is a **glacier**.
A large lump of ice floating in the sea is an **iceberg**.
A finger of ice hanging down is an **icicle**.
Dangerous ice on the road is **black ice**.

idea *noun*
1 I've got an idea!
> OTHER WORDS YOU MIGHT USE ARE (*informal*) **brainwave** **plan** **suggestion** **thought**

2 I have an idea that you are tired.
> OTHER WORDS ARE **belief** **feeling** **impression** **opinion**

ideal *adjective*
The weather was ideal for a picnic.
> OTHER WORDS YOU MIGHT USE ARE **excellent** **just right** **perfect** **suitable**

idle *adjective*
Jo is never idle, even in the holidays.
> OTHER WORDS YOU MIGHT USE ARE **doing nothing** **inactive** **lazy** **unemployed** **unoccupied**

The opposite is **busy**

a
b
c
d
e
f
g
h
i
j
k
l
m
n
o
p
q
r
s
t
u
v
w
x
y
z

ignorant *adjective*
1 ignorant of the truth.
ANOTHER WORD IS **unaware**
The opposite is aware
2 an ignorant fool.
OTHER WORDS ARE **foolish   stupid   unintelligent**
The opposite is clever

ignore *verb*
You get into trouble if you ignore what the teacher says.
OTHER VERBS YOU MIGHT USE ARE **to disobey   to disregard   to neglect   to overlook   to take no notice of**

ill *adjective*
Sam stayed away from school because he was ill.
OTHER WORDS YOU MIGHT USE ARE **indisposed   in poor health   (informal) poorly   sick   unwell**
The opposite is healthy
For other words, see **health**

illegal *adjective*
Stealing is illegal.
OTHER WORDS YOU MIGHT USE ARE **banned   criminal   forbidden   unlawful**
The opposite is legal

illness *noun*
OTHER WORDS YOU MIGHT USE ARE **ailment   (informal) bug   complaint   disease   infection   malady   sickness**
For other words, see **health**

imaginary *adjective*
Unicorns are imaginary animals.
OTHER WORDS YOU MIGHT USE ARE **fictitious   invented   made-up   non-existent   unreal**
The opposite is real

imagine *verb*
You didn't really see a ghost: you only imagined it.
OTHER VERBS YOU MIGHT USE ARE **to dream   to invent   to make up   to picture   to think**

imitate *verb*
The budgie can imitate Jo's voice.
OTHER VERBS YOU MIGHT USE ARE **to copy   to impersonate   to reproduce**

imitation *noun*
It isn't real—it's an imitation.
OTHER WORDS YOU MIGHT USE ARE **copy   counterfeit   fake   forgery   likeness   reproduction**

immediate *adjective*
Granny wants an immediate answer to her invitation.
OTHER WORDS YOU MIGHT USE ARE **instant   prompt**
For more words, see **quick**

impatient *adjective*
We were impatient to begin.
OTHER WORDS YOU MIGHT USE ARE **anxious   eager**
The opposite is patient

impertinent *adjective*
Teachers don't like impertinent comments from the children.
> OTHER WORDS YOU MIGHT USE ARE **cheeky   impolite   improper   impudent   insolent   rude**
The opposite is *polite*

important *adjective*
1 The important thing in swimming is to breathe properly.
> OTHER WORDS YOU MIGHT USE ARE **basic   chief   essential   main   necessary**
2 an important person.
> OTHER WORDS ARE **famous   great   notable   powerful   respected   well-known**
3 an important message.
> OTHER WORDS ARE **serious   urgent**
4 an important event.
> OTHER WORDS ARE **big   major   significant   special**
The opposite is *unimportant*

impression *noun*
I have the impression that you are bored.
> OTHER WORDS YOU MIGHT USE ARE **feeling   idea   opinion**

impressive *adjective*
an impressive occasion.
> OTHER WORDS YOU MIGHT USE ARE **grand   great   magnificent   memorable   spectacular   splendid   wonderful**

improve *verb*
1 Jo's swimming has improved.
> OTHER VERBS YOU MIGHT USE ARE **to develop   to get better   to progress**
2 Go over your work and try to improve it.
> OTHER VERBS ARE **to make better   to revise**

improvise *verb*
We improvised some music.
> OTHER VERBS YOU MIGHT USE ARE **to invent   to make up**

include *verb*
The packet includes everything you need to make a cake.
> OTHER VERBS YOU MIGHT USE ARE **to consist of   to contain**

inconvenient *adjective*
It is inconvenient to visit auntie today.
> OTHER WORDS YOU MIGHT USE ARE **awkward   troublesome**
The opposite is *convenient*

incorrect *adjective*
an incorrect answer.
> OTHER WORDS YOU MIGHT USE ARE **false   inaccurate   mistaken   untrue   wrong**
The opposite is *correct*

increase *verb*
1 They increased the number of children in our class.
> OTHER VERBS YOU MIGHT USE ARE **to add to   to make bigger   to raise**
2 The noise increased as the train got nearer.
> OTHER VERBS ARE **to get louder   to rise**
to increase in size
> OTHER VERBS YOU MIGHT USE ARE **to get bigger   to expand   to swell**
The opposite is *decrease*

incredible *adjective*

His story about dinosaurs was incredible.

OTHER WORDS YOU MIGHT USE ARE **far-fetched** **unbelievable** **unconvincing** **unlikely**

infectious *adjective*

an infectious disease.

ANOTHER WORD IS **catching**

inflate *verb*

to inflate a tyre.

OTHER VERBS YOU MIGHT USE ARE **to blow up** **to pump up**

influence *verb*

1 Does the weather influence the way you behave?

ANOTHER VERB IS **to affect**

2 Don't try to influence the referee!

OTHER VERBS YOU MIGHT USE ARE **to bribe** **to persuade**

inform *verb*

The teacher informed my mother that I was ill.

OTHER VERBS YOU MIGHT USE ARE **to notify** **to tell**

informal *adjective*

1 informal clothes.

OTHER WORDS YOU MIGHT USE ARE **casual** **comfortable**

2 an informal party.

OTHER WORDS ARE **easygoing** **friendly** **relaxed**

The opposite is formal

information *noun*

1 We rang up to get some information about the accident.

OTHER WORDS YOU MIGHT USE ARE **facts** **knowledge** **news**

2 We put the information into the computer.

ANOTHER WORD IS **data**

injure *verb*

Did you injure yourself when you fell over?

OTHER VERBS YOU MIGHT USE ARE **to damage** **to harm** **to hurt**

injury *noun*

For other words, see **wound**

innocent *adjective*

The judge declared that the accused man was innocent.

OTHER WORDS YOU MIGHT USE ARE **blameless** **guiltless**

The opposite is guilty

inquisitive *adjective*

It's rude to be inquisitive about other people's affairs.

OTHER WORDS YOU MIGHT USE ARE **curious** **nosy** **prying**

insect *noun*

VARIOUS INSECTS ARE

ant	**bee**
beetle	**bluebottle**
bumble-bee	**butterfly**
cockroach	**cricket**
daddy-long-legs	**dragonfly**
earwig	**fly**
glow-worm	**gnat**
grasshopper	**hornet**
ladybird	**locust**
mosquito	**moth**
nit	**wasp**

OTHER CRAWLING CREATURES (WHICH ARE NOT PROPER INSECTS) ARE

centipede	**slug**
spider	**worm**

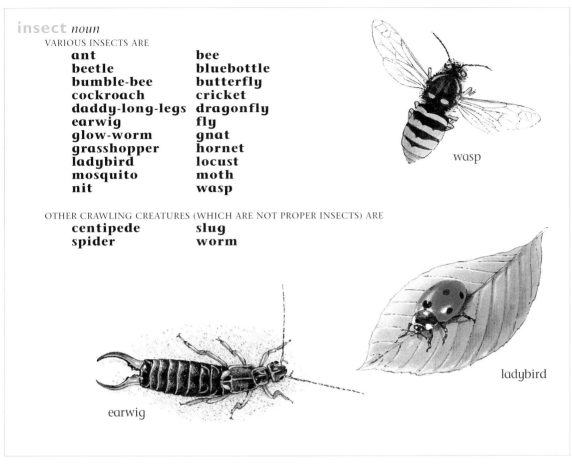

wasp

ladybird

earwig

insolent *adjective*

It is insolent to answer back to a teacher.

OTHER WORDS YOU MIGHT USE ARE **cheeky   impertinent   impolite   improper   impudent   rude**

The opposite is polite

inspect *verb*

The man at the garage inspected the damage to the car.

OTHER VERBS YOU MIGHT USE ARE **to check   to examine   to look at**

instant *adjective*

He didn't keep us waiting, but gave us an instant reply.

OTHER WORDS YOU MIGHT USE ARE **immediate   prompt   quick**

instruct *verb*

1 The policeman instructed us to stay where we were.

OTHER VERBS YOU MIGHT USE ARE **to command   to direct   to order**

2 Our teacher instructed us in how to use the PE equipment.

OTHER VERBS ARE **to coach   to teach   to train**

instrument *noun*

The dentist has an interesting instrument for drilling teeth.

OTHER WORDS YOU MIGHT USE ARE **apparatus   device   gadget   implement   machine   tool**

For musical instruments, see **music**

a b c d e f g h **i** j k l m n o p q r s t u v w x y z

113

insult *verb*

He insulted me by walking away without speaking.

> OTHER VERBS YOU MIGHT USE ARE **to be rude to   to offend   to snub**

intelligent *adjective*

Our dog is so intelligent that she understands what we say.

> OTHER WORDS YOU MIGHT USE ARE **brainy   bright   clever**

The opposite is **stupid**

intend *verb*

Jo intends to learn the piano next year.

> OTHER VERBS YOU MIGHT USE ARE **to aim   to plan   to propose**

intense *adjective*

intense heat. intense pain.

> OTHER WORDS YOU MIGHT USE ARE **extreme   great   severe   strong**

intentional *adjective*

The player was sent off the field for an intentional foul.

> OTHER WORDS YOU MIGHT USE ARE **deliberate   intended**

The opposite is **accidental**

interest *verb*

Dad's stories always interest us.

> OTHER VERBS YOU MIGHT USE ARE **to appeal to   to attract   to fascinate**

The opposite is **bore**

interested *adjective*

> OTHER WORDS YOU MIGHT USE ARE **attentive   curious   keen**
>
> IF YOU ARE TOO INTERESTED, YOU ARE **inquisitive   nosy**

The opposite is **bored**

interfere *verb*

Don't interfere in my business!

> OTHER VERBS YOU MIGHT USE ARE **to intrude   to meddle   to pry**
> (*informal*) **to snoop**

interrupt *verb*

It's rude to interrupt when someone is talking.

> OTHER VERBS YOU MIGHT USE ARE (*informal*) **to butt in   to interfere**

interval *noun*

1 When we went to the pictures, we had ice cream in the interval.

> OTHER WORDS YOU MIGHT USE ARE **break   intermission**

2 There is an interval between the lightning and the thunder.

> OTHER WORDS ARE **gap   pause   rest   space**

introduce *verb*

Jo introduced me to her friend.

> OTHER VERBS YOU MIGHT USE ARE **to make known   to present**

introduction *noun*

1 an introduction to a book.

> OTHER WORDS YOU MIGHT USE ARE **preface   prologue**

2 an introduction to a ballet.

> OTHER WORDS ARE **overture   prelude**

invade *verb*
to invade a foreign country.
OTHER VERBS YOU MIGHT USE ARE **to attack** **to march into** **to occupy**
to overrun **to raid**

invent *verb*
Who invented the first computer?
OTHER VERBS YOU MIGHT USE ARE **to create** **to devise** **to plan** **to put together**
to think up

investigate *verb*
The police spent many weeks investigating the crime.
OTHER VERBS YOU MIGHT USE ARE **to examine** **to explore** **to inquire into**
to study

invisible *adjective*
The door into the secret garden was invisible.
OTHER WORDS YOU MIGHT USE ARE **concealed** **hidden** **undetectable**
The opposite is **visible**

invite *verb*
Jo invited me to her party.
ANOTHER VERB IS **to ask**

irritable *adjective*
Dad gets irritable if we chatter while the football is on.
OTHER WORDS YOU MIGHT USE ARE **annoyed** **bad-tempered** **grumpy**
short-tempered **snappy** **touchy**
For other words, see **angry**

irritate *verb*
The flies irritated the horse.
OTHER VERBS YOU MIGHT USE ARE **to anger** **to annoy** **to bother** **to upset**
to worry

issue *verb*
The teacher issued one pencil to each child.
OTHER VERBS YOU MIGHT USE ARE **to distribute** **to give out** **to pass round**

item *noun*
Have you got any items for the jumble sale?
OTHER WORDS YOU MIGHT USE ARE **article** **object** **thing**

Jj

jab *verb*
He jabbed me with his finger.
OTHER VERBS YOU MIGHT USE ARE **to poke** **to prod** **to stab**

jagged *adjective*

The broken plank had a jagged edge.

OTHER WORDS YOU MIGHT USE ARE **rough   sharp   uneven**

The opposite is smooth

jail *noun*

see **gaol**

jam *verb*

1 I jammed my things into a box.

OTHER VERBS YOU MIGHT USE ARE **to cram   to crush   to squeeze**

2 Cars jammed the street.

OTHER VERBS ARE **to block   to fill**

3 Our back door keeps jamming.

ANOTHER VERB IS **to stick**

jar *noun*

For other things to put things in, see **container**

jealous *adjective*

Jo was a bit jealous when Sam got a lot of money for his birthday.

OTHER WORDS YOU MIGHT USE ARE **bitter   envious   resentful**

jeer *verb*

The crowd jeered at the player who argued with the referee.

OTHER VERBS YOU MIGHT USE ARE **to laugh at   to mock   to sneer at   to taunt**

jet *noun*

a jet of water.

OTHER WORDS YOU MIGHT USE ARE **fountain   spray   spurt   squirt**

---

jewel *noun*

OTHER WORDS YOU MIGHT USE ARE
gem   precious stone

STONES USED IN MAKING JEWELLERY ARE
amber   diamond   emerald   jet   opal   pearl   ruby   sapphire

METALS USED TO MAKE JEWELLERY ARE
gold   platinum   silver

VARIOUS KINDS OF JEWELLERY ARE
**bangle   beads   bracelet   brooch   chain   clasp
earrings   locket   necklace   pendant   ring**

job noun

1 I have some jobs to do for Mum before I come out to play.

OTHER WORDS YOU MIGHT USE ARE

chore   errand   task

2 Sam's cousin has left school and is looking for a job.

OTHER WORDS ARE

employment   occupation   profession   trade   work

SOME OF THE JOBS PEOPLE DO TO EARN THEIR LIVING ARE

accountant	**actor**	**architect**	**artist**
barber	**builder**	**caretaker**	**carpenter**
chef	**chemist**	**cleaner**	**clergyman**
clerk	**cook**	**decorator**	**dentist**
designer	**detective**	**driver**	**doctor**
dustman	**electrician**	**engineer**	**entertainer**
farmer	**fireman**	**gardener**	**hairdresser**
journalist	**lawyer**	**lecturer**	**librarian**
mechanic	**midwife**	**milkman**	**model**
musician	**nurse**	**optician**	**photographer**
pilot	**plumber**	**police officer**	**postman**
receptionist	**reporter**	**scientist**	**secretary**
shopkeeper	**social worker**	**teacher**	**traffic warden**
typist	**vet**	**waiter**	**writer**

join verb

1 to join one thing to another.

OTHER VERBS YOU MIGHT USE ARE   **to attach   to connect   to fasten   to fix   to link**

For other verbs, see **fasten**

2 Two motorways join in a mile.

OTHER VERBS ARE   **to come together   to meet   to merge**

joint noun

JOINTS IN YOUR BODY ARE

ankle   elbow   hip   knee   knuckle   shoulder   wrist

jolt verb

The car jolted along the rough road.

OTHER VERBS YOU MIGHT USE ARE   **to bounce   to bump   to jerk   to shake**

journey noun

KINDS OF JOURNEY ARE

excursion   expedition   outing   tour   trip

A journey in a ship is a **cruise** or a **sail** or a **voyage**.

A journey in a car is a **drive**.

A journey in a plane is a **flight**.

A journey on a horse or bicycle is a **ride**.

A journey on foot is a

hike   ramble   trek   walk

A journey with a special purpose is a **mission**.

For other words, see **travel**

a
b
c
d
e
f
g
h
i
j
k
l
m
n
o
p
q
r
s
t
u
v
w
x
y
z

117

judge *verb*

1 The criminal was judged in a court of law.

OTHER VERBS YOU MIGHT USE ARE **to condemn** **to convict** **to punish** **to sentence**

2 The referee judged that the player was off-side.

OTHER VERBS ARE **to consider** **to decide** **to rule**

jumble *noun*

Dad wanted to know why there was a jumble of clothes on the floor.

OTHER WORDS YOU MIGHT USE ARE **assortment** **chaos** **clutter** **confusion** **mess** **muddle**

jump *verb*

1 We jumped over the fence.

OTHER VERBS YOU MIGHT USE ARE **to bound** **to hop** **to leap** **to skip** **to vault**

2 The cat jumped on the mouse.

OTHER VERBS ARE **to spring** **to pounce**

just *adjective*

The referee's decision was just.

OTHER WORDS YOU MIGHT USE ARE **fair** **honest** **lawful** **proper** **right** **unbiased**

The opposite is unfair

Kk

keen *adjective*

Jo is keen to learn the piano.

OTHER WORDS YOU MIGHT USE ARE **anxious** **eager** **enthusiastic**

keep *verb*

1 I'll keep some sweets for later.

OTHER VERBS YOU MIGHT USE ARE **to save** **to store**

2 If you can't do it straight away, keep trying!

OTHER VERBS ARE **to carry on** **to continue** **to persist**

3 Please keep still.

OTHER VERBS ARE **to remain** **to stay**

4 Mum says it's expensive to keep a family.

OTHER VERBS ARE **to care for** **to feed** **to look after** **to mind** **to provide for** **to support** **to tend**

kill *verb*

OTHER VERBS YOU MIGHT USE ARE
(*informal*) **to finish off**   **to slay**
to kill a famous person
 to assassinate
to kill a criminal
 to execute or **put to death**
to kill a person
 to murder
to kill a lot of people
 to massacre
to kill pests
 to exterminate
to kill an animal that is old or ill
 to put to sleep
to kill an animal for food
 to slaughter

WAYS TO KILL A PERSON ARE
to behead   **to choke**   **to crucify**   **to drown**   **to electrocute**   **to gas**
to hang   **to knife**   **to poison**   **to shoot**   **to stab**   **to strangle**
to suffocate   **to throttle**

kind *adjective*

We are lucky to have kind neighbours.
OTHER WORDS YOU MIGHT USE ARE **considerate**   **friendly**   **good-natured**
helpful   **kind-hearted**   **loving**   **neighbourly**   **sympathetic**
thoughtful   **unselfish**
The opposite is **unkind**

kind *noun*

1 A terrier is a kind of dog.
OTHER WORDS YOU MIGHT USE ARE **breed**   **sort**   **species**   **type**
2 What kind of butter do you buy?
OTHER WORDS ARE **brand**   **make**   **variety**

kitchen *noun*, see next page

kneel *verb*

I kneeled down to tie my shoe.
OTHER VERBS YOU MIGHT USE ARE **to bend**   **to crouch**   **to stoop**

knife *noun*

OTHER WORDS YOU MIGHT USE ARE **carving**   **knife**   **dagger**   **penknife**

knob *noun*

1 the knob on the door.
ANOTHER WORD IS **handle**
2 a knob of butter.
ANOTHER WORD IS **lump**

a
b
c
d
e
f
g
h
i
j
k
l
m
n
o
p
q
r
s
t
u
v
w
x
y
z

kitchen *noun*

THINGS YOU USE IN A KITCHEN TO HEAT OR COOK FOOD ARE

**cooker   electric plate   gas ring   grill   hotplate   kettle
microwave   oven   stove   toaster**

OTHER THINGS YOU USE IN A KITCHEN ARE

baking tin	**blender**	**bowl**	**breadboard**
breadknife	**carving knife**	**casserole**	**chip pan**
crockery	**cutlery**	**dishes**	**dish rack**
dishwasher	**draining board**	**jug**	**mincer**
mixer	**pans**	**percolator**	**pots**
rolling pin	**salt cellar**	**saucepan**	**scales**
sink	**tea towel**	**teapot**	**tin-opener**
tray	**whisk**		

PLACES WHERE YOU KEEP FOOD ARE

freezer	**fridge** or **refrigerator**
larder	**pantry**

knock *verb*

I knocked on the door.
> OTHER VERBS YOU MIGHT USE ARE **to rap   to tap**

For other verbs, see **hit**

know *verb*

1 Sam knows the names of all the kings and queens of England.
> OTHER VERBS YOU MIGHT USE ARE **to recognize   to remember**

2 Mum knows a bit of French.
> ANOTHER VERB IS **to understand**

knowledge *noun*

1 You get a lot of knowledge from an encyclopedia.
> OTHER WORDS YOU MIGHT USE ARE **facts   information**

2 Farmers have a great knowledge of the countryside.
> OTHER WORDS ARE **experience   understanding**

Ll

lag *verb*

If we lag behind we'll miss the bus.
> OTHER VERBS YOU MIGHT USE ARE **to dawdle**   (*informal*) **to hang about   to linger   to loiter   to straggle**

lake *noun*

For other words, see **water**

lame *adjective*

The lame man used a walking stick.
> OTHER WORDS YOU MIGHT USE ARE **crippled   disabled   limping**

land *noun*

1 foreign lands.
> OTHER WORDS YOU MIGHT USE ARE **country   nation**

2 land to grow crops on.
> OTHER WORDS ARE **earth   ground   soil**

land *verb*

1 The plane landed at the airport.
> OTHER VERBS YOU MIGHT USE ARE **to arrive   to come down**

2 The sailors landed on an island.
> OTHER VERBS ARE **to come ashore   to disembark**

large *adjective*

> OTHER WORDS YOU MIGHT USE ARE **big   broad   fat   grand   great   long   roomy   spacious   tall   wide**
>
> WORDS FOR VERY LARGE THINGS ARE **colossal   enormous   giant   gigantic   huge   immense   infinite   massive   mighty   monstrous   tremendous   vast**

The opposite is small

last *adjective*
Our song was the last item in the concert.
OTHER WORDS YOU MIGHT USE ARE **concluding** **final**
The opposite is first

last *verb*
The fine weather lasted all week.
OTHER VERBS YOU MIGHT USE ARE **to continue** **to go on** **to keep on** **to persist** **to remain** **to stay**

late *adjective*
The bus is late.
OTHER WORDS YOU MIGHT USE ARE **delayed** **overdue**
Opposites are early or punctual

lately *adverb*
ANOTHER WORD IS **recently**

laugh *verb*
VARIOUS WAYS WE LAUGH ARE **to chuckle** **to giggle** **to grin** **to smile** **to titter**
TO LAUGH UNKINDLY AT SOMEONE IS **to jeer** **to sneer** **to snigger**
For other verbs, see **mock**

law *noun*
We obey the laws of the country.
OTHER WORDS YOU MIGHT USE ARE **regulation** **rule**

lay *verb*
I laid the papers on the desk.
OTHER VERBS YOU MIGHT USE ARE **to leave** **to place** **to put** **to set down** **to spread**

layer *noun*
There was a layer of ice over the playground.
OTHER WORDS YOU MIGHT USE ARE **coating** **film** **sheet** **skin** **thickness**

lazy *adjective*
That cat leads a lazy life!
ANOTHER WORD IS **idle**
The opposite is busy

lead *verb*
1 The teacher led the children back to the classroom.
OTHER VERBS YOU MIGHT USE ARE **to conduct** **to guide** **to take**
2 The captain led her team with great skill.
OTHER VERBS ARE **to command** **to direct** **to manage**

leak *verb*
Water leaked out of the bucket.
OTHER VERBS YOU MIGHT USE ARE **to drip** **to escape** **to ooze** **to seep** **to trickle**

lean *verb*
The sinking ship leaned to one side.
OTHER VERBS YOU MIGHT USE ARE **to heel over** **to list** **to slant** **to slope** **to tilt**

leap *verb*
Sam leaped over the fence.
OTHER VERBS YOU MIGHT USE ARE **to bound** **to jump** **to spring** **to vault**

learn *verb*

1 We learned a lot about history when we went to the castle.
   OTHER VERBS YOU MIGHT USE ARE **to discover**   **to find out**
2 We learned the song by heart.
   ANOTHER VERB IS   **to memorize**

leave *verb*

1 Don't leave your pets when you go on holiday.
   OTHER VERBS YOU MIGHT USE ARE **to abandon**   **to desert**   **to forsake**
2 The guard blew a whistle to show that the train was ready to leave.
   OTHER VERBS ARE   **to depart**   **to go**   **to set off**
3 Leave the empty milk bottles outside the front door.
   OTHER VERBS ARE   **to deposit**   **to place**   **to put down**   **to set down**

lecture *noun*

A policewoman gave us a lecture on road safety.
   OTHER WORDS YOU MIGHT USE ARE   **lesson**   **speech**   **talk**

leg *noun*

For parts of the body, see **body**

legal *adjective*

Is it legal to park on this road?
   OTHER WORDS YOU MIGHT USE ARE   **allowed**   **lawful**   **permitted**
The opposite is illegal

lend *verb*

Can you lend me a pen?
   ANOTHER VERB IS   **to loan**
If you give something to someone to use for a short time, you **lend** it.
If someone gives something to you to use, you **borrow** it.

length *noun*

OTHER WORDS YOU MIGHT USE ARE   **distance**   **measurement**

let *verb*

1 Sam let Jo ride his bike.
   OTHER VERBS YOU MIGHT USE ARE   **to allow**   **to permit**
2 Aunt Jean lets her caravan to holidaymakers in the summer.
   OTHER VERBS ARE   **to hire**   **to rent**

level *adjective*

1 You need a level field for playing rounders.
   OTHER WORDS YOU MIGHT USE ARE   **even**   **flat**   **horizontal**   **smooth**
2 At half time the scores were level.
   ANOTHER WORD IS   **equal**

licence *noun*

You need a licence to go fishing.
   ANOTHER WORD IS   **permit**

lid *noun*

Put the lid back on the jam.
   OTHER WORDS YOU MIGHT USE ARE   **cap**   **cover**   **top**

lie *noun*

Don't tell lies!
   OTHER WORDS YOU MIGHT USE ARE   **falsehood**   (*informal*) **fib**

lie *verb*

1 Don't believe her—I think she's lying.
OTHER VERBS YOU MIGHT USE ARE **to bluff** (*informal*) **to fib**

2 Sam lay on the sofa.
OTHER VERBS ARE **to lean back** **to recline** **to sprawl**

life *noun*

Our dog is full of life.
OTHER WORDS YOU MIGHT USE ARE **energy** **liveliness** **vitality**

lifelike *adjective*

The wax models were very lifelike.
OTHER WORDS YOU MIGHT USE ARE **natural** **realistic**

lift *verb*

1 Lift the box onto the shelf.
OTHER VERBS YOU MIGHT USE ARE **to hoist** **to raise**

2 Jo lifted baby out of her pram.
ANOTHER VERB IS **to pick up**

light *adjective*

1 a light suitcase.
The opposite is heavy

2 a light room.
OTHER WORDS YOU MIGHT USE ARE **bright** **well-lit**
The opposite is dark

3 light colours.
OTHER WORDS ARE **faint** **pale**
The opposite is strong

light *noun*, see opposite page

like *verb*

1 We like our neighbours.
OTHER VERBS YOU MIGHT USE ARE **to approve of** **to be fond of** **to respect**
For other verbs, see **love**

2 I would like a drink, please.
OTHER VERBS ARE **to enjoy** **to fancy** **to want** **to wish for**
The opposite is hate

likely *adjective*

1 Rain is likely today.
ANOTHER WORD IS **probable**

2 Sam is a likely person to be captain of the team.
OTHER WORDS ARE **appropriate** **suitable**

limp *adjective*

1 limp covers on a book.
OTHER WORDS YOU MIGHT USE ARE **flexible** **soft**
The opposite is stiff

2 limp lettuce.
OTHER WORDS ARE **drooping** **floppy**
The opposite is crisp

limp *verb*

Jo limped because her shoe hurt.
ANOTHER VERB IS **to hobble**
For other words, see **lame**

light *noun*

THINGS WHICH GIVE LIGHT ARE

**bulb   candle   electric light   floodlight   headlight   lamp
lantern   searchlight   spotlight   street light   torch**

LIGHTS USED FOR DECORATION ARE

fairy   lights   illuminations

NATURAL LIGHT IS

daylight   moonlight   starlight   sunlight

DIFFERENT WAYS LIGHT SHINES ARE

**blaze   burn   dazzle   flash   flicker   glare   gleam   glimmer
glint   glisten   glitter   glow   shine   spark   sparkle   twinkle**

line *noun*

1 lines on the road.

OTHER WORDS YOU MIGHT USE ARE **dash   mark   streak   stripe**

2 lines on someone's face.

OTHER WORDS ARE **crease   furrow   wrinkle**

3 a railway line.

OTHER WORDS ARE **rails   route   track**

4 We waited in a line.

OTHER WORDS ARE **column   file   queue   rank   row**

linger *verb*

Don't linger in the playground.

OTHER VERBS YOU MIGHT USE ARE **to dawdle   to delay   (*informal*) to hang about
to loiter   to remain   to stay   to wait about**

link *verb*

Sam can link his keyboard to a computer.

OTHER VERBS YOU MIGHT USE ARE **to attach   to connect   to join**

litter *noun*

We get into trouble if we leave litter round the school.

OTHER WORDS YOU MIGHT USE ARE **clutter   junk   rubbish**

a b c d e f g h i j k **l** m n o p q r s t u v w x y z

little *adjective*

1 Sam's got a little radio that he can put in his pocket.
OTHER WORDS YOU MIGHT USE ARE **compact** **miniature** **minute** **small** **tiny**

2 We had a little chat.
OTHER WORDS ARE **brief** **short**

3 She gave us little helpings.
OTHER WORDS ARE **mean** (*informal*) **measly** **stingy**

4 They had a little argument.
OTHER WORDS ARE **minor** **slight** **trivial** **unimportant**

The opposite is big

live *adjective*

There aren't any live dinosaurs.
OTHER WORDS YOU MIGHT USE ARE **existing** **living**

live *verb*

1 Plants can't live without water.
OTHER VERBS YOU MIGHT USE ARE **to exist** **to remain alive** **to survive**

2 Jo's Granny lives in a flat.
OTHER VERBS ARE **to dwell in** **to inhabit** **to occupy**

lively *adjective*

Those puppies are lively!
OTHER WORDS YOU MIGHT USE ARE **active** **energetic** **frisky**

The opposite is lazy

load *noun*

Can you carry that heavy load?
OTHER WORDS YOU MIGHT USE ARE **burden** **weight**

load *verb*

We loaded the trolley with food.
OTHER VERBS YOU MIGHT USE ARE **to fill** **to pack**

lock *noun*

Mum fitted a lock to the door.
OTHER WORDS YOU MIGHT USE ARE **bolt** **catch** **latch** **padlock**

lock *verb*

Did you lock the door?
OTHER VERBS YOU MIGHT USE ARE **to fasten** **to secure**

logical *adjective*

a logical argument.
OTHER WORDS YOU MIGHT USE ARE **intelligent** **reasonable** **sensible**

lonely *adjective*

1 Jo felt lonely when Sam went away.

OTHER WORDS YOU MIGHT USE ARE **alone   forsaken   friendless   neglected   solitary**

2 We heard a ghost story about a lonely farmhouse.

OTHER WORDS ARE **isolated   remote   secluded**

long *adjective*

It seemed a long journey.

OTHER WORDS YOU MIGHT USE ARE **endless   lengthy**

The opposite is short

long *verb*

I longed for a drink.

OTHER VERBS YOU MIGHT USE ARE **to fancy   to hanker after   to want   to wish for   to yearn for**

look *verb*

1 We looked at the things we had collected on our walk.

OTHER VERBS YOU MIGHT USE ARE **to examine   to study   to survey   to view**

TO LOOK AT SOMETHING QUICKLY **to glance   to peep**

TO LOOK FOR A LONG TIME **to gaze   to stare   to watch**

2 The dog looked friendly.

OTHER VERBS ARE **to appear   to seem**

3 I helped Mum look for her purse.

OTHER VERBS ARE **to hunt   to search for   to seek**

loose *adjective*

1 My tooth is loose.

OTHER WORDS YOU MIGHT USE ARE **shaky   unsteady   wobbly**

2 The animals were all loose.

OTHER WORDS ARE **at liberty   free**

lorry *noun*

For other words, see **travel**

lose *verb*

1 Sam was upset when he lost his watch.

ANOTHER VERB IS **to mislay**

2 Our team lost on Saturday.

A PHRASE IS **to be defeated**

loud *adjective*

The neighbours complained about the loud music.

OTHER WORDS YOU MIGHT USE ARE **deafening   noisy   shrill**

The opposite is quiet

lounge *noun*

OTHER WORDS YOU MIGHT USE ARE **drawing room   living room   sitting room**

love *verb*

OTHER VERBS YOU MIGHT USE ARE **to adore   to be fond of   to be in love with   to care for   to idolize   to like   to treasure   to worship**

lovely *adjective*

For other words, see **beautiful**

low *adjective*

The opposite is high

a
b
c
d
e
f
g
h
i
j
k
l
m
n
o
p
q
r
s
t
u
v
w
x
y
z

loyal *adjective*

Sam is a loyal supporter of his local team.

OTHER WORDS YOU MIGHT USE ARE **devoted**   **faithful**   **reliable**   **trustworthy**

luck *noun*

Sam found his lost watch by luck.

OTHER WORDS YOU MIGHT USE ARE **accident**   **chance**   **coincidence**

lucky *adjective*

I was lucky to find what I wanted.

ANOTHER WORD IS **fortunate**

The opposite is unlucky

luggage *noun*

The driver put our luggage in the back of the car.

DIFFERENT ITEMS OF LUGGAGE MIGHT BE

**bag   box   case   holdall
suitcase   trunk**

lump *noun*

1 Uncle gave Jo a lump of chocolate.

OTHER WORDS YOU MIGHT USE ARE **bar   block   chunk   hunk   piece   slab**

2 Dad got a lump on the head where he hit himself.

OTHER WORDS YOU MIGHT USE ARE **bulge   bump   hump   knob   swelling**

luxury *noun*

That cat lives a life of luxury!

OTHER WORDS YOU MIGHT USE ARE **comfort   ease   pleasure   relaxation**

Mm

machine *noun*

The workshop had a machine for doing woodwork.

OTHER WORDS YOU MIGHT USE ARE **apparatus   instrument   tool**

A word you might use for machines in general is **machinery**

mad *adjective*

1 He behaved so strangely that people said he was mad.

OTHER WORDS YOU MIGHT USE ARE *(informal)* **crazy   insane   mentally ill
unbalanced**

2 He's mad to go out in this rain!

For other words, see **silly**

magic *noun*

1 Can witches really do magic?

OTHER WORDS YOU MIGHT USE ARE **charms** **enchantments** **sorcery** **spells** **witchcraft**

2 The conjuror did some magic.

A PHRASE YOU MIGHT USE IS **conjuring tricks**

magician *noun*

OTHER WORDS YOU MIGHT USE ARE **conjuror** **sorcerer** **wizard**

magnificent *adjective*

a magnificent palace.

OTHER WORDS YOU MIGHT USE ARE **grand** **impressive** **majestic** **noble** **splendid** **stately**

mail *noun*

For other words, see **post**

main *adjective*

The main ingredient of bread is flour.

OTHER WORDS YOU MIGHT USE ARE **basic** **chief** **essential** **important** **principal**

make *verb*, see next page

---

make-up *noun*

KINDS OF MAKE-UP ARE

blusher **eyeliner** **eyeshadow** **face cream** **face powder** **lipstick** **nail varnish**

THINGS PEOPLE USE TO MAKE THEMSELVES SMELL NICER ARE

aftershave **deodorant** **perfume** **scent** **talc** or **talcum powder**

---

male *noun*

THERE ARE SPECIAL WORDS FOR MALE AND FEMALE HUMAN BEINGS AND SOME ANIMALS.

A male human being is a **boy** or **man.**
A male goat is a **billy goat**.
A male pig is a **boar**.
A male deer is a **buck** or **stag**.
A male rabbit is a **buck**.
A male swan is a **cob**.
A male bird is a **cock**.
A male chicken is a **cockerel**.
A male duck is a **drake**.
A male goose is a **gander**.
A male sheep is a **ram**.
A male horse is a **stallion**.
A male cat is a **tom-cat**.

make *verb*

THIS VERB HAS MANY USES. HERE ARE SOME OF THE WAYS YOU CAN USE IT, AND SOME OTHER VERBS YOU COULD CHOOSE

1 I made a plan.
to form   to invent   to produce   to think up
2 We made a den in the garden.
to build   to construct   to create   to erect
3 They make cars in that factory.
to assemble   to manufacture
4 Don't make trouble.
to bring about   to cause   to provoke
5 You can't make me do it.
to compel   to force   to oblige   to order
6 The head made a speech.
to deliver   to give
7 It's easy to make a P into a B.
to alter   to change   to convert   to transform   to turn
8 How can I make some money?
to earn   to get   to obtain   to receive
9 You'll make a good player if you practise.
to become   to change into   to grow into   to turn into
10 Will our team make the final?
to get to   to reach
11 2 and 2 make 4.
to add up to   to come to
12 Mum made an appointment at the doctor's.
to arrange   to fix
13 I can't make out what happened.
to follow   to hear   to see   to understand
14 She made up an excuse.
to invent   to plan   to think up

man *noun*

OTHER WORDS YOU MIGHT USE ARE
a polite word
gentleman
a married man
husband
a man who is not married
bachelor
a man whose wife has died
widower
a man who has children
father
a young man
boy   youth

manage *verb*

1 The head manages the school.
OTHER VERBS YOU MIGHT USE ARE **to be in charge of   to control   to look after   to run**

2 Can you manage a big helping?
OTHER VERBS YOU MIGHT USE ARE **to cope with   to deal with   to handle**

3 Could you manage to help us on Saturday?
ANOTHER VERB IS **to arrange**

manner *noun*

He spoke in a friendly manner.
OTHER WORDS YOU MIGHT USE ARE **fashion   style   way**

---

map *noun*

A simple map is a **diagram** or **plan**.
A map used by sailors is a **chart**.
A book of maps is an **atlas**.

---

mark *noun*

There's a mark on my new dress.
OTHER WORDS YOU MIGHT USE ARE **smear   smudge   spot   stain**

---

market *noun*

DIFFERENT KINDS OF MARKET ARE
auction   bazaar   car boot sale   fair   street market

---

marsh *noun*

We began to sink into the marsh.
OTHER WORDS YOU MIGHT USE ARE **bog   swamp**

marvellous *adjective*

I had a marvellous holiday.
OTHER WORDS YOU MIGHT USE ARE **excellent**   (*informal*) **fabulous   splendid   wonderful**

mash *verb*

We mashed the baby's dinner until it was soft.
OTHER VERBS YOU MIGHT USE ARE **to crush   to pulp   to purée   to smash   to squash**

mass *noun*

There was a mass of rubbish to clear away.
OTHER WORDS YOU MIGHT USE ARE **heap   mound   pile   quantity   stack**

a b c d e f g h i j k l **m** n o p q r s t u v w x y z

match *noun*

a boxing match.

OTHER WORDS YOU MIGHT USE ARE **competition** **contest** **game**

material *noun*

1 building materials.

OTHER WORDS YOU MIGHT USE ARE **stuff** **substances** **things**

2 material to make curtains.

For other words, see **cloth**

---

mathematics *noun*

A short word for mathematics is **maths**.

Working with numbers is also called **arithmetic**.

WORDS FOR THINGS YOU DO IN MATHEMATICS ARE

addition or **adding** **calculation** or **calculating**
counting **division** or **dividing** **investigating**
measuring **multiplication** or **multiplying**
subtraction or **subtracting** or **taking away** **sums**

VERBS YOU MIGHT USE IN MATHS ARE

to add **to add up** **to calculate** **to count**
to divide **to investigate** **to measure** **to multiply**
to subtract **to take away** **to work out**

OTHER WORDS YOU MIGHT USE IN MATHS ARE

angle **answer** **area** **capacity** **diagonal**
difference **digit** **figure** **fraction** **graph**
measurement **minus** **number** **pattern** **plus**
problem **shape** **sum** **symmetry** **times**
total **unit** **volume**

THINGS YOU MIGHT USE TO HELP YOU IN MATHEMATICS ARE

calculator **compasses** **computer**
ruler **set square**

For words you might use when you measure things,
see **measurement**

For names of different shapes, see **shape**

---

matter *noun*

1 We have some matters to discuss.

OTHER WORDS YOU MIGHT USE ARE **business** **subject** **topic**

2 What's the matter?

OTHER WORDS ARE **difficulty** **problem** **trouble**

---

meal *noun*

DIFFERENT MEALS ARE

breakfast **dinner** **high tea** **lunch** **supper** **tea**

A very splendid meal is a **banquet** or **feast**.

A meal where you help yourself is a **buffet**.

A small meal is a **snack**.

A meal you eat out of doors is a **picnic**.

A meal you cook out of doors is a **barbecue**.

mean *adjective*

He's mean with his money.
> OTHER WORDS YOU MIGHT USE ARE **miserly**   (*informal*) **stingy**

The opposite is generous

mean *verb*

1 What does this word mean?
> OTHER VERBS YOU MIGHT USE ARE **to convey**   **to indicate**   **to say**   **to stand for**

2 What do you mean to do?
> OTHER VERBS ARE **to aim**   **to intend**   **to plan**   **to propose**

---

measurement *noun*

> ANOTHER WORD IS
> **size**
>
> OTHER WORDS YOU MIGHT USE ARE
> how long something is: **length**
> how wide something is: **breadth** or **width**
> how tall something is: **height**
> UNITS TO MEASURE LENGTH, BREADTH, OR HEIGHT ARE
> **centimetres**   **metres**   **kilometres**
> OLD UNITS ARE
> **inches**   **feet**   **yards**   **miles**
>
> how big a surface is: **area**
> UNITS TO MEASURE AREA ARE
> **square metres**   **metres**
> OLD UNITS ARE
> **square feet**   **square yards**   **acres**
>
> how much something holds: **volume**
> UNITS TO MEASURE VOLUME ARE
> **cubic centimetres** or **litres**
> OLD UNITS ARE
> **pints** or **gallons**
>
> how heavy something is: **weight**
> UNITS TO MEASURE WEIGHT ARE
> **grams**   **kilograms**   **tonnes**
> OLD UNITS ARE
> **ounces**   **pounds**   **tons**

---

meat *noun*

> DIFFERENT KINDS OF MEAT ARE
> **bacon**   **beef**   **chicken**   **ham**   **lamb**   **pork**   **turkey**   **veal**
> **venison**
>
> YOU CAN BUY MEAT IN THE FORM OF
> **burgers**   **chops**   **joint**   **mince**   **sausage**
> **steak**

medicine *noun*

I need medicine for my cough.
For other words, see **health**

medium *adjective*
Sam is medium height for his age.
OTHER WORDS YOU MIGHT USE ARE **average   middling   normal**

meet *verb*
1 Two roads meet here.
OTHER VERBS YOU MIGHT USE ARE **to come together   to join   to merge**
2 I met my friend in town.
OTHER VERBS ARE **to encounter**   (*informal*) **to run into   to see**
3 All the classes met in the hall.
OTHER VERBS ARE **to assemble   to congregate   to gather**

meeting *noun*
DIFFERENT KINDS OF MEETING ARE **assembly   committee   conference   council**

melt *verb*
The ice melted in the sun.
OTHER VERBS YOU MIGHT USE ARE **to thaw   to unfreeze**

mend *verb*
1 The garage mended the car.
OTHER VERBS YOU MIGHT USE ARE **to fix   to put right   to repair**
2 Dad likes mending old furniture.
OTHER VERBS ARE **to do up   to renovate   to restore**
3 Sam mended his jeans.
OTHER VERBS ARE **to darn   to patch   to sew up   to stitch up**

mention *verb*
I mentioned that I was hungry.
OTHER VERBS YOU MIGHT USE ARE **to comment   to remark   to say**

merciful *adjective*
The judge was merciful and let him off with a warning.
OTHER WORDS YOU MIGHT USE ARE **forgiving   kind   sympathetic**
The opposite is cruel

mercy *noun*
The judge showed mercy.
OTHER WORDS YOU MIGHT USE ARE **forgiveness   pity**

merry *adjective*
a merry tune.
OTHER WORDS YOU MIGHT USE ARE **cheerful   happy   jolly   lively**
The opposite is sad

mess *noun*
Clear up this mess!
OTHER WORDS YOU MIGHT USE ARE **chaos   clutter   confusion   jumble
muddle**

message *noun*
I sent a message that I was busy.
OTHER WORDS YOU MIGHT USE ARE **letter   note**

metal *noun*
DIFFERENT METALS ARE
**aluminium   brass   bronze   copper   gold   iron   lead
platinum   silver   steel   tin   uranium   zinc**

method *noun*
Our teacher showed us a good method for doing multiplication.
OTHER WORDS YOU MIGHT USE ARE **procedure   system   technique   way**

middle *noun*
the middle of the earth.
OTHER WORDS YOU MIGHT USE ARE **centre   core   heart**

mild *adjective*
1 mild weather.
OTHER WORDS YOU MIGHT USE ARE **gentle   pleasant   warm**
2 a mild illness.
ANOTHER WORD IS **slight**
The opposite is severe

mind *noun*
Use your mind!
OTHER WORDS YOU MIGHT USE ARE **brain   intelligence   understanding**

mind *verb*
1 I'll mind the baby.
OTHER VERBS YOU MIGHT USE ARE **to care for   to look after   to tend**
2 Do you mind about missing the party?
OTHER VERBS ARE **to care   to worry**

mine *noun*
a coal mine.
OTHER WORDS YOU MIGHT USE ARE **pit   shaft**
A place where they dig coal from the Earth's surface is an **opencast mine**.
A place where they dig stone is a **quarry**.

mischievous *adjective*
The mischievous puppy stole Dad's slippers.
OTHER WORDS YOU MIGHT USE ARE **badly behaved   naughty**

miserable *adjective*
1 Jo's miserable when Sam is away.
OTHER WORDS YOU MIGHT USE ARE **depressed   gloomy   sad   unhappy   wretched**
The opposite is happy
2 The refugees live in miserable conditions.
OTHER WORDS ARE **awful   bad   pitiful   poor   wretched**

misery *noun*
We can't imagine the misery of the refugees.
OTHER WORDS YOU MIGHT USE ARE **distress   grief   sadness   sorrow   suffering   unhappiness**

mislead *verb*
She misled us and sent us the wrong way.
OTHER VERBS YOU MIGHT USE ARE **to deceive   to fool   to trick**

a
b
c
d
e
f
g
h
i
j
k
l
m
n
o
p
q
r
s
t
u
v
w
x
y
z

miss *verb*

1 If we leave now we'll miss the rush-hour traffic.
OTHER VERBS YOU MIGHT USE ARE **to avoid** **to dodge** **to steer clear of**
2 I missed the bus.
The opposite is catch
3 Jo missed Sam when he was away.
ANOTHER VERB IS **to pine for**
4 You can miss out the questions you don't understand.
OTHER VERBS ARE **to leave out** **to omit** **to skip**

missing *adjective*
Did you find the missing money?
ANOTHER WORD IS **lost**

mist *noun*
ANOTHER WORD IS **haze**
A thick mist is **fog**.

mistake *noun*
spelling mistakes.
OTHER WORDS YOU MIGHT USE ARE **blunder** **error** (*informal*) **slip**

misty *adjective*
a misty view.
OTHER WORDS YOU MIGHT USE ARE **blurred** **dim** **faint** **fuzzy** **hazy**
indistinct **unclear**
The opposite is clear

mix *verb*

1 Mix the flour, fat, and sugar in a bowl.
OTHER VERBS YOU MIGHT USE ARE **to blend** **to combine** **to mingle**
to stir together
2 Don't mix two packs of cards!
OTHER VERBS ARE **to confuse** **to jumble** **to muddle**

mixture *noun*
I had a mixture of sweets.
OTHER WORDS YOU MIGHT USE ARE **assortment** **variety**

moan *verb*
He moaned with pain.
OTHER VERBS YOU MIGHT USE ARE **to groan** **to wail**

mock *verb*
It's unkind to mock other people.
OTHER VERBS YOU MIGHT USE ARE **to laugh at** **to make fun of** **to ridicule**
to sneer at **to taunt** **to tease**

moderate *adjective*
Dad drives at moderate speed.
OTHER WORDS YOU MIGHT USE ARE **medium** **middling** **normal** **ordinary**
reasonable

modern *adjective*

1 Grandad says he doesn't understand modern inventions like computers.
OTHER WORDS YOU MIGHT USE ARE **new** **recent**
The opposite is old
2 Do you like modern clothes?
OTHER WORDS ARE **fashionable** **stylish** (*informal*) **trendy** **up-to-date**
The opposite is old-fashioned

modest *adjective*

1 She was modest about winning the prize.
ANOTHER WORD IS **humble**
The opposite is conceited

2 He was too modest to undress on the beach.
OTHER WORDS YOU MIGHT USE ARE **bashful** **shy**

money *noun*

Money you have in your pocket is **cash** or **change**.
IT MIGHT BE
coins (*informal*) **coppers** **notes** **silver**
People can also buy things with a **cheque** or a **credit card**.

A LOT OF MONEY IS
a fortune **wealth**

MONEY YOU GET FOR WORK YOU DO IS
earnings **income** **pay** **salary** **wages**

Money you get when you retire from work is a **pension**.
Money you save in the bank is your **savings**.
Money people have to pay to the government is **tax**.

monster *noun*
FRIGHTENING CREATURES YOU READ ABOUT IN STORIES ARE
beast **dragon** **giant** **ogre** **troll** **vampire** **werewolf**

month *noun*
THE MONTHS OF THE YEAR ARE
January **February** **March** **April** **May** **June** **July** **August**
September **October** **November** **December**

mood *noun*
Is Dad in a good mood today?
OTHER WORDS YOU MIGHT USE ARE **humour** **temper**

moral *adjective*

a moral person.

OTHER WORDS YOU MIGHT USE ARE **good   honest   truthful   virtuous**

The opposite is **immoral**

motive *noun*

What was the motive for the crime?

OTHER WORDS YOU MIGHT USE ARE **purpose   reason**

---

mountain *noun*

The top of a mountain is the **summit** or **peak**.

A line of mountains is a **range** or **ridge**.

A mountain which sometimes sends out hot liquid, gases, or ash is a **volcano**.

---

move *verb*

THIS VERB HAS MANY USES. HERE ARE SOME OF THE WAYS YOU CAN USE IT, AND SOME OTHER VERBS YOU COULD CHOOSE

1 to move along.
**to come   to fly   to go
to journey   to march   to pass
to tour   to travel   to walk**

2 to move along quickly.
**to canter   to dart   to dash   to fly   to gallop   to hurry   to race
to run   to rush   to shoot   to speed   to streak   to tear**
(*informal*) **to zoom**

3 to move along slowly.
to crawl   to dawdle   to stroll

4 to move along gracefully.
to dance   to glide   to skate   to skim   to slide   to slip

5 to move along clumsily.
to shuffle   to stagger   to stumble   to sway   to totter   to trip

6 to move along stealthily.
to crawl   to creep   to slink   to slither

7 to move away from somewhere.
to depart   to leave   to quit

8 to move back.
to reverse   to withdraw

9 to move downwards.
to descend   to drop   to fall   to sink

10 to move upwards.
  to arise   to climb   to mount   to rise
11 to move in somewhere.
  to enter
12 to move round and round.
  **to revolve   to roll   to rotate   to spin   to turn   to twirl   to twist
  to whirl**
13 to move towards something.
  to advance   to approach

14 to move restlessly.
  **to fidget   to shake   to stir   to toss   to tremble   to twist
  to twitch   to wag   to waggle   to wave**
15 to move things.
  to budge   to carry   to shift   to transport

mud *noun*
There was some mud on the road.
OTHER WORDS YOU MIGHT USE ARE   **clay   dirt   muck   slime**

muddle *verb*
1 Don't muddle the library books.
OTHER VERBS YOU MIGHT USE ARE   **to jumble   to mix up**
2 You muddle me if you talk fast.
OTHER VERBS ARE   **to bewilder   to confuse**

murder *verb*
For other verbs, see **kill**

music *noun*, see next page

mysterious *adjective*
1 The doctors didn't know what to do about my mysterious illness.
OTHER WORDS YOU MIGHT USE ARE   **mystifying   puzzling   strange**
2 The castle looked mysterious in the moonlight.
OTHER WORDS ARE   **eerie   ghostly   magical   weird**

mystery *noun*
The detective solved the mystery.
OTHER WORDS YOU MIGHT USE ARE   **problem   puzzle   riddle**

a
b
c
d
e
f
g
h
i
j
k
l
m
n
o
p
q
r
s
t
u
v
w
x
y
z

music *noun*

DIFFERENT KINDS OF MUSIC ARE

**classical music   music   folk music   jazz   musicals   opera
pop music   rap   reggae   rock**

KINDS OF MUSIC FOR SINGING ARE

**ballad   carol   folk song   hymn   lullaby   pop song   shanty
spiritual**

BRASS INSTRUMENTS ARE

bugle   cornet   horn   trombone   trumpet   tuba

OTHER INSTRUMENTS YOU PLAY BY BLOWING ARE

bagpipes   bassoon   clarinet   flute   harmonica or **mouth organ
oboe   pan pipes   piccolo   recorder   saxophone**

INSTRUMENTS WITH STRINGS THAT YOU PLAY BY PLUCKING ARE

banjo   guitar   harp   sitar

INSTRUMENTS WITH STRINGS THAT YOU CAN PLAY WITH A BOW ARE

cello   double bass   fiddle   viola   violin

violin

INSTRUMENTS YOU PLAY BY PRESSING KEYS ARE

harmonium   harpsichord   keyboard   organ   piano

PERCUSSION INSTRUMENTS ARE

**castanets   chime bars   cymbals   drums   glockenspiel   gong
kettledrum   tambourine   triangle   tubular bells   xylophone**

PEOPLE WHO MAKE MUSIC ARE

composer   conductor   performer   player   singer

PEOPLE WHO PLAY INSTRUMENTS ARE

**drummer   fiddler   guitarist   harpist   organist   percussionist
pianist   piper   trumpeter   violinist**

DIFFERENT SINGING VOICES ARE

alto   bass   soprano   tenor   treble
People who play or sing on their own are **soloists**.
A singer may also be called a **vocalist**.

trumpet

GROUPS OF MUSICIANS ARE

band   choir or **chorus   ensemble   group   orchestra   quartet
quintet   trio**

bagpipes

harp

drum

sitar

Nn

naked *adjective*
OTHER WORDS YOU MIGHT USE ARE **bare   nude   unclothed   undressed**

name *noun*
The name that you are given when you are born is your **first name**.
The name that everyone in your family has is your **surname** or **family name**.
An invented name which friends give you is a **nickname**.
A name you use instead of your real name is an **alias**.
The name of a book is the **title**.
The name of a particular make of goods is the **brand**.

narrow *adjective*
OTHER WORDS YOU MIGHT USE ARE **fine   slim   thin**
The opposite is wide

nasty *adjective*
1 nasty weather.
OTHER WORDS YOU MIGHT USE ARE **bad   dreadful   horrible   unpleasant**
2 a nasty mess.
OTHER WORDS ARE **dirty   disgusting   filthy   foul   revolting**
3 a nasty person.
OTHER WORDS ARE **rude   unfriendly   unkind**
The opposite is nice

nation *noun*
People from many nations take part in the Olympic Games.
OTHER WORDS YOU MIGHT USE ARE **country   race**

natural *adjective*
It's natural to go to sleep when you are tired.
ANOTHER WORD IS **normal**
The opposite is unnatural

naughty *adjective*
We punished the dog because he had been naughty.
OTHER WORDS YOU MIGHT USE ARE **bad   disobedient   mischievous   wicked**
The opposite is well-behaved

near *adjective* and *adverb*
Our house is near to the shops.
ANOTHER WORD IS **close**

nearly *adverb*
I've nearly finished.
OTHER WORDS YOU MIGHT USE ARE **almost   not quite   practically**

neat *adjective*
Jo arranged her books in a neat row.
OTHER WORDS YOU MIGHT USE ARE **orderly   smart   tidy**
The opposite is untidy

necessary *adjective*
It is necessary to water plants in dry weather.
OTHER WORDS YOU MIGHT USE ARE **essential   important   vital**
The opposite is unnecessary

a
b
c
d
e
f
g
h
i
j
k
l
m
n
o
p
q
r
s
t
u
v
w
x
y
z

neck *noun*
For other parts of the body, see **body**

need *verb*
1 We need some butter to make the sandwiches.
    OTHER VERBS YOU MIGHT USE ARE **to require** **to want**
2 The football team needs Sam to play in goal.
    OTHER VERBS ARE **to count on** **to depend on** **to rely on**

neglect *verb*
You mustn't neglect your pets when you go on holiday.
    OTHER VERBS YOU MIGHT USE ARE **to forget** **to ignore** **to overlook**
The opposite is look after

nervous *adjective*
Our dog gets nervous when she hears thunder.
    OTHER WORDS YOU MIGHT USE ARE **anxious** **edgy** **fidgety** **jumpy**
The opposite is calm

neutral *adjective*
The referee has to be neutral.
    OTHER WORDS YOU MIGHT USE ARE **impartial** **unbiased**

new *adjective*
1 new clothes.
    OTHER WORDS YOU MIGHT USE ARE **brand new** **unused**
2 new bread.
    ANOTHER WORD IS **fresh**
3 a new invention.
    OTHER WORDS ARE **modern** **recent** **up-to-date**
The opposite is old

---

nice *adjective*
    THIS WORD HAS MANY USES. HERE ARE SOME OF THE WAYS YOU CAN USE IT, AND SOME OTHER WORDS YOU COULD CHOOSE
1 nice weather.
beautiful **fine** **good** **lovely** **pleasant**
2 nice food.
delicious **enjoyable** **tasty**
3 a nice person.
friendly **kind** **likeable**
The opposite is nasty

---

noble *adjective*
1 a noble deed.
    OTHER WORDS YOU MIGHT USE ARE **brave** **gallant** **heroic** **worthy**
2 a noble palace.
    OTHER WORDS ARE **grand** **majestic** **stately**

noise *noun*
Stop that noise!
    OTHER WORDS YOU MIGHT USE ARE **din** **hubbub** (*informal*) **racket** **row** **rumpus** **uproar**
For kinds of noise, see **sound**

noisy *adjective*
The neighbours complained that our music was too noisy.
OTHER WORDS YOU MIGHT USE ARE **deafening   loud   rowdy**
The opposite is silent

nonsense *noun*
Don't talk nonsense!
ANOTHER WORD IS **rubbish**

normal *adjective*
1 It's quite normal for people to sweat in hot weather.
OTHER WORDS YOU MIGHT USE ARE **common   natural   ordinary   usual**
2 The temperature is normal for this time of year.
ANOTHER WORD IS **average**

nosy *adjective*
The kitten was being nosy and got her head stuck in a tin.
OTHER WORDS YOU MIGHT USE ARE **curious   inquisitive**

nothing *noun*
OTHER WORDS YOU MIGHT USE ARE **nought   zero**
Nothing in cricket is a **duck**.
Nothing in football is **nil**.
Nothing in tennis is **love**.

notice *noun*
We put up a notice about our play.
OTHER WORDS YOU MIGHT USE ARE **advertisement   placard   poster   sign**

notice *verb*
Jo noticed that Mum looked tired.
OTHER VERBS YOU MIGHT USE ARE **to detect   to observe   to see**

nude *adjective*
OTHER WORDS YOU MIGHT USE ARE **bare   naked   unclothed   undressed**

nuisance *noun*
That dog is a nuisance!
OTHER WORDS YOU MIGHT USE ARE **bother   pest   trouble   worry**

number *noun*
We had to add up the numbers.
ANOTHER WORD IS **figure**

nurse *noun*
For people who help us when we are ill, see **health**

nut *noun*
SOME NUTS YOU CAN EAT ARE
almond   brazil   cashew   chestnut   coconut   hazelnut   peanut   walnut

obedient *adjective*
an obedient dog.
ANOTHER WORD IS **well-behaved**
The opposite is disobedient

obey *verb*
You have to obey the rules.
PHRASES YOU MIGHT USE ARE **to abide by   to keep to**
The opposite is disobey

object *verb*
We object to bad language.
PHRASES YOU MIGHT USE ARE **to complain about   to disapprove of
to protest about**

obstinate *adjective*
The donkey was obstinate and refused to move.
OTHER WORDS YOU MIGHT USE ARE **defiant** (*informal*) **pig-headed   stubborn
unhelpful**
The opposite is helpful

obtain *verb*
For other verbs, see **get**

obvious *adjective*
Jo thought the answer to the question was obvious.
OTHER WORDS YOU MIGHT USE ARE **clear   easy to see   plain**

occasional *adjective*
We make occasional visits to the pictures.
OTHER WORDS YOU MIGHT USE ARE **infrequent   rare**
The opposite is regular

occupation *noun*
1 What's your mother's occupation?
OTHER WORDS YOU MIGHT USE ARE **business   employment   job   work**
2 Fishing is a quiet occupation.
OTHER WORDS YOU MIGHT USE ARE **activity   hobby   pastime**

occupy *verb*
1 Six people occupy our house.
OTHER VERBS YOU MIGHT USE ARE **to inhabit   to live in**
2 The soldiers occupied the town.
OTHER VERBS ARE **to capture   to conquer   to invade   to take over**

occur *verb*
A nasty accident occurred today.
OTHER VERBS YOU MIGHT USE ARE **to happen   to take place**

odd *adjective*
1 Jo can't explain her dog's odd behaviour.
OTHER WORDS YOU MIGHT USE ARE **abnormal   curious   funny   peculiar
queer   strange   uncommon   unusual   weird**
The opposite is ordinary
2 Where did this odd sock come from?
OTHER WORDS YOU MIGHT USE ARE **extra   single   spare**

offend *verb*

I offended Jo because I didn't go to her party.
> OTHER VERBS YOU MIGHT USE ARE **to annoy** **to displease** **to insult** **to upset**

The opposite is please

offensive *adjective*

1 There's an offensive smell in the kitchen.
> OTHER WORDS YOU MIGHT USE ARE **disgusting** **foul** **horrible** **nasty** **unpleasant**

2 Don't use offensive language.
> OTHER WORDS ARE **improper** **indecent** **rude**

The opposite is pleasing

offer *verb*

1 I offered some cake to Granny.
> ANOTHER VERB IS **to give**

2 Sam offered to wash up.
> ANOTHER VERB IS **to volunteer**

often *adverb*

> OTHER WORDS YOU MIGHT USE ARE **again and again** **frequently** **regularly** **repeatedly**

The opposite is seldom

old *adjective*

1 an old car.
> OTHER WORDS YOU MIGHT USE ARE **ancient** **old-fashioned**

2 an old man.
> OTHER WORDS ARE **aged** **elderly**

3 an old magazine.
> ANOTHER WORD IS **out-of-date**

4 old bread.
> ANOTHER WORD IS **stale**

5 old clothes.
> OTHER WORDS ARE **shabby** **worn-out**

6 valuable old furniture.
> ANOTHER WORD IS **antique**

The opposite is new

omit *verb*

The captain omitted Sam from the team because he was injured.
> OTHER VERBS YOU MIGHT USE ARE **to drop** **to exclude** **to leave out**

The opposite is include

open *adjective*

Leave the door open.
> OTHER WORDS YOU MIGHT USE ARE **unfastened** **unlocked**

The opposite is shut

open *verb*

Please open the door.
> OTHER VERBS YOU MIGHT USE ARE **to undo** **to unfasten** **to unlock**

The opposite is close

opening *noun*

1 Jo's tortoise crawled through an opening in the fence.
> OTHER WORDS YOU MIGHT USE ARE **break** **crack** **gap** **hole** **space**

2 Sam looks forward to the opening of the football season.
> OTHER WORDS ARE **beginning** **start**

opinion *noun*

It's my opinion that the dog stole the sausages.

> OTHER WORDS YOU MIGHT USE ARE **belief   guess   idea   thought   view**

opposite *adjective*

1 the opposite side of the road.

> ANOTHER WORD IS **facing**

2 the opposite opinion.

> OTHER WORDS YOU MIGHT USE ARE **contrary   different   opposing**

order *verb*

1 He ordered us to stand still.

> OTHER VERBS YOU MIGHT USE ARE **to command   to direct   to instruct   to tell**

2 We ordered fish and chips.

> PHRASES YOU MIGHT USE ARE **to ask for   to send for**

ordinary *adjective*

1 We spent the holiday doing ordinary things.

> OTHER WORDS YOU MIGHT USE ARE **everyday   normal   typical   unexciting   usual**

2 Most of the birds we saw on our walk were just ordinary ones.

> OTHER WORDS ARE **common   familiar   uninteresting   well-known**

3 I want an ordinary portion of chips.

> OTHER WORDS ARE **regular   standard**

The opposite is special

organize *verb*

Our teacher organized a trip to the zoo.

> ANOTHER VERB IS **to arrange**

original *adjective*

Mum said the ideas in Sam's story were very original.

> OTHER WORDS YOU MIGHT USE ARE **fresh   imaginative   new   unusual**

outing *noun*

We went on an outing to the country park.

> OTHER WORDS YOU MIGHT USE ARE **excursion   expedition   trip**

oven *noun*

For things you use to heat or cook food, see **kitchen**

overgrown *adjective*

an overgrown garden.

> OTHER WORDS YOU MIGHT USE ARE **tangled   untidy**

overturn *verb*

The boat overturned.

> ANOTHER VERB IS **to capsize**

own *verb*

Do you own a bike?

> ANOTHER VERB IS **to possess**

to own up

> ANOTHER VERB IS **to confess**

Pp

pack *verb*
We packed everything into the car.
OTHER VERBS YOU MIGHT USE ARE **to load** **to put**

packet *noun*
1 The postman brought an interesting-looking packet.
OTHER WORDS ARE **package** **parcel**
2 I bought a packet of cornflakes.
ANOTHER WORD IS **box**

page *noun*
Jo tore a page out of her notebook.
OTHER WORDS YOU MIGHT USE ARE **leaf** **sheet**

pain *noun*
OTHER WORDS YOU MIGHT USE ARE **ache** **soreness** **sting** **twinge**
VERY BAD PAIN IS **agony** **suffering** **torture**
For other words, see **hurt**

painful *adjective*
The cut on Jo's knee was painful.
OTHER WORDS YOU MIGHT USE ARE **aching** **hurting** **smarting** **sore**
stinging **throbbing**

---

paint *noun*
DIFFERENT KINDS OF PAINT ARE
emulsion **enamel** **gloss** **oil paint** **varnish** **watercolour**

---

pale *adjective*
1 His face went pale when he heard the bad news.
OTHER WORDS YOU MIGHT USE ARE **colourless** **white**
2 Mum decorated the sitting room in pale colours.
OTHER WORDS ARE **faint** **light**

pant *verb*
We were all panting for breath at the end of the race.
OTHER VERBS YOU MIGHT USE ARE **to gasp** **to puff**

---

paper *noun*
DIFFERENT KINDS OF PAPER ARE
card **newspaper** **notepaper** **tissue paper** **toilet paper**
wallpaper **wrapping paper** **writing paper**

---

parcel *noun*
The postman came with a parcel.
OTHER WORDS ARE **package** **packet**

pardon *verb*
The King pardoned the knight who had committed a crime.
OTHER VERBS YOU MIGHT USE ARE **to excuse** **to forgive** **to let off** **to reprieve**
to set free **to spare**

park *noun*
DIFFERENT KINDS OF PARK ARE   **gardens   recreation ground   safari park
wildlife park**

part *noun*
1 I don't want it all, only a part of it.
  OTHER WORDS YOU MIGHT USE ARE   **bit   fraction   piece   portion   section**
2 They sell food in a different part of the shop.
  ANOTHER WORD IS   **department**
3 Granny lives in a nice part of the country.
  OTHER WORDS ARE   **area   district   region**
4 Which part did you have in the nativity play?
  OTHER WORDS ARE   **character   role**

particular *adjective*
1 Jo has her own particular way of writing.
  OTHER WORDS YOU MIGHT USE ARE   **individual   personal**
2 Do you want a particular record, or will any music do?
  ANOTHER WORD IS   **special**
3 The dog is particular about what he eats.
  OTHER WORDS ARE   **choosy   fussy**

partner *noun*
1 You can take a partner with you when you go to the party.
  OTHER WORDS YOU MIGHT USE ARE   **companion   friend**
2 The burglar had a partner.
  ANOTHER WORD IS   **accomplice**

---

party *noun*
DIFFERENT KINDS OF PARTY ARE
**ball   barbecue   birthday party   dance   disco   picnic   social
wedding**

---

pass *verb*
1 We waited for the cars to pass before we crossed the road.
  OTHER VERBS YOU MIGHT USE ARE   **to go by   to move along**
2 Jo's knee hurt when she cut it, but the pain soon passed.
  OTHER VERBS ARE   **to disappear   to go away   to vanish**

passage *noun*
1 We went in through the front door and waited in the passage.
  OTHER WORDS ARE   **corridor   hall**
2 They say there's a secret passage under the castle.
  OTHER WORDS ARE   **tunnel   way**
3 I read my favourite passage from the book.
  OTHER WORDS YOU MIGHT USE ARE   **extract   piece   quotation**

---

path *noun*
We walked along the path.
DIFFERENT KINDS OF PATH ARE
**bridleway   cart track   footpath   pavement   towpath   track
trail**

---

patient *adjective*
Although we had to wait a long time, everyone was very patient.
> ANOTHER WORD IS **calm**

The opposite is impatient

pattern *noun*
1 I like the patterns on the wallpaper.
> OTHER WORDS YOU MIGHT USE ARE **decoration** **design** **shape**

2 Is there a pattern I can copy?
> OTHER WORDS ARE **guide** **model**

pause *noun*
There was a pause before the main film.
> OTHER WORDS YOU MIGHT USE ARE **break** **delay** **gap** **intermission** **interruption** **interval**

pause *verb*
We paused to have a drink.
> OTHER VERBS ARE **to rest** **to stop** **to wait**

---

pay *noun*
> OTHER WORDS YOU MIGHT USE ARE
> **earnings** **income** **payment**

If you are paid by the week, your pay is **wages**.
If you get a regular amount each year, your pay is a **salary**.
The pay for doing one job is a **fee**.

---

pay *verb*
1 Sam paid £10 for his bike.
> OTHER VERBS YOU MIGHT USE ARE **to give** **to hand over** **to spend**

2 When can you pay back the money you owe me?
> OTHER VERBS ARE **to refund** **to repay**

peace *noun*
1 After the war ended there was peace between the two countries.
> ANOTHER WORD YOU MIGHT USE IS **agreement**

The opposite is war

2 We sat by the lake and enjoyed the peace of the evening.
> OTHER WORDS ARE **calmness** **quiet** **stillness**

Opposites are excitement, noise

peaceful *adjective*
It seemed peaceful when the baby went to sleep.
> OTHER WORDS YOU MIGHT USE ARE **calm** **quiet** **restful**

The opposite is noisy

pebble *noun*
> ANOTHER WORD IS **stone**

A lot of pebbles are called **gravel**.
Pebbles on a beach are called **shingle**.

peculiar *adjective*

This drink has a peculiar taste.

OTHER WORDS YOU MIGHT USE ARE **funny   odd   queer   special   strange   unusual**

peel *noun*

the peel of an orange.

OTHER WORDS YOU MIGHT USE ARE **rind   skin**

---

pen *noun*

DIFFERENT KINDS OF PEN ARE

ballpoint   Biro   felt tip   fountain pen   quill pen

---

people *noun*

For other words, see **person**

perfect *adjective*

1 It's a perfect day for a picnic.

OTHER WORDS YOU MIGHT USE ARE **excellent   ideal**

2 Jo's new coat was a perfect fit.

ANOTHER WORD IS **exact**

perform *verb*

Everyone in the class performed in the concert.

OTHER VERBS YOU MIGHT USE ARE **to appear   to take part**

DIFFERENT WAYS TO PERFORM ARE **to act   to dance   to play an instrument   to sing**

For other words, see **entertainment**

perfume *noun*

Mum used some nice perfume when she went to the party.

ANOTHER WORD IS **scent**

For other words, see **smell**

period *noun*

For other words, see **time**

perish *verb*

1 Many birds perish in cold weather.

ANOTHER VERB IS **to die**

2 These pears will perish if you don't use them quickly.

OTHER VERBS YOU MIGHT USE ARE **to decay   to go bad   to rot**

permission *noun*

We had the teacher's permission to go home.

OTHER WORDS YOU MIGHT USE ARE **approval   consent**

permit *noun*

You need a permit to go fishing.

OTHER WORDS YOU MIGHT USE ARE **licence   pass   ticket**

permit *verb*

They don't permit smoking on the bus.

OTHER VERBS YOU MIGHT USE ARE **to agree to   to allow   to approve of**

persist *verb*

If the pain persists you must go to the doctor.

OTHER VERBS YOU MIGHT USE ARE **to carry on   to continue**

person noun

OTHER WORDS YOU MIGHT USE ARE

character **human being** **individual** **mortal**

a fully grown person

adult **grown-up**

a young person

baby **boy** **child** **girl** **infant** **toddler**

a person who is not a child but is not yet grown up

adolescent **juvenile** **teenager**

a woman who is married

wife

an unmarried woman

spinster

a woman whose husband has died

widow

the man who plays a woman in a pantomime

dame

a polite word for a woman

lady

a female child

girl

Female members of a family

aunt **daughter** **grandmother** **mother** **niece** **stepdaughter** **stepmother**

a man who is married

husband

a man who is not married

bachelor

a man whose wife has died

widower

a polite word for a man

gentleman

informal words for a man

bloke **chap** **fellow**

a young man

youth

a male child

boy or **lad**

Male members of a family

father **grandfather** **nephew** **son** **stepfather** **stepson** **uncle**

personal adjective

1 Jo keeps her personal belongings in a drawer in her bedroom.

ANOTHER WORD IS **private**

2 Don't make personal remarks.

OTHER WORDS ARE **cheeky** **impertinent**

persuade verb

We tried to persuade the cat to come down from the tree.

OTHER VERBS YOU MIGHT USE ARE **to coax** **to tempt** **to urge**

pester verb

Don't pester me when I'm busy!

OTHER VERBS YOU MIGHT USE ARE **to annoy** **to bother** **to nag** **to torment** **to trouble** **to worry**

pet *noun*

ANIMALS OFTEN KEPT AS PETS ARE

**budgerigar   canary   cat   dog   ferret   gerbil   goldfish
guinea pig   hamster   mouse   parrot   pigeon   rabbit   rat
tortoise**

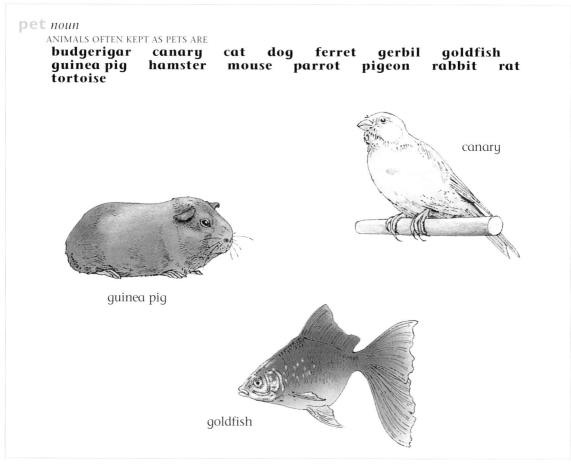

canary

guinea pig

goldfish

phone *verb*

I phoned Granny to ask how she was.

OTHER VERBS YOU MIGHT USE ARE   **to call   to ring   to telephone**

photo, **photograph** *nouns*

DIFFERENT KINDS OF PHOTOGRAPH ARE

enlargement   negative   print   slide or **transparency   snapshot**
For other words, see **camera**

pick *verb*

1 You can pick any flavour of ice cream.

OTHER VERBS YOU MIGHT USE ARE   **to choose   to decide on   to select**

2 We picked Sam to be captain.

OTHER VERBS YOU MIGHT USE ARE   **to elect   to vote for**

3 I picked a lot of blackberries.

OTHER VERBS ARE   **to collect   to gather   to harvest**

picture noun

DIFFERENT KINDS OF PICTURE ARE

cartoon   **collage**   **drawing**   **mosaic**   **mural**   **painting**   **photograph**   **print**   **sketch**   **slide** or **transparency**

A picture of countryside is a **landscape**.
A picture of a person is a **portrait**.
A picture in a book is an **illustration**.

piece noun

1 Sam had a big piece of cake.

OTHER WORDS YOU MIGHT USE ARE   **chunk**   **helping**   **hunk**   **lump**   **portion**   **share**   **slab**   **slice**

2 Mum told Jo to pick up every single piece of the broken cup.

OTHER WORDS ARE   **bit**   **chip**   **fragment**

3 I need a piece of cloth to clean my bike.

OTHER WORDS YOU MIGHT USE ARE   **rag**   **scrap**

pierce verb

The needle pierced my skin.

OTHER VERBS YOU MIGHT USE ARE   **to go through**   **to penetrate**   **to prick**   **to puncture**

pig noun

A male pig is a **boar**.
A female pig is a **sow**.
A baby pig is a **piglet**.

pile noun

Who dumped that pile of rubbish in the yard?

OTHER WORDS YOU MIGHT USE ARE   **heap**   **mound**   **stack**

pillar noun

The roof was held up on pillars.

OTHER WORDS YOU MIGHT USE ARE   **column**   **post**   **support**

pipe noun

a pipe to carry water.

OTHER WORDS YOU MIGHT USE ARE   **hose**   **tube**

pit noun

A pit where miners dig for coal is a **mine** or **coal mine**.
For other words, see **hole**

pity noun

The soldiers showed no pity for their enemies.

OTHER WORDS YOU MIGHT USE ARE   **kindness**   **mercy**   **sympathy**

place noun

1 The map showed the place where the treasure was hidden.

OTHER WORDS YOU MIGHT USE ARE   **location**   **point**   **position**   **site**   **situation**   **spot**

2 This is a nice place to live.

OTHER WORDS ARE   **area**   **district**   **neighbourhood**   **region**

3 Save me a place next to you.

OTHER WORDS ARE   **chair**   **seat**

place *verb*

1 Place your rubbish in the bin.
OTHER VERBS YOU MIGHT USE ARE **to deposit   to leave   to put**

2 Place your work on the table.
OTHER VERBS ARE **to arrange   to lay   to set out**

3 He placed the ladder against the wall.
OTHER VERBS ARE **to lean   to rest   to stand**

plain *adjective*

1 She was wearing a plain dress.
OTHER WORDS YOU MIGHT USE ARE **ordinary   simple**
The opposite is decorated

2 She gave a plain signal.
OTHER WORDS ARE **clear   definite**
The opposite is confusing

plan *noun*

1 Sam has a plan for making a den in the garden.
OTHER WORDS YOU MIGHT USE ARE **idea   project   scheme**

2 We drew a plan of the town to show where we all live.
OTHER WORDS ARE **diagram   map**

plan *verb*

1 We plan to go to the fair on Saturday.
OTHER VERBS YOU MIGHT USE ARE **to aim   to intend**

2 It took weeks to plan our trip.
OTHER VERBS ARE **to arrange   to organize   to prepare for**

plane *noun*
For other words, see **aircraft**

---

planet *noun*
THE PLANETS IN THE SOLAR SYSTEM ARE
**Earth   Jupiter   Mars   Mercury   Neptune   Pluto   Saturn
Uranus   Venus**

---

plant *noun*, see opposite page

play *verb*

1 I play with my friends at the weekend.
OTHER VERBS YOU MIGHT USE ARE **to amuse yourself   to have fun**

2 Jo played a tune on the piano.
ANOTHER VERB IS **to perform**

playful *adjective*
a playful puppy.
OTHER WORDS YOU MIGHT USE ARE **frisky   lively**

plant *noun*

DIFFERENT KINDS OF PLANT ARE

**bulb   cactus   climbing plant   fern   flower   fungus   grass
moss   shrub   tree   water plant   weed**

PLANTS YOU CAN EAT ARE

cereals   herbs   vegetables
You can eat some kinds of **fungus**.
For other words, see **flower, tree, vegetable**

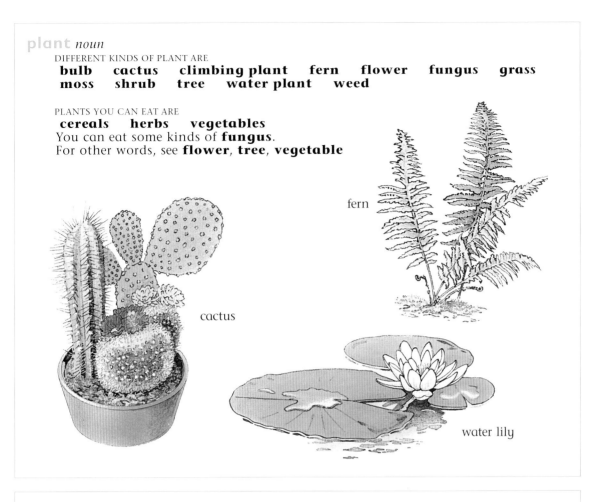

fern

cactus

water lily

pleasant *adjective*

THIS WORD HAS MANY USES. HERE ARE SOME OF THE WAYS YOU CAN USE IT, AND SOME OTHER WORDS YOU COULD CHOOSE

1 a pleasant day out.
enjoyable   nice   pleasing
2 a pleasant person
friendly   kind   likeable
3 pleasant weather.
fine   mild   warm
4 pleasant countryside.
attractive   peaceful   pretty
The opposite is unpleasant

pleased *adjective*

Was Mum pleased when you gave her the present?
OTHER WORDS YOU MIGHT USE ARE **contented   delighted   grateful   satisfied
thankful**
For other words, see **happy**
The opposite is angry

pleasure *noun*

Jo's dog whines with pleasure when you tickle his neck.
OTHER WORDS YOU MIGHT USE ARE **contentment   delight   enjoyment
happiness   satisfaction**

plot *verb*
The robbers plotted to steal some jewels.
OTHER VERBS YOU MIGHT USE ARE **to conspire**   **to plan**   **to scheme**

plunge *verb*
She plunged into the water.
OTHER VERBS YOU MIGHT USE ARE **to dive**   **to drop**   **to jump**   **to leap**

poem *noun*
OTHER WORDS YOU MIGHT USE ARE **poetry**   **rhyme**   **verse**

point *noun*
1 Don't hurt yourself on the sharp point.
OTHER WORDS YOU MIGHT USE ARE **spike**   **tip**
2 We marked the exact point on the map.
OTHER WORDS ARE **location**   **place**   **position**   **spot**

point *verb*
1 The signpost points the way you have to go.
OTHER VERBS YOU MIGHT USE ARE **to indicate**   **to show**
2 Don't point that arrow at me!
OTHER VERBS ARE **to aim**   **to direct**

pointed *adjective*
a pointed stick.
ANOTHER WORD IS **sharp**
The opposite is blunt

poisonous *adjective*
Some toadstools are poisonous.
OTHER WORDS YOU MIGHT USE ARE **deadly**   **harmful**

poke *verb*
He poked me in the back with a stick.
OTHER VERBS YOU MIGHT USE ARE **to dig**   **to jab**   **to prod**

pole *noun*
We pinned our flag to a pole.
OTHER WORDS YOU MIGHT USE ARE **post**   **rod**   **stick**

---

police *noun*
DIFFERENT NAMES FOR PEOPLE WHO WORK IN THE POLICE ARE
constable   **detective**   **inspector**   **officer**   **policeman**
policewoman   **sergeant**

---

polish *verb*
Jo helped to polish the car.
ANOTHER VERB IS **to shine**
For ways to clean things, see **clean**

polite *adjective*
a polite boy.
OTHER WORDS YOU MIGHT USE ARE **considerate**   **respectful**   **well-mannered**
The opposite is rude

> **pool** *noun*
> A large pool is a **pond** or **lake**.
> A small pool is a **puddle**.
> A pool made to swim in is a **swimming pool**.

poor *adjective*
1 The poor family didn't have enough to eat.
OTHER WORDS YOU MIGHT USE ARE **hard up   needy   penniless
   poverty-stricken**
The opposite is rich
2 Our teacher was angry because we had done poor work.
For other words, see **bad**

poorly *adjective*
Jo stayed at home because she was poorly.
OTHER WORDS YOU MIGHT USE ARE **ill   sick   unwell**
The opposite is healthy

popular *adjective*
We sang some popular carols at our concert.
OTHER WORDS YOU MIGHT USE ARE **famous   favourite   well-known**

port *noun*
The ship entered port.
For other words, see **harbour**

portion *noun*
Can I have another portion of pie?
OTHER WORDS YOU MIGHT USE ARE **helping   piece   share   slice**

positive *adjective*
Are you positive you saw a ghost?
OTHER WORDS YOU MIGHT USE ARE **certain   convinced   definite   sure**

possess *verb*
Sam only possesses one pair of jeans.
OTHER VERBS YOU MIGHT USE ARE **to have   to own**

possessions *noun*
Jo keeps her personal possessions in her bedroom.
OTHER WORDS YOU MIGHT USE ARE **belongings   property**

possible *adjective*
The opposite is impossible

post *noun*
1 Dad put up some posts to support the fence.
OTHER WORDS YOU MIGHT USE ARE **column   pillar   pole   prop   support**
2 The postman brought the post.
ANOTHER WORD IS **mail**
THINGS YOU GET IN THE MAIL ARE **letter   packet   parcel   postcard**

poster *noun*
We put up a poster to tell people about our concert.
OTHER WORDS YOU MIGHT USE ARE **advertisement   notice   placard   sign**

a
b
c
d
e
f
g
h
i
j
k
l
m
n
o
p
q
r
s
t
u
v
w
x
y
z

postpone *verb*
They postponed sports day because it was raining.
A PHRASE IS **to put off**

pottery *noun*
OTHER WORDS YOU MIGHT USE ARE **crockery   earthenware**
For other words, see **china**

---

poultry *noun*
DIFFERENT KINDS OF POULTRY ARE
chicken   cockerel   duck   goose   hen   rooster   turkey

---

pour *verb*
1 Water poured through the hole.
OTHER VERBS YOU MIGHT USE ARE **to flow   to gush   to run   to stream**
2 I poured the cold tea into the sink.
OTHER VERBS ARE **to empty   to tip**

power *noun*
1 The police have the power to arrest criminals.
OTHER WORDS YOU MIGHT USE ARE **ability   authority   right**
2 Those big waves have the power to knock you over.
OTHER WORDS ARE **energy   force   might   strength**

powerful *adjective*
a powerful giant.
OTHER WORDS YOU MIGHT USE ARE **mighty   strong**
The opposite is weak

practical *adjective*
a practical tool.
OTHER WORDS YOU MIGHT USE ARE **efficient   handy   useful**
The opposite is useless

practically *adverb*
I've practically finished.
OTHER WORDS YOU MIGHT USE ARE **almost   nearly**

---

practise *verb*
If you practise for a concert, you **rehearse**.
If you practise at a sport, you **train** for it.
If you practise for a test, you **revise**.

---

praise *verb*
Our teacher praised us for working hard today.
OTHER VERBS YOU MIGHT USE ARE **to compliment   to congratulate**
The opposite is scold

precious *adjective*
precious jewels.
OTHER WORDS YOU MIGHT USE ARE **costly   dear   expensive   priceless
valuable**
The opposite is worthless

precise *adjective*
What is the precise time?
OTHER WORDS YOU MIGHT USE ARE **accurate   correct   exact   right**

prepare *verb*
Jo asked Sam to help her prepare for her party.
OTHER VERBS YOU MIGHT USE ARE **to get ready   to make arrangements   to organize   to plan**

present *noun*
Jo got a present from Grandad.
ANOTHER WORD IS **gift**

present *verb*
1 The head presented the prizes on sports day.
OTHER VERBS YOU MIGHT USE ARE **to award   to give   to hand over**
2 Sam presented the songs to the audience.
ANOTHER VERB IS **to introduce**
3 We presented a nativity play at Christmas.
OTHER VERBS ARE **to act   to perform   to put on**

preserve *verb*
1 You can preserve food in a freezer.
OTHER VERBS YOU MIGHT USE ARE **to keep   to save**
2 The museum put the old book in a glass case to preserve it.
OTHER VERBS ARE **to look after   to protect**

press *verb*
1 Press the bell.
ANOTHER VERB IS **to push**
2 Sam pressed his best trousers.
OTHER VERBS YOU MIGHT USE ARE **to flatten   to iron   to smooth**

---

pretend *verb*
There are different ways of pretending.
You can **act** or **play** a part in a play.
You can **disguise** yourself as someone else.
You can **imitate** or **impersonate** someone.
You can **deceive** or **trick** someone.

---

pretty *adjective*
a pretty dress.
OTHER WORDS YOU MIGHT USE ARE **attractive   beautiful   lovely**
The opposite is ugly

prevent *verb*
The snow prevented us from going to Granny's.
OTHER VERBS YOU MIGHT USE ARE **to hinder   to stop**

previously *adverb*
OTHER WORDS YOU MIGHT USE ARE **before   earlier**

price *noun*
Before you buy anything, ask what the price is.
OTHER WORDS YOU MIGHT USE ARE **charge   cost   fee   payment**
The price you pay to ride in a bus or train is the **fare**.

a
b
c
d
e
f
g
h
i
j
k
l
m
n
o
p
q
r
s
t
u
v
w
x
y
z

159

prick *verb*

The doctor pricked my thumb with a needle.

OTHER VERBS YOU MIGHT USE ARE **to pierce** **to puncture**

principal *adjective*

This map only shows the principal towns.

OTHER WORDS YOU MIGHT USE ARE **chief** **important** **main**

principles *noun*

Sam taught Jo the principles of chess.

OTHER WORDS YOU MIGHT USE ARE **laws** **rules** **theory**

---

prison *noun*

ANOTHER WORD IS

gaol or **jail**

A small room where someone can be locked up is a **cell**.

A prison in a castle is a **dungeon**.

---

prisoner *noun*

ANOTHER WORD IS

captive

A person you keep prisoner until you get what you want is a **hostage**.

---

private *adjective*

1 Jo keeps her private things in a drawer in her bedroom.

OTHER WORDS YOU MIGHT USE ARE **personal** **secret**

2 We found a private spot for a picnic.

OTHER WORDS ARE **hidden** **quiet** **secluded**

The opposite is **public**

problem *noun*

1 If you have a problem, tell the teacher.

OTHER WORDS YOU MIGHT USE ARE **difficulty** **worry**

2 The detective had a hard problem to solve.

OTHER WORDS ARE **mystery** **puzzle** **question** **riddle**

procession *noun*

There was a big procession through the middle of town.

OTHER WORDS YOU MIGHT USE ARE **march** **parade**

prod *verb*

Someone prodded me in the back.

OTHER VERBS YOU MIGHT USE ARE **to dig** **to jab** **to poke** **to push**

produce *verb*

1 The factory down the road produces television sets.

OTHER VERBS YOU MIGHT USE ARE **to make** **to manufacture**

2 Grandad's garden produces lots of vegetables.

OTHER VERBS ARE **to grow** **to yield**

3 We produce a magazine every term.

OTHER VERBS ARE **to issue** **to publish**

4 The cat produced four kittens.

OTHER VERBS ARE **to bear** **to give birth to**

5 The conjuror produced a rabbit from a hat.

OTHER VERBS YOU MIGHT USE ARE **to bring out** **to present**

160

progress *noun*
  to make progress
    OTHER WORDS YOU MIGHT USE ARE **advance**   **move**   **forward**   **proceed**

prohibited *adjective*
  Smoking is prohibited on the bus.
    OTHER WORDS YOU MIGHT USE ARE **banned**   **forbidden**   **illegal**
  The opposite is allowed

promise *verb*
  You promised to come to my party.
    OTHER VERBS YOU MIGHT USE ARE **to agree**   **to give your word**   **to guarantee**
      to swear   **to vow**

promptly *adverb*
  1 Mum replied promptly to Granny's letter.
    OTHER WORDS YOU MIGHT USE ARE **immediately**   **quickly**
  2 The train arrived promptly.
    OTHER WORDS ARE **on time**   **punctually**

prop *verb*
  Jo propped her bike against the wall.
    OTHER VERBS YOU MIGHT USE ARE **to lean**   **to rest**   **to stand**   **to support**

proper *adjective*
  1 Put the library books back in their proper places.
    OTHER WORDS YOU MIGHT USE ARE **appropriate**   **correct**   **right**   **suitable**
      usual
  The opposite is wrong
  2 I think it would be proper for you to apologize.
    OTHER WORDS ARE **decent**   **polite**   **respectable**
  The opposite is rude

protect *verb*
  1 The mother bird tried to protect her babies.
    OTHER VERBS YOU MIGHT USE ARE **to defend**   **to guard**   **to keep safe**
      to look after
  2 The hedge protected us from the wind.
    OTHER VERBS ARE **to screen**   **to shield**

protest *verb*
  We protested when they put up the bus fares.
    OTHER VERBS YOU MIGHT USE ARE **to complain**   **to object**

proud *adjective*
  1 He was too proud to admit that he was wrong.
    OTHER WORDS YOU MIGHT USE ARE **boastful**   (*informal*) **cocky**   **conceited**
      (*informal*) **stuck up**   **vain**
  The opposite is modest
  2 Mum was proud when Jo won a prize.
    OTHER WORDS ARE **happy**   **pleased**

prove *verb*
  They proved that he was guilty.
    OTHER VERBS YOU MIGHT USE ARE **to demonstrate**   **to show**

provide *verb*
  Our teacher provided the paper for us to draw on.
    OTHER VERBS YOU MIGHT USE ARE **to give**   **to supply**

a
b
c
d
e
f
g
h
i
j
k
l
m
n
o
p
q
r
s
t
u
v
w
x
y
z

161

provoke *verb*
If you provoke the dog, he may bite you.
OTHER VERBS YOU MIGHT USE ARE **to anger**   **to annoy**   **to tease**   **to torment**
to upset   **to worry**

pry *verb*
Don't pry in my affairs!
OTHER WORDS YOU MIGHT USE ARE **to interfere**   (*informal*) **to poke your nose into**

publish *verb*
We publish a magazine every term.
OTHER VERBS YOU MIGHT USE ARE **to bring out**   **to issue**   **to produce**

pudding *noun*
Sam ate so much first course that he didn't have room for pudding.
OTHER WORDS YOU MIGHT USE ARE   (*informal*) **afters**   **dessert**   **sweet**

pull *verb*
1 We pulled the heavy box across the floor.
OTHER VERBS YOU MIGHT USE ARE **to drag**   **to haul**   **to tug**
2 The car was pulling a caravan.
ANOTHER VERB IS **to tow**
3 The horse was pulling a cart.
ANOTHER VERB IS **to draw**

punch *verb*
For other ways to hit, see **hit**

punctual *adjective*
The train was punctual.
OTHER WORDS YOU MIGHT USE ARE **on time**   **prompt**
The opposite is late

punctuation *noun*
DIFFERENT PUNCTUATION MARKS ARE
apostrophe '
brackets ( )
colon :
comma ,
dash –
exclamation mark !
full stop .
hyphen -
question mark ?
semi-colon ;
speech marks " "

punishment *noun*
DIFFERENT KINDS OF PUNISHMENT ARE
a beating   **detention**   **execution**   **a fine**   **gaol** (or **jail**) or **prison**
an imposition   **a penalty**

pupil *noun*
OTHER WORDS YOU MIGHT USE ARE **schoolboy**   **schoolgirl**   **student**

162

pure *adjective*
pure water.
> OTHER WORDS YOU MIGHT USE ARE **clean   clear   natural**
The opposite is **dirty**

purpose *noun*
He must have a particular purpose to go out in that storm.
> OTHER WORDS YOU MIGHT USE ARE **aim   intention   object   plan   reason**

---

purse *noun*
Jo put her money in a purse.
> OTHER THINGS YOU KEEP MONEY IN ARE
> **handbag   money box   piggy bank   pocket   wallet**

---

pursue *verb*
The police pursued the robbers across the town.
> OTHER VERBS YOU MIGHT USE ARE **to chase   to follow   to hunt**

push *verb*
1 The door will open if you push harder.
> OTHER VERBS YOU MIGHT USE ARE **to press   to shove**
2 I pushed my clothes into a drawer.
> OTHER VERBS ARE **to crush   to force   to squeeze**

put *verb*
1 Put your dirty cups in the sink.
> OTHER VERBS YOU MIGHT USE ARE **to deposit   to leave   to pile   to place   to stack**
2 We put our pictures where everyone could see them.
> OTHER VERBS ARE **to arrange   to lay   to position   to set out**
to put something off
> ANOTHER VERB IS **to postpone**
to put up with something
> ANOTHER VERB IS **to endure**

puzzle *noun*
Can you solve this puzzle?
> OTHER WORDS YOU MIGHT USE ARE **mystery   problem   question   riddle**

puzzle *verb*
The riddle puzzled me.
> OTHER VERBS YOU MIGHT USE ARE **to bewilder   to confuse   to mystify   to perplex**

Qq

quaint *adjective*
a quaint thatched cottage.
> OTHER WORDS YOU MIGHT USE ARE **old-fashioned   picturesque**

quake *verb*

Jack quaked with fear when he saw the giant.

OTHER VERBS YOU MIGHT USE ARE **to quiver**   **to shake**   **to shudder**   **to tremble**

quality *noun*

Our butcher only sells meat of the best quality.

OTHER WORDS YOU MIGHT USE ARE **class**   **grade**   **standard**   **value**

quantity *noun*

In hot weather the shop sells a large quantity of ice cream.

OTHER WORDS YOU MIGHT USE ARE **amount**   **volume**

quarrel *verb*

Jo and Sam sometimes quarrel, but they soon make it up.

OTHER VERBS YOU MIGHT USE ARE **to argue**   **to disagree**   **to fall out**   **to fight**
to squabble

queer *adjective*

1 queer shapes. a queer smell.

OTHER WORDS YOU MIGHT USE ARE   (*informal*) **funny**   **odd**   **peculiar**   **strange**
unusual

2 I feel rather queer.
For other words, see **ill**

queue *noun*

A queue of cars waited at the level crossing.

OTHER WORDS YOU MIGHT USE ARE **line**   **row**

quick *adjective*

1 a quick journey.

OTHER WORDS YOU MIGHT USE ARE **fast**   **rapid**   **speedy**   **swift**

2 a quick dance.

ANOTHER WORD IS **lively**

3 a quick reply.

OTHER WORDS ARE **instant**   **prompt**

The opposite is slow

4 The bus came to a quick halt.

OTHER WORDS ARE **hasty**   **sudden**

quiet *adjective*

1 Our teacher told us to be quiet.

ANOTHER WORD IS **silent**

2 I listened to some quiet music.

OTHER WORDS ARE **low**   **soft**

The opposite is noisy

quite *adverb*

1 I'm not quite sure.

OTHER WORDS YOU MIGHT USE ARE **absolutely**   **completely**   **entirely**   **totally**

2 I'm quite cold.

OTHER WORDS ARE **fairly**   **moderately**   (*informal*) **pretty**   **rather**

quiver *verb*

For other verbs, see **quake**

Rr

radio *noun*

An old-fashioned word is **wireless**.

SOME PROGRAMMES YOU HEAR ON THE RADIO ARE

**chat shows   interviews   music   news   phone-in programmes
plays   sport   stories   talks   weather forecasts**

rail *noun*

There was a rail to stop people falling into the water.

OTHER WORDS YOU MIGHT USE ARE   **bar   railing**

railway *noun*

KINDS OF RAILWAY ARE

**branch line   main line   metro   mountain railway
narrow gauge railway   tramline   underground**

KINDS OF TRAIN ARE

diesel   electric train   express   freight train or **goods train
steam train   tram**

PARTS OF A TRAIN ARE

**buffet car   carriage   coach   locomotive   sleeping car
steam engine   wagon**

PARTS OF A RAILWAY LINE MIGHT BE

electric rail   overhead wires   points   sleepers   rails

ALONG THE RAILWAY YOU MIGHT SEE

**cutting   embankment   junction   level crossing   sidings   signals
signal box   station   tunnel**

THINGS YOU SEE AT A STATION ARE

booking office or **ticket office   buffet   platform   timetable
waiting room**

PEOPLE WHO WORK ON THE RAILWAY ARE

**booking clerk   conductor   driver   guard   porter   signalman
ticket collector**

rain *noun*

Very heavy rain is a **downpour**.
A short period of rain is a **shower**.
Rain coming down in very small drops is **drizzle**.
For other words, see **weather**

raise *verb*

1 A crane raised the car out of the ditch.
OTHER VERBS YOU MIGHT USE ARE   **to hoist   to lift   to pick up**
2 We raised money for charity.
OTHER VERBS ARE   **to collect   to get   to make**

rapid *adjective*

OTHER WORDS YOU MIGHT USE ARE   **fast   quick   speedy   swift**
The opposite is slow

rare *adjective*

Pandas are rare animals.

OTHER WORDS YOU MIGHT USE ARE **scarce   uncommon**

The opposite is common

rather *adverb*

I was rather ill yesterday.

OTHER WORDS YOU MIGHT USE ARE **fairly   moderately   (informal) pretty   quite**

ravenous *adjective*

We were so ravenous that we ate everything!

OTHER WORDS YOU MIGHT USE ARE **famished   hungry   starving**

ray *noun*

A ray of light shone through the crack in the door.

OTHER WORDS YOU MIGHT USE ARE **beam   shaft**

reach *verb*

1 I will hold you if you reach out your hand.

ANOTHER VERB IS **to stretch**

2 We can have something to eat when we reach home.

OTHER VERBS YOU MIGHT USE ARE **to arrive at   to get to**

ready *adjective*

1 Are you ready to go?

OTHER WORDS YOU MIGHT USE ARE **prepared   willing**

2 Have you got your money ready?

OTHER WORDS ARE **available   handy**

real *adjective*

1 Are those real diamonds?

ANOTHER WORD IS **genuine**

The opposite is artificial

2 You can trust Sam: he's a real friend.

ANOTHER WORD IS **true**

The opposite is false

realistic *adjective*

The acting was very realistic.

OTHER WORDS YOU MIGHT USE ARE **lifelike   natural**

realize *verb*

I suddenly realized that everyone was waiting for me.

OTHER VERBS YOU MIGHT USE ARE **to know   to see   to sense   to understand**

rear *noun*

He crashed into the rear of a bus.

OTHER WORDS YOU MIGHT USE ARE **back   end**

The opposite is front

rear *verb*

Our cat reared four kittens.

OTHER VERBS YOU MIGHT USE ARE **to bring up   to care for   to look after**

reason *noun*

Was there any reason for Sam's funny behaviour?

OTHER WORDS YOU MIGHT USE ARE **cause   excuse   explanation**

The reason why someone commits a crime is the **motive**.

reasonable *adjective*

1 Dad paid a reasonable price for his car.
OTHER WORDS YOU MIGHT USE ARE **fair   moderate**
2 You can't have a reasonable argument with a tiny baby.
OTHER WORDS ARE **intelligent   logical   sensible**

rebel *verb*

The soldiers rebelled because they were so hungry.
OTHER VERBS YOU MIGHT USE ARE **to disobey   to revolt**
If sailors rebel on a ship, the word is **mutiny**.

receive *verb*

1 I received ten birthday cards.
ANOTHER VERB IS **to get**
2 He received £2 for doing odd jobs.
ANOTHER VERB IS **to earn**

recent *adjective*

Have you got any recent CDs?
OTHER WORDS YOU MIGHT USE ARE **new   up-to-date**
The opposite is old

reckless *adjective*

Reckless drivers can kill people.
OTHER WORDS YOU MIGHT USE ARE **careless   thoughtless**
The opposite is careful

reckon *verb*

1 Jo reckoned how much the shopping cost.
OTHER VERBS YOU MIGHT USE ARE **to add up   to calculate   to count
to work out**
2 I reckon our side will win.
OTHER VERBS ARE **to believe   to feel sure   to think**

recognize *verb*

Would you recognize that man if you saw him again?
OTHER VERBS YOU MIGHT USE ARE **to identify   to know   to remember**

recommend *verb*

Mum recommends the restaurant down the road.
OTHER VERBS YOU MIGHT USE ARE **to approve of   to praise   to speak well of**

---

record *noun*

1 We kept a record of the birds we saw on holiday.
OTHER WORDS YOU MIGHT USE ARE
account   description   diary   log
2 Dad has lots of old pop records.
KINDS OF GRAMOPHONE RECORD ARE
album   LP   single
OTHER KINDS OF RECORDING ARE
cassette   compact disc or **CD   tape   video**

---

recover *verb*

1 Mum recovered slowly after her operation.
OTHER VERBS YOU MIGHT USE ARE **to get better   to heal   to improve**
2 Did you recover your lost watch?
OTHER VERBS ARE **to find   to get back   to retrieve   to trace**

reduce *verb*
She reduced speed when she saw the police car.
OTHER VERBS YOU MIGHT USE ARE **to cut   to decrease   to lessen**

refer *verb*
1 Did Dad refer to the broken window?
OTHER VERBS YOU MIGHT USE ARE **to comment on   to mention**
2 I referred to the dictionary to find the spelling.
OTHER VERBS ARE **to consult   to look up   to turn to**

refresh *verb*
The drink refreshed us.
OTHER VERBS YOU MIGHT USE ARE **to cool   to quench the thirst   to revive**

refuse *noun*
Put the refuse in the bin.
OTHER WORDS YOU MIGHT USE ARE **junk   rubbish   waste**

refuse *verb*
Why did Jo refuse to go to her friend's party?
ANOTHER VERB IS **to decline**
The opposite is agree

regard *verb*
We regard Sam as the best swimmer in the school.
OTHER VERBS YOU MIGHT USE ARE **to consider   to think of**

region *noun*
The South Pole is a cold region.
OTHER WORDS YOU MIGHT USE ARE **area   district   place   zone**

regret *verb*
Jo regretted saying nasty things about her friend.
OTHER VERBS YOU MIGHT USE ARE **to be sad about   to be sorry for   to repent**

regular *adjective*
1 Did the postman come at the regular time today?
OTHER WORDS YOU MIGHT USE ARE **customary   normal   usual**
2 The drummer kept a regular rhythm.
OTHER WORDS ARE **even   steady**

rehearse *verb*
We rehearsed for the concert all afternoon.
OTHER VERBS YOU MIGHT USE ARE **to practise   to prepare**

reject *verb*
Jo rejected the invitation to her friend's party.
OTHER VERBS YOU MIGHT USE ARE **to refuse   to turn down**
The opposite is accept

rejoice *verb*
The crowd rejoiced when their team won the cup.
OTHER VERBS YOU MIGHT USE ARE **to be happy   to celebrate**

relation *noun*
For other words, see **family**

relax *verb*
I like to relax in a hot bath.
OTHER VERBS YOU MIGHT USE ARE **to rest   to unwind**

release *verb*
They released the animals from the cage.
OTHER VERBS YOU MIGHT USE ARE **to free**   **to let loose**   **to let out**   **to liberate**
to set free

reliable *adjective*
You can trust Sam: he's a reliable friend.
OTHER WORDS YOU MIGHT USE ARE **faithful**   **loyal**   **trustworthy**

relief *noun*
The pills gave me some relief from my headache.
OTHER WORDS YOU MIGHT USE ARE **comfort**   **ease**   **help**

relieved *adjective*
We were relieved to hear that Jo's accident was not serious.
OTHER WORDS YOU MIGHT USE ARE **glad**   **happy**   **thankful**

---

religion *noun*
OTHER WORDS YOU MIGHT USE ARE
belief   **creed**   **faith**

SOME RELIGIONS ARE
Buddhism   **Christianity**   **Hinduism**   **Judaism**   **Islam**   **Sikhism**

PEOPLE WHO FOLLOW A RELIGION ARE
Buddhist   **Christian**   **Hindu**   **Jewish**   **Muslim**   **Sikh**

KINDS OF RELIGIOUS SERVICE ARE
baptism or **christening**   **cremation**   **funeral**   **Holy Communion**
mass   **prayers**   **wedding**   **worship**

PARTS OF A MEETING FOR WORSHIP MIGHT BE
anthem   **blessing**   **collection** or **offering**   **confession**   **devotions**
hymn   **meditation**   **prayers**   **psalm**   **reading from scripture**
sermon

PLACES WHERE PEOPLE WORSHIP ARE
cathedral   **chapel**   **church**   **mosque**   **pagoda**   **shrine**
synagogue   **temple**

RELIGIOUS LEADERS AND TEACHERS ARE
archbishop   **ayatollah**   **bishop**   **cardinal**   **chaplain**   **clergyman**
curate   **druid**   **guru**   **imam**   **lama**   **minister**   **missionary**
parson   **pope**   **priest**   **prophet**   **rabbi**   **rector**   **vicar**

ADJECTIVES YOU MIGHT USE TO DESCRIBE RELIGIOUS THINGS ARE
blessed   **consecrated**   **divine**   **holy**   **sacred**

ADJECTIVES YOU MIGHT USE TO DESCRIBE RELIGIOUS PEOPLE ARE
devout   **pious**

A person who thinks there is no God is an **atheist**.
A person who says you can't know whether there is a God or not is an **agnostic**.

---

reluctant *adjective*
I was reluctant to walk home because it was raining.
OTHER WORDS YOU MIGHT USE ARE **hesitant**   **unwilling**
The opposite is enthusiastic

rely *verb*

You can rely on Jo to do her best.

OTHER VERBS YOU MIGHT USE ARE *(informal)* **to bank on** **to count on** **to depend on** **to trust**

remain *verb*

He told me to remain where I was.

OTHER VERBS YOU MIGHT USE ARE **to stay** **to stop**

remains *noun*

1 We explored the remains of the castle.

ANOTHER WORD IS **ruins**

2 What shall we do with the remains of this stew?

OTHER WORDS ARE *(informal)* **leftovers** **remainder** **rest**

3 His remains were buried near the church.

OTHER WORDS ARE **body** **corpse**

remark *verb*

I remarked that it was a nice day.

OTHER VERBS YOU MIGHT USE ARE **to comment** **to mention** **to say**

remarkable *adjective*

Our team had a remarkable victory.

OTHER WORDS YOU MIGHT USE ARE **amazing** **extraordinary** **special** **surprising** **unusual**

remedy *noun*

Do you know a remedy for a cold?

OTHER WORDS YOU MIGHT USE ARE **cure** **medicine** **treatment**

remember *verb*

Do you remember our holiday last year?

OTHER WORDS YOU MIGHT USE ARE **to recall** **to recollect**

The opposite is **forget**

remind *verb*

Jo reminded Mum to buy some sugar.

A PHRASE YOU MIGHT USE IS **to jog someone's memory**

remove *verb*

1 Please remove this rubbish.

OTHER VERBS YOU MIGHT USE ARE **to carry away** **to get rid of** **to move** **to shift** **to take away**

2 The dentist removed a tooth.

OTHER VERBS ARE **to extract** **to take out**

3 What removes oil from clothes?

ANOTHER VERB IS **to wash off**

repair *verb*

OTHER VERBS YOU MIGHT USE ARE *(informal)* **to fix** **to mend** **to put right**

to repair clothes **to darn** **to patch** **to sew up**

to repair something old or broken **to do up** **to renovate** **to restore**

repeat *verb*

Don't repeat everything I say!

OTHER VERBS YOU MIGHT USE ARE **to go over** **to say again**

reply *verb*

I replied to Granny's letter.

OTHER VERBS YOU MIGHT USE ARE **to answer** **to respond to**

report *verb*

1 We reported that we had finished our work.
OTHER VERBS YOU MIGHT USE ARE **to announce   to declare   to state**

2 I reported him to the police.
OTHER VERBS ARE **to complain about   to inform against**   (*informal*) **to tell of**

reproduce *verb*

1 Sam can reproduce a lot of bird calls.
OTHER VERBS YOU MIGHT USE ARE **to imitate   to mimic**

2 We reproduced our work on the copier in the school office.
OTHER VERBS ARE **to copy   to duplicate   to photocopy**

3 Rabbits reproduce very quickly.
OTHER VERBS ARE **to breed   to multiply**

reptile *noun*, see next page

request *verb*

When the work got too hard, we requested help from our teacher.
OTHER VERBS YOU MIGHT USE ARE **to appeal for   to ask for   to beg for**

require *verb*

We required 3 more runs to win.
OTHER VERBS ARE **to be short of   to need   to want**

rescue *verb*

Robin Hood rescued the prisoners from the Sheriff's castle.
OTHER VERBS YOU MIGHT USE ARE **to free   to liberate   to release   to save   to set free**

resemble *verb*

Sam resembles his father.
OTHER VERBS YOU MIGHT USE ARE **to be similar to   to look like**

reserve *noun*

We have two reserves who can play on Saturday if necessary.
OTHER WORDS ARE **deputy   stand-in   substitute**

reserve *verb*

1 Jo reserved some sandwiches for people who came late.
OTHER VERBS YOU MIGHT USE ARE **to keep   to save**

2 We reserved our seats on the train.
ANOTHER WORD IS **to book**

resign *verb*

The manager resigned because the team was doing so badly.
OTHER VERBS YOU MIGHT USE ARE **to give up   to leave**   (*informal*) **to quit**

resist *verb*

He made things worse because he resisted the police.
OTHER VERBS YOU MIGHT USE ARE **to defy   to oppose   to stand up to**

respect *noun*

We should show respect to people who work hard for us.
OTHER WORDS YOU MIGHT USE ARE **admiration   consideration**
The respect you show towards religious things is **reverence**.

a
b
c
d
e
f
g
h
i
j
k
l
m
n
o
p
q
r
s
t
u
v
w
x
y
z

reptile *noun*

DIFFERENT KINDS OF REPTILE ARE

alligator   **crocodile**   **lizard**   **snake**   **tortoise**   **turtle**

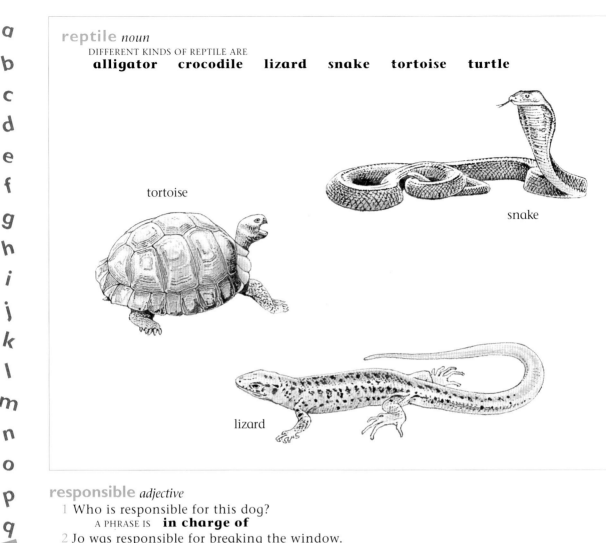

tortoise

snake

lizard

responsible *adjective*

1 Who is responsible for this dog?
    A PHRASE IS   **in charge of**
2 Jo was responsible for breaking the window.
    A PHRASE IS   **guilty of**
3 We need a responsible person to look after the money.
    OTHER WORDS ARE   **dependable**   **honest**   **reliable**   **trustworthy**

rest *noun*

1 Let's have a rest for a minute.
    OTHER WORDS YOU MIGHT USE ARE   **break**   **pause**
2 If you have finished, the dog will eat the rest.
    ANOTHER WORD IS   **remainder**

rest *verb*

1 Halfway up the hill we sat down to rest.
    OTHER VERBS YOU MIGHT USE ARE   **to relax**   (*informal*) **to take it easy**
  When you are resting you might   **doze**   **lie down**   **sleep**   (*informal*) **take a nap**
2 Rest the ladder against the wall.
    OTHER VERBS YOU MIGHT USE ARE   **to lean**   **to prop**   **to stand**   **to support**

restore *verb*

Uncle David restores old cars.
    OTHER VERBS YOU MIGHT USE ARE   (*informal*) **to do up**   **to mend**   **to renovate**
        to repair

result *noun*

The result of getting up late was that I missed the bus.
> OTHER WORDS YOU MIGHT USE ARE **consequence** **effect**

retreat *verb*

The soldiers retreated when they knew that they were losing.
> OTHER VERBS YOU MIGHT USE ARE **to go back** **to move back** **to run away**

return *verb*

1 We returned at tea time.
> OTHER VERBS YOU MIGHT USE ARE **to come back** **to go back**

2 Jo returned the pen I lent her.
> OTHER VERBS ARE **to give back** **to repay**

reveal *verb*

1 We drew back the curtain and revealed the stage.
> OTHER VERBS YOU MIGHT USE ARE **to disclose** **to show**

2 Don't ever reveal our secret!
> PHRASES ARE **to let out** **to make known**

reverse *verb*

Dad damaged the car when he reversed into a wall.
> OTHER VERBS ARE **to back** **to go backwards**

revolt *verb*

The players revolted because they thought the rules were not fair.
> OTHER VERBS YOU MIGHT USE ARE **to disobey** **to rebel**

When sailors revolt the word is **mutiny**.

revolting *adjective*

The food was so revolting that nobody would eat it.
> OTHER WORDS YOU MIGHT USE ARE **disgusting** **foul** **horrible** **nasty** **unattractive**

The opposite is attractive

rhythm *noun*

Sam likes music with a strong rhythm.
> OTHER WORDS YOU MIGHT USE ARE **beat** **pulse**

rich *adjective*

Rich people can buy what they want.
> OTHER WORDS YOU MIGHT USE ARE **prosperous** **wealthy** **well-off**

The opposite is poor

ride *verb*

For other verbs, see **travel**

ridiculous *adjective*

We laughed at his ridiculous hat.
> OTHER WORDS YOU MIGHT USE ARE **absurd** **comic** **funny** **silly** **stupid**

a
b
c
d
e
f
g
h
i
j
k
l
m
n
o
p
q
r
s
t
u
v
w
x
y
z

right *adjective*

1 Most people use their right hand to write with.
The opposite is **left**

2 All Jo's answers were right.
OTHER WORDS YOU MIGHT USE ARE **accurate   correct**

3 Is that the right time?
OTHER WORDS ARE **exact   precise   proper   true**

4 It's right to own up when you've been naughty.
OTHER WORDS ARE **fair   honest   moral**

5 A thesaurus helps you to find the right word.
OTHER WORDS ARE **appropriate   suitable**
The opposite is **wrong**

ring *noun*

We all stood in a ring.
ANOTHER WORD IS **circle**

ring *verb*

1 I heard a bell ring.
Loud bells **peal**.
A small bell **tinkles**.
An annoying noisy bell **jangles**.
A clock **chimes**.

2 We ring Granny every Sunday.
OTHER WORDS ARE
to call   to phone   to telephone

riot *noun*

The police were called to control the riot.
OTHER WORDS YOU MIGHT USE ARE **disorder   disturbance   mutiny   revolt**

rip *verb*

Sam ripped his jeans.
OTHER VERBS YOU MIGHT USE ARE **to split   to tear**

rise *verb*

1 I watched the balloon rise into the sky.
OTHER VERBS YOU MIGHT USE ARE **to ascend   to climb   to go up   to lift**
The opposite is **fall**

2 Bus fares are going to rise next week.
ANOTHER VERB IS **to increase**

3 We all rose when the teacher came into the room.
OTHER VERBS ARE **to get up   to stand**

risk *noun*

There's a risk of rain today.
OTHER WORDS YOU MIGHT USE ARE **chance   danger   possibility**

rival *noun*

The team we played on Saturday were our old rivals.
OTHER WORDS YOU MIGHT USE ARE **enemy   opponent**

river *noun*

For other words, see **water**

road *noun*

BIG ROADS FOR MOTOR TRAFFIC ARE
bypass   **motorway**   **ring road**

OTHER WORDS YOU MIGHT USE ARE
a road with houses along it is a **street**
a road with trees along it is an **avenue**
a narrow road between buildings is an **alley**
a road where you can only drive one way is a **one-way street**
a road closed at one end is a **cul-de-sac**
a road that goes up to a house is a **drive**
a narrow road in the country is a **lane**
a rough road in the country is a **track** or **cart track**
a path for horses is a **bridleway**
a path along a canal is a **towpath**

robber *noun*

ANOTHER WORD IS
thief
DIFFERENT KINDS OF ROBBER ARE
burglar   **highwayman**   **mugger**   **pickpocket**   **shoplifter**
For other words, see **steal**

rock *noun*
ANOTHER WORD IS   **stone**
A big piece of rock is a **boulder**.

rock *verb*
1 The boat rocked gently in the breeze.
OTHER VERBS YOU MIGHT USE ARE   **to sway**   **to swing**
2 The boat rocked violently in the storm.
OTHER VERBS ARE   **to roll**   **to toss**

rod *noun*
The climbing frame is made of iron rods.
OTHER WORDS YOU MIGHT USE ARE   **bar**   **pole**   **rail**

rodent *noun*
THESE ANIMALS ARE RODENTS:
gerbil   **hamster**   **mouse**   **rat**   **squirrel**

room *noun*
For different rooms, see **home**

rope *noun*
OTHER WORDS YOU CAN USE ARE **cord** **line**

rotten *adjective*
1 rotten wood.
OTHER WORDS YOU MIGHT USE ARE **decayed** **decomposed**
2 rotten food.
OTHER WORDS ARE **bad** **mouldy** **smelly**
3 Sam is rotten at tennis!
OTHER WORDS ARE **bad** **hopeless** **incompetent** **useless**

rough *adjective*
1 We jolted along the rough road.
OTHER WORDS YOU MIGHT USE ARE **bumpy** **uneven**
The opposite is smooth
2 Sandpaper feels rough.
OTHER WORDS ARE **coarse** **harsh** **scratchy**
The opposite is soft
3 The sea was very rough.
OTHER WORDS ARE **stormy** **wild**
The opposite is calm
4 I don't like rough games.
OTHER WORDS ARE **bad-tempered** **boisterous** **rowdy** **violent**
The opposite is gentle
5 At a rough guess it will cost £100 to mend the car.
ANOTHER WORD IS **approximate**
The opposite is exact

---

round *adjective*
Most coins are round.
ANOTHER WORD IS
circular
A flat round shape is a **disc**.
A solid round shape is a **ball** or **globe** or **sphere**.

---

route *noun*
Sam knows a quick route into town.
ANOTHER WORD IS **way**

row *noun* (rhymes with *cow*)
1 Sam and Jo hardly ever have a row.
OTHER WORDS YOU MIGHT USE ARE **disagreement** **quarrel** **squabble**
2 What was that row in the night?
OTHER WORDS ARE **commotion** **din** **noise** **uproar**

row *noun* (rhymes with *toe*)
We stood in a straight row.
OTHER WORDS YOU MIGHT USE ARE **file** **line** **queue**

rubbish *noun*
Throw away that rubbish.
OTHER WORDS YOU MIGHT USE ARE (*informal*) **junk** **litter** **refuse** **scrap** **waste**

rude *adjective*

That rude girl shouted at us.
> OTHER WORDS YOU MIGHT USE ARE **bad-mannered cheeky disrespectful impertinent impolite impudent insulting offensive**

The opposite is **polite**

ruin *verb*

The storm ruined the flowers in the garden.
> OTHER VERBS YOU MIGHT USE ARE **to destroy to spoil to wreck**

rule *noun*

When you play a game, you must obey the rules.
> OTHER WORDS YOU MIGHT USE ARE **law regulation**

---

rule *verb*

In the old days, the king used to rule the country.
> OTHER VERBS YOU MIGHT USE ARE
> **to control to govern to lead to manage to run**

> DIFFERENT WORDS FOR PEOPLE WHO RULE OVER THEIR SUBJECTS MIGHT BE
> **dictator emperor empress governor king monarch queen president prince princess rajah sovereign sultan tyrant tzar**

Some countries are ruled by a **government** with a **prime minister**.

---

rumour *noun*

It's not fair to spread stories that are only rumour.
> ANOTHER WORD IS **gossip**

---

run *verb*

> DIFFERENT WAYS TO RUN ARE
> **to jog to race to scamper to sprint**

For other words, see **rush**

> DIFFERENT WAYS A HORSE RUNS ARE
> **canter gallop trot**

---

runny *adjective*

The jelly hasn't set yet—it's still runny.
> OTHER WORDS YOU MIGHT USE ARE **liquid sloppy watery**

rush *verb*

Jo was hungry, so she rushed home for something to eat.
> OTHER VERBS YOU MIGHT USE ARE **to dash to hurry to speed**

For other verbs, see **run**

a
b
c
d
e
f
g
h
i
j
k
l
m
n
o
p
q
r
s
t
u
v
w
x
y
z

Ss

sacred *adjective*

The Bible and the Koran are sacred books.

OTHER WORDS YOU MIGHT USE ARE **holy   religious**

sad *adjective*

1 a sad look on someone's face.

OTHER WORDS YOU MIGHT USE ARE **depressed   disappointed   gloomy
heartbroken   melancholy   miserable   mournful   sorrowful
tearful   troubled   unhappy   wretched**

2 sad news.

OTHER WORDS YOU MIGHT USE ARE **depressing   disappointing   distressing
tragic   upsetting**

The opposite is happy

safe *adjective*

1 When we got indoors, we felt safe from the storm.

OTHER WORDS YOU MIGHT USE ARE **protected   secure**

2 We were glad to get home safe.

ANOTHER WORD IS **unharmed**

3 Is the dog safe?

OTHER WORDS YOU MIGHT USE ARE **harmless   tame**

sailor *noun*

ANOTHER WORD IS **seaman**

The sailors who sail a ship are the **crew**.

---

salad *noun*

THINGS YOU EAT IN SALAD ARE

**beetroot   celery   cress   cucumber
lettuce   mustard and cress   onion
potato   radish   tomato
watercress**

---

sample *noun*

Jo showed Dad samples of her work.

OTHER WORDS YOU MIGHT USE ARE **example   specimen**

satisfactory *adjective*

We can go out to play if our work is satisfactory.

OTHER WORDS YOU MIGHT USE ARE **acceptable   all right   good enough**

satisfy *verb*

He's always grumpy: nothing satisfies him.

OTHER VERBS YOU MIGHT USE ARE **to content   to make happy   to please**

a b c d e f g h i j k l m n o p q r s t u v w x y z

savage *adjective*

a savage attack.
> OTHER WORDS YOU MIGHT USE ARE **bloodthirsty   brutal   cruel   fierce   heartless   ruthless   vicious   violent**

The opposite is gentle

save *verb*

1 Robin Hood saved the prisoners.
> OTHER VERBS YOU MIGHT USE ARE **to free   to liberate   to release   to rescue   to set free**

2 I saved some sweets for later.
> OTHER VERBS ARE **to keep   to preserve   to put aside**

say *verb*

For other verbs, see **talk**

saying *noun*

'I don't believe it' is a common saying.
> OTHER WORDS YOU MIGHT USE ARE **expression   phrase   remark**

A saying that is supposed to teach a moral, like 'Many hands make light work', is a **proverb**.

scarce *adjective*

1 Water is scarce in the desert.
> A PHRASE IS **in short supply**

The opposite is plentiful

2 Snakes are scarce in England.
> OTHER WORDS ARE **rare   uncommon**

The opposite is common

scarcely *adverb*

I could scarcely believe my eyes!
> OTHER WORDS YOU MIGHT USE ARE **barely   hardly   only just**

scare *verb*

The sudden noise scared me.
> OTHER VERBS ARE **to alarm   to frighten   to shock   to startle   to terrify   to upset**

scatter *verb*

The baby always scatters her toys round the room.
> OTHER VERBS YOU MIGHT USE ARE **to spread   to throw about**

scent *noun*

the scent of roses.
> OTHER WORDS YOU MIGHT USE ARE **fragrance   perfume   smell**

---

school *noun*

DIFFERENT KINDS OF SCHOOL ARE
> **boarding school   comprehensive school   first school
> infant school   junior school   kindergarten   middle school
> nursery school   play group   primary school   secondary school**

For other words, see **educate**, **teach**

---

a
b
c
d
e
f
g
h
i
j
k
l
m
n
o
p
q
r
s
t
u
v
w
x
y
z

science *noun*

DIFFERENT KINDS OF SCIENCE ARE

**astronomy   biology   botany   chemistry   electronics
engineering   geology   physics   psychology   technology
zoology**

scold *verb*

Jo scolded the dog for eating her chocolate.

OTHER VERBS YOU MIGHT USE ARE **to reprimand**   (*informal*) **to tell off**
(*informal*) **to tick off**

scramble *verb*

I scrambled over the rocks.

OTHER VERBS YOU MIGHT USE ARE **to clamber   to climb   to crawl**

scrap *noun*

1 We put scraps of food out for the birds.

OTHER WORDS YOU MIGHT USE ARE **bit   crumb   piece**

2 Dad took some scrap to the tip.

OTHER WORDS YOU MIGHT USE ARE   (*informal*) **junk   rubbish   waste**

scrape *verb*

1 I scraped my knee on the stones.

OTHER VERBS YOU MIGHT USE ARE **to graze   to scratch**

2 Jo scraped the mud off her shoe.

OTHER VERBS ARE **to clean   to rub   to scrub**

scratch *verb*

Dad scratched the car on the gate.

OTHER VERBS YOU MIGHT USE ARE **to damage   to graze   to scrape**

scream *verb*

Everyone screamed when the ride went faster and faster.

OTHER VERBS ARE **to cry out   to howl   to screech   to shriek   to squeal
to yell**

sculpture *noun*

OTHER WORDS ARE **carvings   statues**

sea *noun*

ANOTHER WORD IS **ocean**

seal *verb*

Remember to seal the envelope.

OTHER VERBS YOU MIGHT USE ARE **to close   to fasten   to stick down**

search *verb*

I was searching for my watch.

OTHER VERBS YOU MIGHT USE ARE **to hunt for   to look for**

seaside *noun*

We had a trip to the seaside.

OTHER WORDS YOU MIGHT USE ARE

beach   coast

Another word for beach is **shore**.

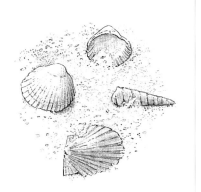

THINGS YOU MIGHT SEE AT THE SEASIDE ARE

**breakwater   cliffs   pier   promenade
rocks   rock pools   sand   sand dunes
shingle   waves**

THINGS YOU MIGHT FIND ARE

pebbles   seaweed   shellfish   shells

season *noun*

THE SEASONS OF THE YEAR ARE

spring   summer   autumn   winter

seat *noun*

DIFFERENT THINGS YOU SIT ON ARE

**armchair   bench   chair   deckchair   pew   pouffe
rocking chair   settee   sofa   stool**

The seat a king or queen sits on for official occasions is a **throne**.

secret *adjective*

1 a secret diary.

OTHER WORDS YOU MIGHT USE ARE   **intimate   personal   private**

2 a secret place.

OTHER WORDS ARE   **concealed   hidden   unknown**

The opposite is public

secure *adjective*

Make sure the ladder is secure before you climb it.

OTHER WORDS YOU MIGHT USE ARE   **firm   fixed   safe   steady**

The opposite is loose

a
b
c
d
e
f
g
h
i
j
k
l
m
n
o
p
q
r
s
t
u
v
w
x
y
z

181

see *verb*

1 Did you see anyone you know?
OTHER VERBS YOU MIGHT USE ARE **to make out**   **to notice**   **to recognize**   **to spot**
To see someone or something very briefly is to **glimpse** it.
2 We saw a good film.
OTHER VERBS ARE **to look at**   **to view**   **to watch**
3 If you see an accident, tell the police.
ANOTHER VERB IS **to witness**

seem *verb*

Granny seems better today.
OTHER VERBS YOU MIGHT USE ARE **to appear**   **to look**

seize *verb*

1 I seized the end of the rope.
OTHER VERBS YOU MIGHT USE ARE (*informal*) **to grab**   **to hold**   **to snatch**
2 The police seized the thief.
OTHER VERBS ARE **to arrest**   **to capture**   **to catch**

seldom *adverb*

It seldom snows in May.
ANOTHER WORD IS **rarely**
The opposite is often

select *verb*

1 You can select some sweets from the tin.
OTHER VERBS YOU MIGHT USE ARE **to choose**   **to pick**
2 We selected Jo to be captain.
OTHER VERBS ARE **to appoint**   **to decide on**   **to vote for**

selfish *adjective*

It's selfish to keep the best sweets for yourself.
OTHER WORDS YOU MIGHT USE ARE **greedy**   **mean**   **thoughtless**
The opposite is generous

send *verb*

We sent a parcel to Grandad.
OTHER VERBS YOU MIGHT USE ARE **to dispatch**   **to post**

sense *noun*

1 If you've got any sense, you won't go out in the rain.
OTHER WORDS YOU MIGHT USE ARE
intelligence   **wisdom**
2 We use our five senses to recognize things.
OUR FIVE SENSES ARE
hearing   **sight**   **smell**   **taste**   **touch**

sensible *adjective*

Sensible people stay in when it rains.
OTHER WORDS YOU MIGHT USE ARE **reasonable**   **thoughtful**   **wise**
The opposite is silly

sensitive *adjective*

Jo has a sensitive skin.
OTHER WORDS YOU MIGHT USE ARE **delicate**   **soft**   **tender**

separate *adjective*
1 They kept the sick children separate from the rest of us.
   OTHER WORDS ARE **apart   divided   isolated   segregated**
2 The infants are in a separate building from the juniors.
   OTHER WORDS ARE **detached   different   distinct**

series *noun*
We had a series of accidents.
   OTHER WORDS ARE **row   sequence   string   succession**

serious *adjective*
1 Sam takes a serious interest in his work.
   OTHER WORDS YOU MIGHT USE ARE **careful   sincere   thoughtful**
2 She had a serious look on her face.
   OTHER WORDS ARE **grave   sad   solemn**
3 Several people were hurt in the serious accident.
   OTHER WORDS ARE **awful   bad   dreadful   severe   terrible**

---

service *noun*
   KINDS OF RELIGIOUS SERVICE ARE
   baptism or **christening   funeral   Holy Communion   mass   prayers
   wedding service   worship**
   For other words, see **religion**

---

set *verb*
1 Has the glue set yet?
   ANOTHER VERB IS **to harden**
2 We set out our work for the parents to see.
   OTHER VERBS YOU MIGHT USE ARE **to arrange   to lay out   to put out**
3 We set off at breakfast time.
   OTHER VERBS ARE **to depart   to start**

settle *verb*
Have you settled on what to do?
   OTHER VERBS YOU MIGHT USE ARE **to agree   to decide   to fix**

severe *adjective*
1 a severe teacher.
   OTHER WORDS YOU MIGHT USE ARE **stern   strict**
2 a severe illness.
   OTHER WORDS ARE **bad   serious**
The opposite is mild

sew *verb*
   ANOTHER WORD IS **to stitch**
   To sew up a hole is **to darn**.
   To sew with loose stitches is **to tack**.

sewing *noun*
   OTHER WORDS ARE **embroidery   needlework**

shabby *adjective*
shabby clothes.
   OTHER WORDS YOU MIGHT USE ARE **faded   old   ragged   **(informal)** scruffy
   worn**
The opposite is smart

shade *noun*

1 We sat in the shade of a tree.

ANOTHER WORD IS **shadow**

2 My coat is a pretty shade of red.

OTHER WORDS YOU MIGHT USE ARE **colour** **hue** **tinge**

shady *adjective*

We sat down in a shady place.

OTHER WORDS YOU MIGHT USE ARE **shaded** **shadowy**

shaggy *adjective*

The dog had a shaggy coat.

OTHER WORDS YOU MIGHT USE ARE **hairy** **rough** **woolly**

shake *verb*

1 I shook with fear.

OTHER VERBS YOU MIGHT USE ARE **to quake** **to quiver** **to shiver** **to shudder** **to tremble**

2 The house shook in the earthquake.

OTHER VERBS ARE **to rock** **to sway** **to vibrate** **to wobble**

shallow *adjective*

The opposite is deep

shame *noun*

We'll never forget the shame of losing 14–0!

OTHER WORDS YOU MIGHT USE ARE **disgrace** **embarrassment**

shape *noun,* see opposite page

share *noun*

1 We all had a share of the money.

OTHER WORDS YOU MIGHT USE ARE **fraction** **part**

2 Mum made sure that everyone had a fair share of the pudding.

OTHER WORDS ARE **helping** **portion** **ration**

share *verb*

We shared the food between us.

OTHER VERBS YOU MIGHT USE ARE **to deal out** **to distribute** **to divide** **to split**

sharp *adjective*

1 a sharp stick.

ANOTHER WORD IS **pointed**

2 a sharp knife.

OTHER WORDS YOU MIGHT USE ARE **keen** **razor-sharp**

The opposite is blunt

3 a sharp bend in the road.

ANOTHER WORD IS **sudden**

4 a sharp girl.

OTHER WORDS ARE **bright** **clever** **intelligent** **quick** **smart**

The opposite is dull

shed *verb*

A lorry shed its load on the motorway.

OTHER VERBS ARE **to drop** **to scatter**

shape noun

OTHER WORDS YOU MIGHT USE ARE

form   outline

DIFFERENT SHAPES ARE

circle   heptagon   hexagon   oblong   octagon
oval   pentagon   rectangle   semicircle   spiral
square   triangle

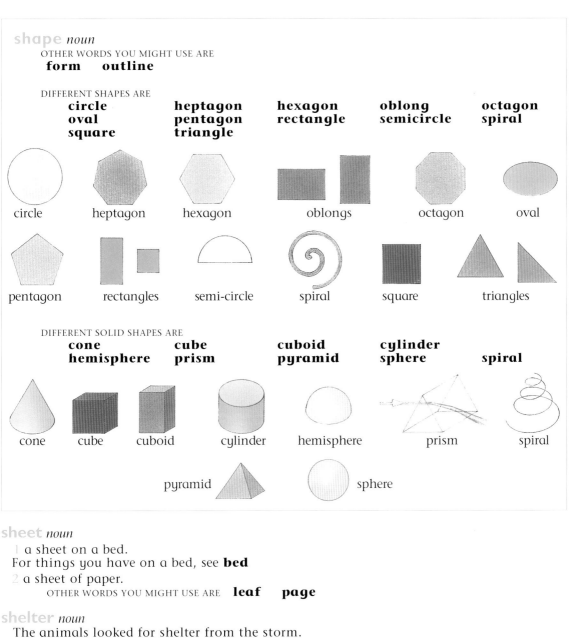

circle   heptagon   hexagon   oblongs   octagon   oval

pentagon   rectangles   semi-circle spiral   square   triangles

DIFFERENT SOLID SHAPES ARE

cone   cube   cuboid   cylinder
hemisphere prism   pyramid   sphere   spiral

cone   cube   cuboid   cylinder   hemisphere   prism   spiral

pyramid   sphere

sheet noun

1 a sheet on a bed.
For things you have on a bed, see **bed**
2 a sheet of paper.

OTHER WORDS YOU MIGHT USE ARE   **leaf   page**

shelter noun

The animals looked for shelter from the storm.

OTHER WORDS ARE   **cover   protection   refuge   safety**

shelter verb

The hedge sheltered us from the wind.

OTHER VERBS YOU MIGHT USE ARE   **to guard   to hide   to protect   to shield**

shift verb

For other verbs, see **move**

shine verb

Things shine in different ways.

THEY CAN:

blaze   burn   dazzle   flash   flicker   glare   gleam   glimmer
glint   glisten   glitter   glow   shine   sparkle twinkle

shiny *adjective*

a shiny new coin.

> OTHER WORDS YOU MIGHT USE ARE **bright   gleaming   glossy   polished   shining**

The opposite is **dull**

shiver *verb*

I was shivering with cold.

> OTHER VERBS YOU MIGHT USE ARE **to quiver   to shake   to shudder   to tremble**

shock *verb*

1 The explosion shocked everyone.

> OTHER VERBS YOU MIGHT USE ARE **to alarm   to frighten   to startle   to stun   to surprise**

2 The swearing shocked us.

> OTHER VERBS ARE **to disgust   to offend   to upset**

---

shoe *noun*

> THINGS YOU WEAR ON YOUR FEET ARE
> **boots   clogs   plimsolls   sandals   slippers   trainers   wellingtons**

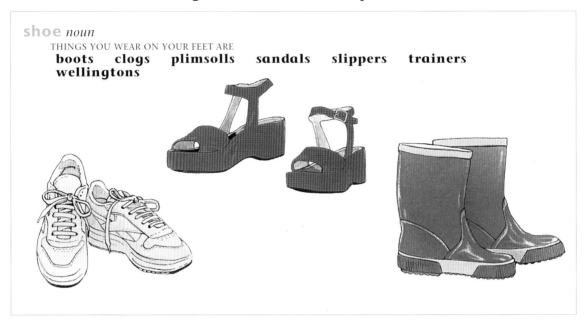

---

shoot *verb*

He shot at the target.

> OTHER VERBS YOU MIGHT USE ARE **to aim   to fire**

---

shop *noun*

> ANOTHER WORD IS
> **store**
>
> BIG SHOPS THAT SELL ALL KINDS OF GOODS ARE
> **department store   hypermarket   supermarket**
>
> DIFFERENT KINDS OF SHOP ARE

baker	**bank**	**barber**	**book shop**
butcher	**chemist**	**clothes shop**	**dairy**
delicatessen	**DIY shop**	**fishmonger**	**florist**
greengrocer	**grocer**	**hairdresser**	**ironmonger**
jeweller	**launderette**	**newsagent**	**off-licence**
post office	**shoe shop**		

short *adjective*

1 a short poem.
> ANOTHER WORD IS **brief**

The opposite is long

2 a short person.
> OTHER WORDS ARE **little** **small**

The opposite is tall

shout *verb*

Sam shouted so loud that the people next door heard him.
> OTHER VERBS YOU MIGHT USE ARE **to call** **to cry out** **to roar** **to scream** **to shriek** **to yell**

show *noun*

an art show.
> OTHER WORDS ARE **display** **exhibition**

show *verb*

1 We showed our work to the visitors.
> OTHER VERBS YOU MIGHT USE ARE **to display** **to exhibit** **to present**

2 She showed me how to do it.
> OTHER VERBS ARE **to explain** **to teach** **to tell**

3 We drew pictures to show how people used to dress in Victorian times.
> OTHER VERBS ARE **to illustrate** **to portray** **to represent**

shrill *adjective*

a shrill whistle.
> OTHER WORDS YOU MIGHT USE ARE **high** **piercing** **sharp**

shrivel *verb*

The plants shrivelled in the heat.
> OTHER VERBS YOU MIGHT USE ARE **to dry up** **to shrink** **to wither**

shudder *verb*

I shuddered when I thought of the monster.
> OTHER VERBS YOU MIGHT USE ARE **to quake** **to quiver** **to shake** **to tremble**

shut *verb*

Shut the door.
> OTHER VERBS ARE **to close** **to fasten** **to lock** **to seal**

To shut a door loudly is to **slam** it.
The opposite is open

shy *adjective*

He was too shy to say that he knew the answer.
> OTHER WORDS YOU MIGHT USE ARE **bashful** **modest** **nervous** **timid**

The opposite is bold

sick *adjective*

Jo was away from school because she was sick.
> OTHER WORDS YOU MIGHT USE ARE **ill** (*informal*) **poorly** **unwell**

to be sick
> OTHER WORDS ARE (*informal*) **throw up** **vomit**

For other words, see **health**

a
b
c
d
e
f
g
h
i
j
k
l
m
n
o
p
q
r
s
t
u
v
w
x
y
z

side *noun*

1 A cube has six sides.
  OTHER WORDS ARE **face   surface**
2 I stood at the side of the road.
  ANOTHER WORD IS **edge**
A grassy side of a road is a **verge**

sight *noun*

1 The optician says that Sam has good sight.
  OTHER WORDS YOU MIGHT USE ARE **eyesight   vision**
2 The hills are a lovely sight.
  OTHER WORDS ARE **scene   spectacle**

sign *noun*

1 He gave a sign that it was my turn.
  OTHER WORDS YOU MIGHT USE ARE **hint   reminder   signal**
2 The doctor said that spots might be a sign of measles.
  OTHER WORDS ARE **indication   symptom**

silent *adjective*

1 During the night the house is completely silent.
  OTHER WORDS YOU MIGHT USE ARE **quiet   soundless**
The opposite is noisy
2 Sam was silent when he heard the bad news.
  OTHER WORDS ARE **dumb   speechless**

silky *adjective*

The cat has a silky coat.
  OTHER WORDS YOU MIGHT USE ARE **sleek   smooth   soft**
The opposite is rough

silly *adjective*

It's silly to go out in the rain.
  OTHER WORDS ARE (*informal*) **daft   foolish   ridiculous   senseless   stupid**
The opposite is sensible

similar *adjective*

The two girls had similar dresses.
  ANOTHER WORD IS **matching**
The opposite is different

simple *adjective*

1 a simple problem.
  OTHER WORDS YOU MIGHT USE ARE **clear   easy   straightforward**
The opposite is complicated
2 a simple dress.
  ANOTHER WORD IS **plain**

sincere *adjective*

He was sincere when he said he was glad to see us.
  OTHER WORDS YOU MIGHT USE ARE **genuine   honest   truthful**
The opposite is dishonest

singer *noun*
ANOTHER WORD IS
vocalist
A group of singers is a **choir** or a **chorus**.
Someone who sings on their own is a **soloist**.
SINGERS WITH DIFFERENT KINDS OF VOICE ARE
alto   bass   contralto   soprano   tenor   treble
For other words to do with music, see **music**

single *adjective*
There wasn't a single sweet left!
ANOTHER WORD IS **solitary**

site *noun*
We found a nice site to put up the tent.
OTHER WORDS YOU MIGHT USE ARE   **plot   position   situation   spot**

situation *noun*
1 My house is in a nice situation.
OTHER WORDS YOU MIGHT USE ARE   **place   position   spot**
2 I was in an awkward situation when I lost my money.
ANOTHER WORD IS   **position**

size *noun*
For other words, see **measurement**

skate *verb*
He skated gracefully over the ice.
OTHER VERBS YOU MIGHT USE ARE   **to glide   to skim   to slide**

skeleton *noun*
For other parts of the body, see **body**

skid *verb*
The car skidded on the ice.
OTHER VERBS YOU CAN USE ARE   **to slide   to slip**

skilful *adjective*
a skilful player.
OTHER WORDS YOU MIGHT USE ARE   **clever   expert   talented**

skill *noun*
Sam admired the player's skill.
OTHER WORDS YOU MIGHT USE ARE   **ability   cleverness   talent**

skin *noun*
WORDS FOR ANIMALS' SKIN ARE   **fur   hide**
Words for the skin of an orange are **peel** or **rind**.

skip *verb*
The lambs skipped about the field.
OTHER VERBS ARE   **to dance   to frisk   to hop   to jump   to leap   to prance   to spring**

slanting *adjective*
a slanting line.
OTHER WORDS ARE   **sloping   tilting**

a
b
c
d
e
f
g
h
i
j
k
l
m
n
o
p
q
r
s
t
u
v
w
x
y
z

sledge *noun*
OTHER WORDS ARE **sleigh** **toboggan**

---

sleep *verb*
DIFFERENT WAYS TO GO TO SLEEP ARE
to doze (*informal*) **to drop off** **to nod off** **to slumber** **to snooze**
(*informal*) **to take a nap**
When animals sleep for a long time in the winter, they **hibernate**.

---

sleepy *adjective*
I was sleepy so I went to bed.
OTHER WORDS YOU MIGHT USE ARE **drowsy** **tired** **weary**

slender *adjective*
She has a slender figure.
ANOTHER WORD IS **graceful**
For other words, see **slim**

slide *verb*
We slid on the ice.
OTHER VERBS YOU MIGHT USE ARE **to glide** **to skate** **to skid** **to slip**

slight *adjective*
a slight accident.
OTHER WORDS YOU MIGHT USE ARE **minor** **small** **unimportant**
The opposite is **serious**

slim *adjective*
He could get through the hole in the fence because he was so slim.
OTHER WORDS YOU MIGHT USE ARE **lean** **slender** **slight** **thin**
The opposite is **fat**

slip *verb*
Sam slipped and fell over.
OTHER VERBS YOU MIGHT USE ARE **to skid** **to slide**

slippery *adjective*
Take care: the floor is slippery.
OTHER WORDS ARE **greasy** **icy** **oily** **slimy** **slithery** **smooth**

slope *noun*
It's hard to run up a steep slope.
OTHER WORDS ARE **bank** **gradient** **hill** **ramp** **rise**

slope *verb*
The beach slopes down to the sea.
ANOTHER VERB IS **to slant**

slot *noun*
I put a coin in the slot.
OTHER WORDS YOU MIGHT USE ARE **groove** **opening** **slit**

slow *adjective*
1 There was a slow change in the weather.
ANOTHER WORD IS **gradual**
2 I'm sorry I'm late, but my watch is slow.
The opposite is **fast**

sly *adjective*
They say the fox is a sly animal.
OTHER WORDS ARE **crafty** **cunning** (*informal*) **sneaky** **wily**

smack *verb*
For other verbs, see **hit**

small *adjective*
1 The book was small enough to put in my pocket.
OTHER WORDS YOU MIGHT USE ARE **compact** **little** **minute** **tiny**
2 Sam made a small model of the castle.
ANOTHER WORD IS **miniature**
3 She gave us small helpings.
OTHER WORDS ARE **mean** (*informal*) **measly** **stingy**
4 We had a small problem.
OTHER WORDS ARE **minor** **slight** **unimportant**
The opposite is big

smart *adjective*
1 He looked smart in his new clothes.
OTHER WORDS YOU MIGHT USE ARE **neat** **posh** **tidy** **well-dressed**
The opposite is untidy
2 That's a smart dog if he understands what you say.
OTHER WORDS YOU MIGHT USE ARE **bright** **clever** **intelligent**
The opposite is stupid

smart *verb*
The wasp sting made Sam's hand smart.
OTHER VERBS YOU MIGHT USE ARE **to hurt** **to sting** **to throb**

smear *verb*
I smeared ointment on the sore place.
OTHER VERBS YOU MIGHT USE ARE **to rub** **to spread** **to wipe**

smell *noun*
ANOTHER WORD IS **odour**
WORDS FOR A NICE SMELL ARE **aroma** **fragrance** **perfume** **scent**
A word for a nasty smell is **stink**.
A word for a slight smell is **whiff**.

smile *verb*
For other verbs, see **laugh**

smoke *noun*
the smoke from an engine.
OTHER WORDS YOU MIGHT USE ARE **exhaust** **fumes**

smooth *adjective*
1 a smooth surface.
OTHER WORDS YOU MIGHT USE ARE **even** **flat** **level**
The opposite is rough
2 a smooth sea.
ANOTHER WORD IS **calm**
The opposite is stormy

smudge *verb*
I smudged the wet paint.
OTHER WORDS YOU MIGHT USE ARE **to smear** **to streak**

a
b
c
d
e
f
g
h
i
j
k
l
m
n
o
p
q
r
s
t
u
v
w
x
y
z

snatch *verb*

The dog snatched the sandwich out of my hand.

OTHER VERBS YOU MIGHT USE ARE **to grab**   **to seize**   **to take**

sneak *verb*

She sneaked up behind me and made me jump.

OTHER VERBS YOU MIGHT USE ARE **to creep**   **to steal**

soft *adjective*

1 The baby cuddled a soft toy.

OTHER WORDS TO DESCRIBE SOFT THINGS ARE **flexible**   **floppy**   **limp**   **spongy**   **springy**   **squashy**

The opposite is hard

2 Jo's dress is made of soft material.

OTHER WORDS YOU MIGHT USE ARE **silky**   **smooth**   **velvety**

The opposite is rough

3 They played soft music when we went into church.

OTHER WORDS YOU MIGHT USE ARE **gentle**   **low**   **quiet**   **restful**

The opposite is loud

soil *noun*

Sam planted his seeds in the soil.

OTHER WORDS YOU MIGHT USE ARE **earth**   **ground**

---

soldier *noun*

ANOTHER WORD IS

serviceman or **servicewoman**

Soldiers who go on horseback are the **cavalry**.

Soldiers who go on foot are the **infantry**.

A soldier trained for specially daring raids is a **commando**.

A soldier trained to fight on land or at sea is a **marine**.

A soldier who goes into battle by parachute is a **paratrooper**.

WORDS FOR A LOT OF SOLDIERS ARE

army   **troops**

For other fighters, see **fight**

---

solemn *adjective*

They looked solemn when they heard the news.

OTHER WORDS YOU MIGHT USE ARE **grave**   **serious**   **thoughtful**

solid *adjective*

1 Cricket balls are solid.

The opposite is hollow

2 We were glad to get out of the mud onto solid ground.

OTHER WORDS YOU MIGHT USE ARE **firm**   **hard**

The opposite is soft

solution *noun*

Did you get the solution to the puzzle?

OTHER WORDS YOU MIGHT USE ARE **answer**   **explanation**

solve *verb*

Jo solved the puzzle in a couple of minutes.

OTHER VERBS YOU MIGHT USE ARE **to answer**   **to explain**   **to work out**

song *noun*

DIFFERENT KINDS OF MUSIC FOR SINGING ARE

ballad   carol   folk song   hymn   lullaby   pop song   shanty

For other words to do with music, see **music**

soothe *verb*

Quiet music soothes your nerves.

OTHER VERBS YOU MIGHT USE ARE   **to calm   to comfort   to relax**

The opposite is disturb

sore *adjective*

Jo had a sore place on her knee.

OTHER WORDS YOU MIGHT USE ARE   **aching   inflamed   painful   raw   red   tender**

sorrow *noun*

Jo was full of sorrow when her cat died.

OTHER WORDS YOU MIGHT USE ARE   **grief   misery   sadness   unhappiness**

sorry *adjective*

1 He was sorry when he saw the damage he had done.

OTHER WORDS ARE   **apologetic   ashamed   regretful   repentant**

2 Jo was sorry for the sick boy.

OTHER WORDS ARE   **sad   sympathetic**

sort *noun*

1 Which sort of cake do you like?

OTHER WORDS YOU MIGHT USE ARE   **brand   kind   type   variety**

2 What sort of dog is that?

OTHER WORDS ARE   **breed   species**

sort *verb*

Sam sorted the library books.

OTHER VERBS YOU MIGHT USE ARE   **to arrange   to classify   to organize**

sound *adjective*

1 Jo's dog is in a sound condition.

OTHER WORDS YOU MIGHT USE ARE   **healthy   strong**

2 The teacher said we had done sound work.

OTHER WORDS YOU MIGHT USE ARE   **correct   good   reasonable**

sound *noun*, see next page

sour *adjective*

a sour taste.

OTHER WORDS YOU MIGHT USE ARE   **acid   sharp   tangy   tart**

The opposite is sweet

source *noun*

the source of a river.

OTHER WORDS ARE   **beginning   origin   starting point**

a
b
c
d
e
f
g
h
i
j
k
l
m
n
o
p
q
r
s
t
u
v
w
x
y
z

193

sound *noun* and *verb*

DIFFERENT SOUNDS WE CAN MAKE ARE

bawl	boo	clap	cry	groan
hiccup	hiss	jeer	lisp	moan
scream	shout	shriek	sigh	sniff
snore	sob	wail	whistle	yell

For other sounds we make, see **talk**

DIFFERENT SOUNDS ANIMALS MAKE ARE

bark	bellow	bleat	bray	croak
growl	grunt	howl	jabber	low
miaow	moo	neigh	purr	roar
screech	snarl	snort	squeak	squeal
whine	whinny	yap		

SOUNDS DIFFERENT BIRDS MAKE ARE

cackle	chirp	cluck	coo	crow
hoot	quack	screech	squawk	twitter
warble				

SOUNDS INSECTS MAKE ARE

buzz	drone	hum	murmur

DIFFERENT SOUNDS THINGS MAKE ARE

bang	blare	bleep	boom	chime
clang	clank	clash	clatter	click
clink	crack	crackle	crash	creak
jangle	jingle	peal	ping	plop
pop	rattle	ring	rumble	rustle
sizzle	slam	snap	splutter	swish
throb	thud	thunder	tick	tinkle
twang	whiz			

For other words, see **music**, **noise**

space *noun*

1 Give me a bit of space.
   ANOTHER WORD IS   **room**
2 Write your answer in the space.
   ANOTHER WORD IS   **blank**
3 What goes in that empty space?
   OTHER WORDS YOU MIGHT USE ARE   **gap**   **hole**   **opening**

spacecraft *noun*

DIFFERENT KINDS OF SPACECRAFT ARE   **rocket**   **spaceship**   **space**   **shuttle**

spare *adjective*

Take some spare socks in case you get your feet wet.
   OTHER WORDS YOU MIGHT USE ARE   **additional**   **extra**

spare *verb*

The cruel soldier would not spare his enemy.
   OTHER VERBS YOU MIGHT USE ARE   **to be merciful to**   **to forgive**   **to let off**
      to pardon   **to reprieve**   **to save**

sparkle *verb*

The firework sparkled in the dark.
   OTHER VERBS YOU MIGHT USE ARE   **to flash**   **to spark**

speak *verb*
For other verbs, see **talk**

---

spear *noun*
A spear used by knights in old times was a **lance**.
A spear used to kill whales is a **harpoon**.
A spear you throw as a sport is a **javelin**.

---

special *adjective*
1 Your birthday is a special day.
    ANOTHER WORD IS **important**
2 Petrol has a special smell.
    OTHER WORDS ARE **different   distinct**
3 Jo has tea in her special mug.
    OTHER WORDS YOU MIGHT USE ARE **individual   particular   personal**

specimen *noun*
Show me a specimen of your work.
    OTHER WORDS YOU MIGHT USE ARE **example   illustration   sample**

speck *noun*
a speck of dust.
    OTHER WORDS ARE **bit   dot   grain   spot**

speckled *adjective*
a speckled pattern.
    OTHER WORDS ARE **dotted   mottled   spotty**

spectacular *adjective*
a spectacular fireworks display.
    OTHER WORDS YOU MIGHT USE ARE **big   exciting   impressive**

speech *noun*
We listened to the speech.
    OTHER WORDS YOU MIGHT USE ARE **lecture   talk**

speed *noun*
We walked at an ordinary speed.
    OTHER WORDS YOU MIGHT USE ARE **pace   rate**

spell *noun*
a magic spell.
    OTHER WORDS YOU MIGHT USE ARE **charm   enchantment**

spend *verb*

1 How much money did you spend?
OTHER VERBS YOU MIGHT USE ARE **to pay** **to use**

2 We spent a nice day by the sea.
ANOTHER VERB IS **to pass**

spike *noun*

There were spikes along the top of the railings.
OTHER WORDS YOU MIGHT USE ARE **point** **prong**

spill *verb*

Who spilt the milk on the carpet?
OTHER VERBS YOU MIGHT USE ARE **to drop** **to slop** **to tip** **to upset**

spin *verb*

The top spun round and round.
OTHER VERBS ARE **to revolve** **to turn** **to twirl** **to whirl**

---

spirit *noun*

Another word for your spirit is your **soul**.

SPIRITS YOU READ ABOUT IN STORIES ARE

demon	**devil**	**fairy**	**genie**
ghost	**gremlin**	**imp**	**phantom**
poltergeist	(*informal*) **spook**		

---

spiteful *adjective*

Jo doesn't like people who make spiteful remarks.
OTHER WORDS YOU MIGHT USE ARE (*informal*) **catty** **hurtful** **nasty** **unkind**
The opposite is kind

splash *verb*

The car splashed water over us.
OTHER VERBS YOU MIGHT USE ARE **to shower** **to slop** **to spatter**

splendid *adjective*

1 The soldiers wore splendid uniforms.
OTHER WORDS YOU MIGHT USE ARE **brilliant** **gorgeous** **grand** **impressive** **magnificent**

2 We had a splendid holiday.
For other words, see **good**

split *verb*

1 He split the log with an axe.
OTHER VERBS YOU MIGHT USE ARE **to chop** **to crack** **to cut** **to slice**

2 We split into two teams.
OTHER VERBS ARE **to divide** **to separate**

spoil *verb*

The stain has spoilt my new dress.
OTHER VERBS YOU MIGHT USE ARE **to damage** (*informal*) **to mess up** **to ruin** **to wreck**

sport *noun*

DIFFERENT SPORTS ARE

athletics	baseball	basketball	boxing
climbing	cricket	cycling	darts
fishing	football	golf	gymnastics
hockey	ice hockey	rounders	rugby
running	sailing	showjumping	skating
skiing	snooker	soccer	squash
surfing	swimming	table tennis	tennis
volleyball	water-skiing	windsurfing	wrestling
yachting			

spot *noun*

1 You've got a dirty spot on your new trousers.
OTHER WORDS YOU MIGHT USE ARE
blot   dot   mark   speck   stain

2 I've got spots on my face.
DIFFERENT KINDS OF SPOTS ARE
boil   freckle   mole   pimple
A spot on your eyelid is a **sty**.
A large number of spots is a **rash**.

3 Here's a nice spot for a picnic.
OTHER WORDS ARE
place   position   situation

spray *verb*
The bus sprayed us with water when it went through the puddle.
OTHER VERBS YOU MIGHT USE ARE **to scatter   to shower   to spatter   to splash   to sprinkle**

spread *verb*
We spread the map on the table.
OTHER VERBS YOU MIGHT USE ARE **to lay out   to open out   to unfold**

spring *verb*
1 The cat crouched, ready to spring on the mouse.
OTHER VERBS YOU MIGHT USE ARE **to jump   to leap   to pounce**

2 Weeds sprang up all over the garden.
OTHER VERBS ARE **to grow   to shoot**

sprout *verb*
The seeds began to sprout.
OTHER VERBS YOU MIGHT USE ARE **to grow   to shoot up   to spring up**

squabble *verb*
Those boys are always squabbling.
OTHER VERBS YOU MIGHT USE ARE **to argue   to fight   to quarrel**

squeeze *verb*
1 I squeezed an orange to make some juice.
OTHER VERBS YOU MIGHT USE ARE **to crush   to press**

2 They squeezed us into a little room.
OTHER VERBS ARE **to crowd   to push   to shove   to squash**

squirt *verb*
Water squirted out of the hole.
OTHER VERBS YOU MIGHT USE ARE **to pour   to spout   to spurt   to stream**

stack *noun*
a stack of books.
OTHER WORDS ARE **heap   mound   pile**

stage *noun*
1 We stood on the stage to sing.
ANOTHER WORD IS **platform**

2 The baby is at the crawling stage.
OTHER WORDS ARE **period   phase**

stain *noun*

What's that stain on your shirt?

OTHER WORDS ARE **blot** **mark** **smudge** **spot**

stairs *noun*

OTHER WORDS YOU MIGHT USE ARE **staircase** **steps**

stale *adjective*

1 stale bread.

OTHER WORDS YOU MIGHT USE ARE **dry** **old**

2 stale news.

ANOTHER WORD IS **out-of-date**

The opposite is *fresh*

stalk *noun*

a flower on a stalk.

ANOTHER WORD IS **stem**

stand *verb*

1 We all stood when the visitors arrived.

OTHER VERBS YOU MIGHT USE ARE **to get up** **to rise**

2 I stood my books on the shelf.

OTHER VERBS ARE **to arrange** **to place** **to position**

standard *noun*

Our teacher expects a high standard of work.

OTHER WORDS YOU MIGHT USE ARE **level** **quality**

stare *verb*

For other verbs, see **look**

start *verb*

1 What time does the film start?

OTHER VERBS YOU MIGHT USE ARE **to begin** **to commence**

2 Our teacher has started a chess club.

OTHER VERBS ARE **to create** **to introduce** **to set up**

3 They started on their journey at dawn.

OTHER VERBS ARE **to depart** **to embark** **to set off** **to set out**

startle *verb*

The explosion startled us.

OTHER VERBS YOU MIGHT USE ARE **to alarm** **to frighten** **to shock** **to surprise** **to upset**

starving *adjective*

For other words, see **hungry**

state *verb*

Dad stated that he had no money.

OTHER VERBS YOU MIGHT USE ARE **to announce** **to declare** **to report** **to say**

statement *noun*

The police issued a statement about the burglary.

OTHER WORDS YOU MIGHT USE ARE **announcement** **communication**

statue *noun*

We saw some statues in the museum.

OTHER WORDS YOU MIGHT USE ARE **carving** **figure** **sculpture**

a
b
c
d
e
f
g
h
i
j
k
l
m
n
o
p
q
r
s
t
u
v
w
x
y
z

stay *verb*

1 Stay here until I come back.
OTHER VERBS YOU MIGHT USE ARE **to remain   to stop   to wait**

2 Stay on the path.
OTHER VERBS ARE **to carry on   to continue   to keep on**

3 Jo went to stay with Granny.
ANOTHER WORD IS **to visit**

steady *adjective*

1 Make sure the ladder is steady.
OTHER WORDS YOU MIGHT USE ARE **firm   secure   solid**

2 The music had a steady rhythm.
OTHER WORDS ARE **constant   continuous   even   regular**

---

steal *verb*
OTHER VERBS YOU MIGHT USE ARE
(*informal*) **to pinch   to take**
Someone who steals things is a **robber** or a **thief**.
Someone who steals things from someone's house is a **burglar**.
Someone who steals things in a riot is a **looter**.
Someone who steals things from a shop is a **shoplifter**.
Someone who steals by attacking people in the street is a **mugger**.
Someone who steals things out of your pocket is a **pickpocket**.
Someone who used to steal things from travellers was a **highwayman**.

---

step *noun*

1 We all moved forwards one step.
OTHER WORDS YOU MIGHT USE ARE **pace   stride**

2 I climbed up the steps.
ANOTHER WORD IS **stair**

stern *adjective*

She had a stern look on her face.
OTHER WORDS YOU MIGHT USE ARE **angry   grim   severe   strict**

---

stick *noun*
DIFFERENT KINDS OF STICK ARE:
a long straight stick
pole   rod
a stick that is part of a plant
branch   stalk   twig
a stick used in a relay race or by the conductor of a band
baton
a stick used to support plants
bamboo   cane
a stick used as a weapon
club   truncheon
a stick used to help someone walk
crutch   walking stick
a magician's stick
wand

---

stick *verb*

1 The door has stuck.
   ANOTHER VERB IS **to jam**

2 This glue will stick plastic.
   OTHER VERBS YOU MIGHT USE ARE **to fasten**   **to fix**   **to glue**

3 She stuck a pin in me!
   OTHER VERBS ARE **to jab**   **to stab**

stiff *adjective*

1 stiff cardboard.
   OTHER WORDS YOU MIGHT USE ARE **hard**   **rigid**

2 stiff paste.
   ANOTHER WORD IS **thick**

still *adjective*

It was a very still evening.
   OTHER WORDS ARE **calm**   **peaceful**   **quiet**

stir *verb*

1 Sam stirred the cake mixture.
   OTHER VERBS YOU MIGHT USE ARE **to beat**   **to mix**   **to whisk**

2 Mum called Jo and said it was time to stir.
   OTHER VERBS ARE **to get going**   **to get up**   **to move**

stomach *noun*

AN INFORMAL WORD IS **tummy**
A word some people think is impolite is **belly**.

stone *noun*

DIFFERENT KINDS OF STONE ARE **boulder**   **cobble**   **gravel**   **jewel**   **pebble**   **rock**

stoop *verb*

I stooped down to pull up my sock.
   OTHER VERBS YOU MIGHT USE ARE **to bend**   **to bow**   **to crouch**   **to kneel**

stop *verb*

1 The policeman stopped the traffic.
   OTHER VERBS YOU MIGHT USE ARE **to check**   **to halt**   **to hold up**

2 The bus stopped.
   OTHER VERBS ARE **to draw up**   **to halt**   **to pull up**

3 The noise suddenly stopped.
   OTHER VERBS ARE **to cease**   **to end**   **to finish**

4 You can stop for tea.
   ANOTHER VERB IS **to stay**

store *verb*

We store food in the fridge.
   OTHER VERBS YOU MIGHT USE ARE **to keep**   **to put away**   **to save**

a
b
c
d
e
f
g
h
i
j
k
l
m
n
o
p
q
r
s
t
u
v
w
x
y
z

201

storm *noun*
> DIFFERENT KINDS OF STORM:
> a violent storm
> **tempest**
> a snow storm
> **blizzard**
> a storm with a lot of wind
> **gale   hurricane   tornado   whirlwind**
> a storm with a lot of rain
> **deluge   downpour   rainstorm**
> a storm with thunder and lightning
> **thunderstorm**
> For other words, see **weather**

story *noun*
> OTHER WORDS YOU MIGHT USE ARE
> **narrative   tale**
>
> DIFFERENT KINDS OF STORY ARE
> **adventure story   comedy   fable   fairy tale   fantasy   folk tale
> legend   love story   myth   novel   parable   romance**

stout *adjective*
a stout person.
> OTHER WORDS YOU MIGHT USE ARE   **fat   overweight   plump**   (*informal*) **tubby**
The opposite is **thin**

straight *adjective*
a straight line. a straight road.
> ANOTHER WORD IS   **direct**
The opposite is **crooked**

strain *verb*
1 He strained to escape from the monster's grip.
> OTHER VERBS YOU MIGHT USE ARE   **to make an effort   to struggle   to try hard**
2 Jo strained a muscle when she was running.
> OTHER VERBS ARE   **to damage   to hurt   to injure**
3 Don't strain yourself!
> OTHER VERBS ARE   **to exhaust   to tire out   to wear out**

strange *adjective*
1 When I woke up I was in a strange place.
> OTHER WORDS YOU MIGHT USE ARE   **different   foreign   new   unfamiliar
> unknown**
The opposite is **familiar**
2 A strange thing happened.
> OTHER WORDS ARE   **curious   extraordinary   funny   mysterious   odd
> peculiar   puzzling   queer   surprising   unusual**
The opposite is **ordinary**

stranger *noun*
Please show me the way, because I am a stranger here.
A stranger might be a **foreigner** or a **visitor**.

stray *verb*
Whatever you do, don't stray in the forest.
> OTHER VERBS YOU MIGHT USE ARE **to get lost**   **to roam about**   **to wander**

streak *noun*
The plane left a white streak in the sky.
> OTHER WORDS YOU MIGHT USE ARE **line**   **stripe**

stream *noun*
We paddled across a stream.
> ANOTHER WORD IS **brook**
A big stream is a **river**.
For other words, see **water**

strength *noun*
Have you got the strength to lift this box?
> OTHER WORDS ARE **force**   **might**   **power**

strengthen *verb*
Dad put in some posts to strengthen the fence.
> OTHER VERBS YOU MIGHT USE ARE **to reinforce**   **to support**
The opposite is weaken

stretch *verb*
You can stretch elastic.
> OTHER VERBS YOU MIGHT USE ARE **to lengthen**   **to pull out**

strict *adjective*
a strict teacher.
> OTHER WORDS YOU MIGHT USE ARE **firm**   **severe**   **stern**

---

string *noun*
> OTHER THINGS YOU MIGHT USE TO TIE THINGS UP ARE
> **cord**   **lace**   **line**   **ribbon**   **rope**   **wire**

---

strip *verb*
We stripped off our clothes to go swimming.
> OTHER VERBS YOU MIGHT USE ARE **to peel off**   **to remove**   **to take off**

stripe *noun*
Sam's football shirt has red and white stripes.
> OTHER WORDS ARE **band**   **line**   **strip**

strong *adjective*
1 a strong person.
OTHER WORDS YOU MIGHT USE ARE **healthy** **muscular** **sturdy** **tough** **wiry**
2 a strong rope. strong walking shoes.
OTHER WORDS ARE **sound** **stout** **thick**
The opposite is weak

struggle *verb*
1 The thief struggled to get away.
OTHER VERBS YOU MIGHT USE ARE **to fight** **to wrestle**
2 We struggled to put the tent up.
OTHER VERBS ARE **to exert yourself** **to make an effort** **to strive** **to try**

stubborn *adjective*
The stubborn animal refused to move.
OTHER WORDS YOU MIGHT USE ARE **defiant** **disobedient** **obstinate**

study *verb*
1 Mum is studying for an exam.
OTHER VERBS YOU MIGHT USE ARE **to learn** **to revise** (*informal*) **to swot**
2 The police studied the evidence.
OTHER VERBS ARE **to analyse** **to consider** **to examine** **to investigate**
to think about

stuff *noun*
1 What's this stuff in the jar?
ANOTHER WORD IS **substance**
2 What's that stuff in the attic?
OTHER WORDS ARE **articles** **odds and ends** **things**
3 I put my stuff in a box.
OTHER WORDS ARE **belongings** **possessions**

stuffy *adjective*
a stuffy room.
OTHER WORDS YOU MIGHT USE ARE **close** **muggy** **stifling** **warm**

stumble *verb*
I stumbled over a big stone.
OTHER VERBS YOU MIGHT USE ARE **to blunder** **to stagger** **to trip**

stun *verb*
1 The hit on the head stunned her.
OTHER VERBS YOU MIGHT USE ARE **to daze** **to knock out**
2 The unexpected news stunned us.
OTHER VERBS ARE **to amaze** **to astonish** **to shock** **to surprise**

stupid *adjective*
1 a stupid idea.
OTHER WORDS YOU MIGHT USE ARE **crazy** **foolish** **idiotic** **silly**
2 a stupid person.
OTHER WORDS ARE **dense** **dim** **dull** **slow** (*informal*) **thick**
The opposite is clever

style *noun*
Jo likes the new style of dancing.
OTHER WORDS YOU MIGHT USE ARE **fashion** **way**

subject *noun*
Sam chose an interesting subject for his project.
OTHER WORDS YOU MIGHT USE ARE **theme topic**

submit *verb*
1 The wrestler submitted to his opponent.
OTHER VERBS YOU MIGHT USE ARE **to give in to surrender to yield**
2 We must submit our work today.
OTHER VERBS ARE **to give in to hand in to present**

substance *noun*
What's this sticky substance?
OTHER WORDS YOU MIGHT USE ARE **material stuff**

subtract *verb*
Our teacher subtracts marks for untidy work.
OTHER VERBS YOU MIGHT USE ARE **to deduct to take away**

succeed *verb*
1 Jo succeeded in winning the race.
OTHER VERBS YOU MIGHT USE ARE **to be successful to do well**
2 Did your plan succeed?
ANOTHER VERB IS **to work**

sudden *adjective*
The car came to a sudden halt.
OTHER WORDS YOU MIGHT USE ARE **abrupt hasty quick unexpected**
The opposite is gradual

suffer *verb*
I hate to see animals suffer pain.
OTHER VERBS YOU MIGHT USE ARE **to bear to endure to go through
to put up with to stand**

suffering *noun*
For other words, see **pain**

sufficient *adjective*
Have you got sufficient money for your journey?
OTHER WORDS YOU MIGHT USE ARE **adequate enough**

suggest *verb*
What do you suggest we should do?
OTHER VERBS YOU MIGHT USE ARE **to advise to propose to recommend**

suitable *adjective*
Is this dress suitable for a wedding?
OTHER WORDS YOU MIGHT USE ARE **appropriate proper right**

sulky *adjective*
After Mum told him off he was sulky for hours.
OTHER WORDS ARE **bad-tempered cross gloomy moody sullen**
The opposite is cheerful

sunny *adjective*
sunny weather.
OTHER WORDS YOU MIGHT USE ARE **bright clear cloudless fine**

supply *noun*
There's a supply of paper in the cupboard.
OTHER WORDS YOU MIGHT USE ARE **reserve stock**

a
b
c
d
e
f
g
h
i
j
k
l
m
n
o
p
q
r
s
t
u
v
w
x
y
z

supply *verb*

We took our own sandwiches, and our teacher supplied the drinks.

OTHER VERBS YOU MIGHT USE ARE **to contribute   to give   to provide**

support *verb*

1 Those pillars support the roof.

OTHER VERBS YOU MIGHT USE ARE **to bear   to hold up   to prop up**

2 Our friends supported us when we were in trouble.

OTHER VERBS ARE **to aid   to assist   to encourage   to help   to stand up for**

supporter *noun*

Sam is a supporter of the local team.

OTHER WORDS ARE **fan   follower**

suppose *verb*

Let's suppose that Jo's the queen.

OTHER VERBS YOU MIGHT USE ARE **to assume   to believe   to imagine   to pretend**

sure *adjective*

1 I'm sure he will come.

OTHER WORDS YOU MIGHT USE ARE **certain   confident   convinced   definite   positive**

2 He's sure to come.

ANOTHER WORD IS **bound**

surprise *verb*

The unexpected news surprised us.

OTHER VERBS YOU MIGHT USE ARE **to amaze   to astonish   to shock   to startle   to stun**

surrender *verb*

After a long fight, the army surrendered.

OTHER VERBS YOU MIGHT USE ARE **to give in   to submit   to yield**

survey *noun*

We did a survey to find out who comes to school by car.

OTHER WORDS YOU MIGHT USE ARE **investigation   study**

survive *verb*

Some plants don't survive through the winter.

OTHER VERBS YOU MIGHT USE ARE **to keep going   to last   to live**

suspect *verb*

Mum suspects that I broke her mug.

OTHER VERBS ARE **to guess   to have a feeling   to think**

swamp *noun*

The lorry got stuck in the swamp.

OTHER WORDS ARE **bog   marsh**

swear *verb*

1 Do you swear that you'll tell the truth?

OTHER VERBS YOU MIGHT USE ARE **to give your word   to promise   to vow**

2 He swore when he hit his finger.

ANOTHER VERB IS **to curse**

sweep *verb*

I swept the floor.

ANOTHER VERB IS **to brush**

For ways to clean things, see **clean**

sweet *adjective*
For other words to describe how things taste, see **taste**
The opposite is sour

swell *verb*
You can see the tyre swell while you pump it up.
OTHER VERBS ARE **to blow up**   **to bulge**   **to get bigger**   **to grow**   **to puff up**

swelling *noun*
I got a nasty swelling where the wasp stung me.
OTHER WORDS YOU MIGHT USE ARE **bulge**   **bump**   **lump**

swift *adjective*
a swift journey.
OTHER WORDS YOU MIGHT USE ARE **fast**   **quick**   **rapid**   **speedy**
The opposite is slow

swindle *verb*
He swindled us and made us pay too much.
OTHER VERBS YOU MIGHT USE ARE **to cheat**   **to deceive**   **to fool**   **to trick**

swing *verb*
The branches swung to and fro in the wind.
ANOTHER VERB IS **to sway**

switch *verb*
I switched places with my friend.
OTHER VERBS YOU MIGHT USE ARE **to change**   **to exchange**   **to swap**

swoop *verb*
The owl swooped down on its prey.
OTHER VERBS ARE **to dive**   **to pounce**

sympathy *noun*
He didn't have much sympathy when I was ill!
OTHER WORDS YOU MIGHT USE ARE **consideration**   **feeling**   **mercy**   **pity**

symptom *noun*
Spots might be a symptom of measles.
OTHER WORDS ARE **indication**   **sign**

a
b
c
d
e
f
g
h
i
j
k
l
m
n
o
p
q
r
s
t
u
v
w
x
y
z

Tt

take *verb*

1 Take my hand.
OTHER VERBS YOU MIGHT USE ARE **to clasp**   **to get hold of**   **to grasp**   **to hold**   **to seize**

2 The bus takes you into town.
OTHER VERBS ARE **to bring**   **to carry**   **to transport**

3 The army took many prisoners.
OTHER VERBS ARE **to capture**   **to catch**   **to seize**

4 The burglar took the jewels.
OTHER VERBS ARE **to remove**   **to steal**

5 The dentist took out one of my teeth.
OTHER VERBS ARE **to extract**   **to remove**

talent *noun*

Sam has great talent in football.
OTHER WORDS YOU MIGHT USE ARE **ability**   **skill**

talented *adjective*

Jo is a talented musician.
OTHER WORDS YOU MIGHT USE ARE **clever**   **expert**   **gifted**   **skilful**

talk *noun*

1 I had a nice talk with Granny.
OTHER WORDS YOU MIGHT USE ARE **chat**   **conversation**   **discussion**

2 The head gave us a long talk.
OTHER WORDS ARE **address**   **lecture**   **speech**

---

talk *verb*

OTHER VERBS YOU MIGHT USE ARE
to communicate   **to express yourself**   **to say something**   **to speak**

THERE ARE DIFFERENT WAYS OF TALKING. YOU CAN

call out	**chat**	**chatter**	**exclaim**
gossip	**have a conversation**		**lisp**
mumble	**murmur**	**mutter**	**prattle**
recite a poem	**scream**	**screech**	**shout**
shriek	**snap at someone**		**snarl**
splutter	**stammer**	**stutter**	**whisper**
yell			

---

tall *adjective*

a tall tower.
ANOTHER WORD IS **high**
The opposite is low or short

tame *adjective*

These animals are very tame.
OTHER WORDS YOU MIGHT USE ARE **gentle**   **meek**   **obedient**   **safe**
The opposite is dangerous or wild

tangled *adjective*

tangled string.
OTHER WORDS YOU MIGHT USE ARE **knotted**   **muddled**   **twisted**

tank *noun*
A tank to keep fish in is an **aquarium**.

tap *verb*
She tapped on the door.
> OTHER VERBS YOU MIGHT USE ARE **to knock** **to rap**

task *noun*
> OTHER WORDS YOU MIGHT USE ARE **job** **work**

---

taste *noun*
1 Do you like the taste of this?
ANOTHER WORD IS
flavour
2 Can I have a taste of your ice cream?
OTHER WORDS YOU MIGHT USE ARE
bit **lick** **mouthful** **nibble** **piece**

WORDS TO DESCRIBE THINGS THAT TASTE NICE ARE
appetizing **delicious** **luscious** **tasty**

WORDS TO DESCRIBE THINGS THAT TASTE NASTY ARE
bad (*informal*) **off** **stale** **uneatable**

OTHER WORDS TO DESCRIBE HOW THINGS TASTE ARE
acid **bitter** **creamy** **fruity** **hot** **meaty** **peppery** **salty**
savoury **sharp** **sour** **spicy** **sugary** **sweet** **tangy**

---

taste *verb*
Taste a bit of this!
> OTHER VERBS YOU MIGHT USE ARE **to nibble** **to sample** **to sip** **to try**

---

teach *verb*
> OTHER WORDS YOU MIGHT USE ARE
> to teach someone in school **educate**
> to teach someone to do a job **instruct** **train**
> to teach someone to be good at a sport **coach**

---

teacher *noun*
DIFFERENT KINDS OF TEACHER ARE **lecturer** **professor** **schoolteacher** **tutor**
a person who teaches us to play games properly **coach** **trainer**
a person who teaches you how to do a particular thing **instructor**

team *noun*
a football team.
> ANOTHER WORD IS **side**

tear *verb*
Sam tore his jeans.
> OTHER VERBS ARE **to rip** **to slit** **to split**

tease *verb*
If you tease the cat she'll scratch.
> OTHER VERBS YOU MIGHT USE ARE **to annoy** **to laugh at** **to make fun of**
> **to pester** **to torment**

telephone *verb*

I telephoned Grandad to ask him to come to tea.
OTHER VERBS YOU MIGHT USE ARE **to call   to dial   to phone   to ring**

---

television *noun*

DIFFERENT KINDS OF TV PROGRAMME ARE

**cartoons   chat shows   comedy   commercials   films   interviews
music   nature programmes   news   plays   quiz shows   serials
sport**

---

tell *verb*

1 He told me he'd be home for tea.
OTHER VERBS YOU MIGHT USE ARE **to inform   to promise**
2 Our teacher told the story.
OTHER VERBS ARE **to narrate   to relate**
3 I told the police what happened.
OTHER VERBS ARE **to describe to someone   to explain to someone**
4 Mum told us to stop shouting.
OTHER VERBS ARE **to command   to instruct   to order**
to tell someone off
OTHER VERBS YOU MIGHT USE ARE **to reprimand   to scold   (*informal*) to tick off**

temper *noun*

1 Is Dad in a good temper?
ANOTHER WORD IS **mood**
2 Baby yells when she's in a temper.
OTHER WORDS YOU MIGHT USE ARE **rage   tantrum**
to lose your temper
A PHRASE IS **get angry**

tend *verb*

1 Grandad tends to fall asleep in the evening.
A PHRASE YOU MIGHT USE IS **to be liable to**
2 Nurses tend sick people.
OTHER VERBS YOU MIGHT USE ARE **to care for   to look after   to mind**

tender *adjective*

1 I gave the baby a tender smile.
OTHER WORDS YOU MIGHT USE ARE **affectionate   fond   gentle   kind   loving**
The opposite is **cruel**
2 The baby has tender skin.
OTHER WORDS ARE **delicate   soft**
The opposite is **tough**
3 I had a tender place where I hit my head.
OTHER WORDS ARE **sensitive   sore**

terrible *adjective*

There was a terrible storm.
OTHER WORDS YOU MIGHT USE ARE **alarming   awful   bad   dreadful
frightening   horrible   (*informal*) scary   terrific**

terrific *adjective*

1 I had a terrific idea.
For other words, see **good**
2 There was a terrific storm.
For other words, see **terrible**

terrify *verb*

The dog terrified the baby.

OTHER VERBS YOU MIGHT USE ARE **to alarm** **to frighten** **to scare** **to upset**

terror *noun*

People ran away from the fire in terror.

OTHER WORDS YOU MIGHT USE ARE **alarm** **fear** **fright** **panic**

test *noun*

1 a spelling test. a driving test.

ANOTHER WORD IS **exam** or **examination**

2 a scientific test.

OTHER WORDS YOU MIGHT USE ARE **experiment** **research** **trial**

thankful *adjective*

I was thankful it wasn't raining.

OTHER WORDS YOU MIGHT USE ARE **grateful** **pleased**

thaw *verb*

The snow thawed when the sun came out.

OTHER VERBS YOU MIGHT USE ARE **to melt** **to unfreeze**

The opposite is freeze

theatre *noun*

We went to the theatre for a Christmas treat.

OTHER WORDS YOU MIGHT USE ARE

performance **show**

THINGS YOU SEE IN A THEATRE ARE

ballet **comedy** **drama** **musical** **opera** **pantomime** **play**

For other words, see **entertainment**

thick *adjective*

1 a thick line.

OTHER WORDS YOU MIGHT USE ARE **broad** **wide**

2 a thick slice of cake.

AN INFORMAL WORD IS **chunky**

The opposite is thin

3 thick gravy.

The opposite is runny

thief *noun*

For different kinds of thief, see **steal**

thin *adjective*

1 a thin line.

OTHER WORDS YOU MIGHT USE ARE **fine** **narrow**

The opposite is thick

2 a thin person.

KIND WORDS YOU MIGHT USE ARE **lean** **slender** **slim**

AN UNKIND WORD IS **skinny**

The opposite is fat

3 thin gravy.

OTHER WORDS ARE **runny** **watery**

The opposite is thick

a
b
c
d
e
f
g
h
i
j
k
l
m
n
o
p
q
r
s
t
u
v
w
x
y
z

thing *noun*

1 What are these things in the cupboard?
OTHER WORDS YOU MIGHT USE ARE **article** **item** **object**

2 I've got several things on my mind.
OTHER WORDS ARE **idea** **thought** **worry**

3 I saw a funny thing today.
ANOTHER WORD IS **happening**

think *verb*

1 If you think, you won't make a mistake.
OTHER VERBS YOU MIGHT USE ARE **to attend** **to concentrate**

2 We thought about what to do.
OTHER VERBS ARE **to consider** **to reflect**

3 I think you are right.
OTHER VERBS ARE **to believe** **to feel** **to guess** **to suppose**

thorough *adjective*

1 a thorough job.
OTHER WORDS YOU MIGHT USE ARE **careful** **proper**

2 a thorough mess.
OTHER WORDS ARE **absolute** **complete** **utter**

thoughtful *adjective*

1 You look thoughtful today.
OTHER WORDS YOU MIGHT USE ARE **serious** **solemn**

2 It's thoughtful of you to wash up.
OTHER WORDS ARE **considerate** **friendly** **helpful** **unselfish**

threaten *verb*

For other verbs, see **frighten**

thrilling *adjective*

The band played thrilling music.
OTHER WORDS ARE **exciting** **rousing** **stirring**

throw *verb*

She threw a stone and broke the glass.
OTHER VERBS YOU MIGHT USE ARE **to bowl** **to cast** (*informal*) **to chuck** **to fling** **to hurl** **to lob** **to pitch** **to sling** **to toss**

tidy *adjective*

Mum asked Jo to make her room tidy.
OTHER WORDS YOU MIGHT USE ARE **neat** **orderly** **smart** **trim**

tie *verb*

1 Can you tie this string?
ANOTHER VERB IS **to knot**

2 I tied a bandage round my leg.
OTHER VERBS YOU MIGHT USE ARE **to bind** **to fasten** **to fix** **to wind**

3 They tied up the boat.
OTHER VERBS ARE **to anchor** **to moor**

4 The farmer tied up the bull.
ANOTHER VERB IS **to tether**

tight *adjective*

1 Make sure the lid is tight.
>OTHER WORDS YOU MIGHT USE ARE **firm   fixed   secure**

2 These shoes are a bit tight.
>OTHER WORDS ARE **close-fitting   small**

The opposite is loose

tilt *verb*

The boat tilted to one side.
>OTHER VERBS ARE **to lean   to slant   to slope   to tip**

---

time *noun*

1 Is this a good time to ring Granny?

OTHER WORDS YOU MIGHT USE ARE

moment   opportunity

2 Shakespeare lived in the time of Elizabeth I.

OTHER WORDS ARE

age   era   period

UNITS USED TO MEASURE TIME ARE

centuries   days   fortnights   hours   minutes   months   seconds   weeks   years

DIFFERENT TIMES OF THE DAY ARE

afternoon   bedtime   dawn   dusk   evening   midday   midnight   morning   night   noon   sunrise   sunset   twilight

THE SEASONS OF THE YEAR ARE

spring   summer   autumn   winter

SPECIAL TIMES OF THE YEAR ARE

an anniversary   your birthday   Christmas   Diwali   Easter   Hallowe'en   Hogmanay   Midsummer   New Year   Passover   Ramadan   St Valentine's Day   Yom Kippur

THINGS WE USE TO MEASURE TIME ARE

calendar   clock   digital watch   hourglass   sundial   watch

---

timid *adjective*

He was too timid to ask for more.
>OTHER WORDS ARE **cowardly   fearful   nervous   shy**

The opposite is brave

tiny *adjective*

Some insects are tiny.
>OTHER WORDS ARE **little   microscopic   minute   small**

The opposite is big

tip *noun*

1 the tip of a pencil.
>OTHER WORDS ARE **end   point**

2 the tip of an iceberg.
>OTHER WORDS ARE **head   top**

tip *verb*

A big wave tipped the boat over.
>OTHER VERBS YOU MIGHT USE ARE **to capsize   to overturn   to turn over   to upset**

tired *adjective*

1 We were tired after our walk.
other words you might use are **exhausted   weary   worn out**

2 Go to bed: you look tired.
other words are **drowsy   sleepy**

tiring *adjective*

tiring work.
other words you might use are **exhausting   hard**
The opposite is easy

toilet *noun*

other words you might use are **lavatory**   (*informal*) **loo   WC**

token *noun*

I've got a token for a free drink.
other words are **counter   coupon   voucher**

tomb *noun*

other words are **grave   gravestone   memorial   monument   tombstone**

tone *noun*

Her voice had a gentle tone.
other words you might use are **expression   note   sound**

---

tool *noun*

Dad has tools for every job.
other words you might use are

device	**gadget**	**implement**	**instrument**

tools used for woodwork are

chisel	**clamp**	**drill**	**hammer**
pincers	**plane**	**saw**	**vice**

tools you might use on the car are

jack	**lever**	**oil can**	**pliers**
screwdriver	**spanner**		

tools used in the garden are

broom	**fork**	**hoe**	**lawnmower**
rake	**shears**	**spade**	**trowel**
watering can			

other tools people use are

axe	**chopper**	**crowbar**	**file**
ladder	**pick**	**shovel**	**sledgehammer**
wrench			

spanner

saw

hammer

top *noun*
1 the top of a hill.
OTHER WORDS YOU MIGHT USE ARE **head** **peak** **summit** **tip**
The opposite is bottom
2 the top of a jar.
OTHER WORDS ARE **cap** **cover** **lid**

topic *noun*
We all wrote about different topics.
OTHER WORDS YOU MIGHT USE ARE **subject** **theme**

torment *verb*
1 I hate it when people torment animals.
OTHER VERBS YOU MIGHT USE ARE **to annoy** **to distress** **to tease**
2 Sam saw a big boy tormenting some little ones.
OTHER VERBS ARE **to bully** **to victimize**

torture *verb*
It's horrible to think of people torturing each other.
OTHER VERBS ARE **to be cruel to** **to hurt**

total *adjective*
Because it rained, the picnic was a total disaster.
OTHER WORDS YOU MIGHT USE ARE **absolute** **complete**

total *noun*
Count the money and tell me the total.
OTHER WORDS ARE **amount** **answer** **sum**

---

touch *verb*
OTHER VERBS YOU MIGHT USE ARE
to contact **to feel** **to handle**

DIFFERENT WAYS TO TOUCH PEOPLE OR ANIMALS ARE
to caress **to cuddle** **to embrace** **to fondle** **to kiss** **to pat**
to rub **to stroke** **to tickle**

DIFFERENT WAYS TO TOUCH THINGS ARE
to fiddle with **to fidget with** **to finger** **to handle** **to hold**

---

tough *adjective*
You need tough shoes to walk in the hills.
OTHER WORDS YOU MIGHT USE ARE **hard-wearing** **stout** **strong** **sturdy**

tour *verb*
We toured the castle before we had our picnic.
OTHER VERBS ARE **to go round** **to visit**

tow *verb*
The car was towing a caravan.
OTHER VERBS YOU MIGHT USE ARE **to haul** **to pull**

a
b
c
d
e
f
g
h
i
j
k
l
m
n
o
p
q
r
s
t
u
v
w
x
y
z

town *noun*

A big town is a **city**.
A small town is a **village**.
The areas at the edge of a town are the **outskirts** or **suburbs**.

THINGS YOU OFTEN FIND IN A TOWN ARE

bank	**bus station**	**café**	**car park**
church	**cinema**	**college**	**factory**
flats	**hotel**	**leisure centre**	**library**
museum	**offices**	**park**	**police station**
post office	**railway station**	**school**	**shopping centre**
supermarket	**theatre**	**town hall**	

For other words, see **shop**

IN THE OUTSKIRTS OF A TOWN YOU MIGHT FIND

housing estate   **industrial estate**   **retail park**

track *verb*

The hounds tracked the fox across the fields.

OTHER VERBS YOU MIGHT USE ARE   **to chase**   **to follow**   **to hunt**   **to pursue**
to trail

traffic *noun*

TRAFFIC YOU SEE ON THE ROADS INCLUDES

bicycles   **buses**   **cars**   **coaches**   **lorries**
motorbikes or **motorcycles**   **taxis**   **vans**
For other words, see **travel**

tragedy *noun*

The plane crash was a terrible tragedy.

OTHER WORDS YOU MIGHT USE ARE   **calamity**   **catastrophe**   **disaster**
misfortune

trail *noun*

For other words, see **path**

trail *verb*

1 The police trailed him for miles.
For other verbs, see **track**
2 Jo's scarf is so long that it trails in the mud.

ANOTHER VERB IS   **to drag**

train *noun*

We went to London on the train.
For other words, see **railway**

train *verb*

1 Jo's Dad trains the school team.

OTHER VERBS YOU MIGHT USE ARE   **to coach**   **to instruct**   **to teach**
2 The team trains every Thursday.

OTHER VERBS ARE   **to exercise**   **to practise**

trainer *noun*

1 Sam's feet are too big for his old trainers.
For other things you wear on your feet, see **shoe**
2 Our team has a new trainer.
ANOTHER WORD IS **coach**

transfer *verb*

1 A bus transferred us from the airport to the hotel.
OTHER VERBS YOU MIGHT USE ARE **to carry** **to take** **to transport**
2 The goalkeeper was transferred to another team.
OTHER VERBS ARE **to move** **to switch**

transform *verb*

The fairy transformed the pumpkin into a coach.
OTHER VERBS YOU MIGHT USE ARE **to change** **to turn**

transport *noun*

For different kinds of transport, see **travel**

trap *verb*

We trapped the mouse in a box.
OTHER VERBS YOU MIGHT USE ARE **to capture** **to catch** **to corner**

travel *noun*, see next page

treacherous *adjective*

Take care: that dog's treacherous.
OTHER WORDS YOU MIGHT USE ARE **dangerous** **untrustworthy**
The opposite is loyal

tread *verb*

Don't tread on the flowers.
OTHER VERBS YOU MIGHT USE ARE **to step** **to trample** **to walk**

treat *verb*

1 Treat your pets well.
OTHER VERBS YOU MIGHT USE ARE **to care for** **to look after**
2 How shall we treat this problem?
OTHER VERBS ARE **to attend to** **to deal with** **to tackle**

tree *noun*, see next page

tremble *verb*

I trembled with fear.
OTHER VERBS YOU MIGHT USE ARE **to quake** **to quiver** **to shake** **to shiver**
to shudder

tremendous *adjective*

1 We heard a tremendous explosion.
OTHER WORDS ARE **alarming** **awful** **fearful** **frightful** **terrible**
terrific
2 Granny gave us tremendous helpings of dinner.
OTHER WORDS ARE **big** **enormous** **huge** **large**

a
b
c
d
e
f
g
h
i
j
k
l
m
n
o
p
q
r
s
t
u
v
w
x
y
z

travel *verb*

DIFFERENT WAYS TO TRAVEL ARE

cruise	cycle	drive	fly
hitch-hike	ride	sail	walk

DIFFERENT KINDS OF JOURNEY ARE

cruise	drive	expedition	flight
hike	outing	pilgrimage	ramble
ride	safari	tour	trek
trip	voyage	walk	

A person who travels is a **traveller**.

OTHER WORDS FOR PEOPLE WHO TRAVEL ARE

a person who drives a car: **motorist**

a person who travels while someone else drives: **passenger**

a person who goes on foot

  hiker   pedestrian   rambler   walker

a person who travels to work every day: **commuter**

a traveller to a holy place: **pilgrim**

a person who travels on holiday

  holidaymaker   tourist

a person who travels in a boat

  sailor   yachtsman   yachtswoman

a person who travels to find somewhere new: **explorer**

people who travel about because that's how they like to live

  gypsies   nomads   tramps   travellers

Something you travel in is a **vehicle**.

DIFFERENT VEHICLES THAT PEOPLE TRAVEL IN ON THE ROADS ARE

bus	car	coach	jeep
minibus	motorbike or motorcycle		taxi
tram			

OTHER FORMS OF TRANSPORT FOR PASSENGERS ARE

aeroplane	bicycle	ferry	railway
underground			

WAYS PEOPLE USED TO TRAVEL ARE

carriage	horse	stagecoach

VEHICLES THAT CARRY GOODS ARE

articulated lorry		cart	lorry
pick-up truck	truck	van	wagon

OTHER KINDS OF TRANSPORT FOR GOODS ARE

aircraft	goods train	ship

VEHICLES MADE TO DO SPECIAL JOBS ARE

ambulance	bulldozer	caravan	digger
dustcart	fire engine	horsebox	milk float
police car	steamroller	tanker	tractor

For other words, see
  **aircraft, boat, car,
  railway**

tree *noun*

DIFFERENT KINDS OF TREE ARE

ash	beech	birch	cedar	chestnut
elm	fir	holly	larch	lime
maple	oak	palm tree	pine	plane
poplar	sycamore	willow	yew	

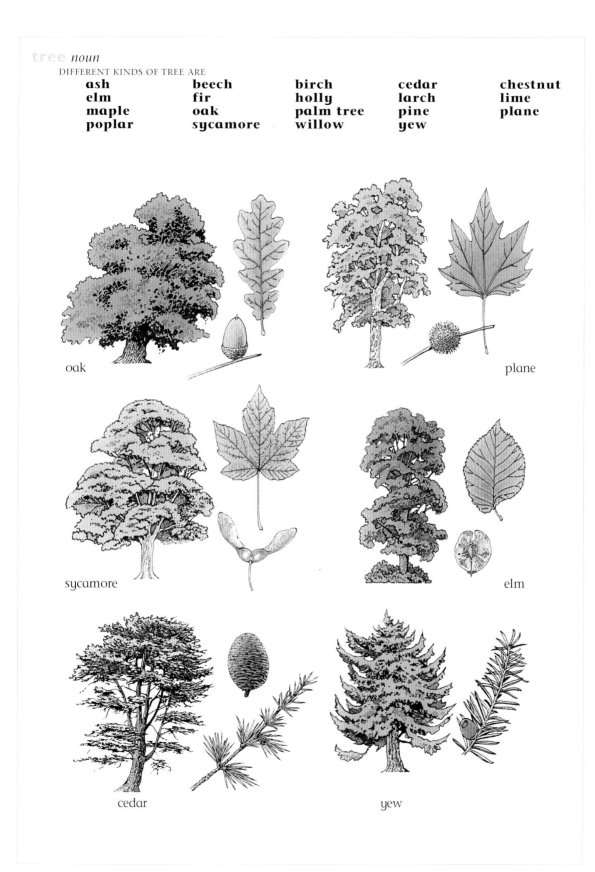

oak

plane

sycamore

elm

cedar

yew

trick *noun*

1 That was a nasty trick!
OTHER WORDS YOU MIGHT USE ARE **cheat   deception   fraud   hoax**
2 The dolphins did some amazing tricks.
ANOTHER WORD IS **stunt**

trick *verb*

He tricked us into buying rubbish.
OTHER VERBS YOU MIGHT USE ARE **to cheat   to fool   to hoax   to mislead   to swindle**

trickle *verb*

Water trickled out of the crack.
OTHER VERBS YOU MIGHT USE ARE **to dribble   to drip   to leak   to ooze   to run   to seep**

trip *noun*

a trip to the seaside.
OTHER WORDS YOU MIGHT USE ARE **excursion   expedition   outing   visit**
For other words, see **travel**

trouble *noun*

1 Mum has had a lot of trouble lately.
OTHER WORDS YOU MIGHT USE ARE **distress   grief   hardship   misery   misfortune   problems   sadness   worry**
2 There was some trouble in the playground at dinner time.
OTHER WORDS ARE **bother   commotion   disorder   fighting   fuss   row**
3 Sam takes trouble with his work.
OTHER WORDS ARE **care   effort**

trouble *verb*

Do wasps trouble you?
OTHER VERBS YOU MIGHT USE ARE **to annoy   to bother   to upset   to worry**

trousers *noun*

For other words, see **clothes**

true *adjective*

1 Is that story true?
OTHER WORDS YOU MIGHT USE ARE **correct   factual   genuine   real**
2 Jo is a true friend.
OTHER WORDS ARE **faithful   loyal   reliable   trustworthy**

trust *verb*

You can trust Jo to do her best.
PHRASES YOU MIGHT USE ARE (*informal*) **to bank on   to be sure of   to count on   to depend on   to have faith in   to rely on**

try *verb*

1 Sam tried to swim ten lengths.
OTHER VERBS ARE **to aim   to attempt   to endeavour   to exert yourself   to make an effort   to strive**
2 Can I try the cake?
ANOTHER VERB IS **to sample**
3 Try the brakes before you ride your bike.
OTHER VERBS ARE **to experiment with   to test**

tube *noun*

ANOTHER WORD IS **pipe**
A tube to take water from the tap to where you want it is a **hose**.

tune *noun*
Jo played a well-known tune.
ANOTHER WORD IS **melody**

tunnel *noun*
A tunnel that a rabbit makes is a **burrow**.
A tunnel under a road is a **subway** or **underpass**.

turn *noun*
It's your turn to play next.
OTHER WORDS ARE **chance   go   opportunity**

turn *verb*
1 The wheel began to turn.
OTHER VERBS YOU MIGHT USE ARE **to revolve   to rotate   to spin   to twirl   to whirl**
For other verbs, see **twist**
2 Tadpoles turn into frogs.
OTHER VERBS ARE **to become   to change into**
3 We turned the attic into a playroom.
OTHER VERBS ARE **to convert   to transform**

twinkle *verb*
The lights twinkled in the distance.
OTHER VERBS ARE **to flicker   to shine   to sparkle**
For other verbs, see **light**

twist *verb*
1 The road twisted up the hill.
OTHER VERBS YOU MIGHT USE ARE **to bend   to curve   to zigzag**
2 I twisted the wires round each other.
OTHER VERBS ARE **to coil   to curl   to loop   to turn   to wind**

type *noun*
1 What type of music do you like?
OTHER WORDS YOU MIGHT USE ARE **kind   sort**
2 What type of dog is that?
OTHER WORDS ARE **breed   species   variety**

typical *adjective*
In England, showers are typical April weather.
OTHER WORDS YOU MIGHT USE ARE **common   normal   ordinary   usual**
The opposite is unusual

Uu

ugly *adjective*
We screamed when we saw the ugly monster.
OTHER WORDS YOU MIGHT USE ARE **foul   frightful   hideous   monstrous   repulsive   unattractive**
The opposite is beautiful

uncommon *adjective*

Eagles are uncommon in this country.
OTHER WORDS YOU MIGHT USE ARE **infrequent   rare   unusual**
The opposite is common

unconscious *adjective*

If you are unconscious, you may be **knocked out** or you may have **fainted**.
The opposite is conscious

understand *verb*

Do you understand what I mean?
OTHER VERBS YOU MIGHT USE ARE **to follow   to grasp   to know   to realize   to see**

undo *verb*

Jo undid the parcel.
OTHER VERBS YOU MIGHT USE ARE **to unfasten   to untie**

unemployed *adjective*

PHRASES ARE **on the dole   out of work**

uneven *adjective*

1 We jolted along the uneven road.
OTHER WORDS YOU MIGHT USE ARE **bumpy   rough**
The opposite is smooth
2 The music had an uneven beat.
ANOTHER WORD IS **irregular**
The opposite is regular

unfair *adjective*

1 It's unfair if she gets more than me.
OTHER WORDS YOU MIGHT USE ARE **unjust   unreasonable   wrong**
2 We complained that the referee was unfair.
OTHER WORDS YOU MIGHT USE ARE **biased   prejudiced**
The opposite is fair

unfriendly *adjective*

Mum was upset by our neighbour's unfriendly remarks.
OTHER WORDS YOU MIGHT USE ARE **aggressive   angry   disagreeable   hostile   nasty   offensive   rude**
For other words, see **unkind**
The opposite is friendly

unhappy *adjective*

He was unhappy after his dog died.
OTHER WORDS ARE **depressed   gloomy   glum   heartbroken   miserable   sorrowful   tearful   troubled   wretched**
The opposite is happy

unite *verb*

We united to sing the last song.
OTHER VERBS YOU MIGHT USE ARE **to combine   to join together**

unkind *adjective*

Jo hates to see people being unkind to animals.
OTHER WORDS ARE **cruel   heartless   spiteful   thoughtless**
For other words, see **unfriendly**
The opposite is kind

unlikely *adjective*
I don't believe his unlikely story.
> OTHER WORDS YOU MIGHT USE ARE **far-fetched   improbable   incredible   unconvincing**

The opposite is *likely*

unlucky *adjective*
We were unlucky to miss the bus.
> ANOTHER WORD IS **unfortunate**

The opposite is *lucky*

unpleasant *adjective*
1 The accident was an unpleasant experience.
> OTHER WORDS YOU MIGHT USE ARE **awful   dreadful   frightening   painful   terrible   upsetting**

2 I hate touching unpleasant things.
> OTHER WORDS ARE **disgusting   horrible   nasty   objectionable**

3 The noisy neighbours were very unpleasant.
> OTHER WORDS ARE **rude   unfriendly**

The opposite is *pleasant*

untidy *adjective*
1 Our teacher hates untidy work.
> OTHER WORDS YOU MIGHT USE ARE **careless   disorganized   scruffy**

2 Everything was in an untidy pile on the floor.
> OTHER WORDS ARE **confused   disorderly   jumbled   muddled**

The opposite is *tidy*

unusual *adjective*
It's unusual to have snow in May.
> OTHER WORDS YOU MIGHT USE ARE **extraordinary   odd   peculiar   strange   surprising   uncommon**

The opposite is *common*

upset *verb*
1 The thunder upset the dog.
> OTHER VERBS YOU MIGHT USE ARE **to alarm   to bother   to distress   to frighten   to trouble   to worry**

2 Sam upset the milk.
> OTHER VERBS ARE **to knock over   to overturn   to spill**

urge *noun*
I had an urge to giggle.
> OTHER WORDS ARE **desire   wish**

urge *verb*
Mum urged us to be quick.
> OTHER VERBS YOU MIGHT USE ARE **to appeal to   to beg   to encourage   to entreat   to plead with**

use *verb*
1 They used the most up-to-date machines to dig the tunnel.
> ANOTHER VERB IS **to employ**

2 Have we used all the milk?
> OTHER VERBS YOU MIGHT USE ARE **to consume   to finish**

a b c d e f g h i j k l m n o p q r s t **u** v w x y z

useful *adjective*

1 Dad's penknife is a useful tool.
OTHER WORDS YOU MIGHT USE ARE **convenient handy practical**
2 Sam is a useful member of the team.
OTHER WORDS ARE **helpful valuable**
The opposite is useless

useless *adjective*

1 A car is useless without petrol.
ANOTHER WORD IS **unusable**
2 He was a useless goalkeeper.
OTHER WORDS ARE **incompetent worthless**
The opposite is useful

usual *adjective*

1 Ten o'clock is my usual bedtime.
OTHER WORDS YOU MIGHT USE ARE **normal ordinary regular**
2 It's usual to put milk in tea.
OTHER WORDS ARE **common expected typical**
The opposite is unusual

Vv

vague *adjective*

1 He made some vague comments, but nothing definite.
OTHER WORDS YOU MIGHT USE ARE **broad general**
2 He was a vague sort of person.
OTHER WORDS ARE **absent-minded forgetful scatterbrained**
The opposite is definite

vain *adjective*

He's so vain that he's always looking in the mirror.
OTHER WORDS ARE **boastful conceited proud**
The opposite is modest

valuable *adjective*

1 valuable jewels.
OTHER WORDS YOU MIGHT USE ARE **expensive precious priceless**
The opposite is worthless
2 He gave me some valuable advice.
OTHER WORDS ARE **helpful useful worthwhile**
The opposite is useless

vanish *verb*

The robber vanished into the crowd.
ANOTHER VERB IS **to disappear**

variety *noun*

1 There's a variety of things to eat.
OTHER WORDS YOU MIGHT USE ARE **assortment mixture**
2 Mum grows many varieties of flowers.
OTHER WORDS ARE **kind sort type**

various *adjective*
We made various sandwiches.
>OTHER WORDS YOU MIGHT USE ARE **assorted   different   mixed**

vary *verb*
The date of Easter varies each year.
>OTHER VERBS YOU MIGHT USE ARE **to alter   to change**

---

vegetable *noun*
>VEGETABLES PEOPLE EAT INCLUDE

>**asparagus   beans**
>**Brussels sprouts   cabbage**
>**carrot   cauliflower**
>**greens   leek**
>**marrow   onion**
>**parsnip   pea**
>**potato   pumpkin**
>**spinach   swede**
>**turnip**

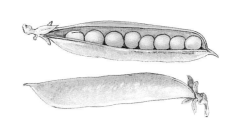

---

vehicle *noun*
For other words, see **travel**

version *noun*
1 Jo's version of the accident is different from Sam's.
>OTHER WORDS YOU MIGHT USE ARE **account   description   story**
2 Mum makes a vegetarian version of shepherd's pie.
>OTHER WORDS ARE **kind   sort   type**

vertical *adjective*
The opposite is horizontal

vibrate *verb*
When the engine started we felt the boat vibrate.
>OTHER VERBS YOU MIGHT USE ARE **to quiver   to shake   to shudder   to throb**

victory *noun*
We celebrated our team's victory.
>OTHER WORDS YOU MIGHT USE ARE **success   triumph   win**
The opposite is defeat

view *verb*
We viewed the the stars through a telescope.
>OTHER VERBS YOU MIGHT USE ARE **to look at   to watch**

villain *noun*
I guessed he was the villain at the very beginning of the film.
>OTHER WORDS ARE *(informal)* **baddy   rascal   scoundrel**
The opposite is hero

violent *adjective*
1 a violent attack.
>OTHER WORDS ARE **cruel   ferocious   fierce   savage**
2 a violent storm.
>OTHER WORDS ARE **rough   severe   strong**
The opposite is gentle

a
b
c
d
e
f
g
h
i
j
k
l
m
n
o
p
q
r
s
t
u
v
w
x
y
z

visible *adjective*
Is the ink stain still visible?
OTHER WORDS ARE **clear   noticeable   obvious   plain**
The opposite is invisible

visit *verb*
Granny visited us on Sunday.
OTHER VERBS YOU MIGHT USE ARE **to call**   (*informal*) **to drop in**

visitor *noun*
Are you expecting a visitor?
OTHER WORDS ARE **caller   guest**

vivid *adjective*
1 vivid colours.
OTHER WORDS YOU MIGHT USE ARE **bright   brilliant   colourful**
2 a vivid imagination.
ANOTHER WORD IS **lively**
3 a vivid dream.
OTHER WORDS ARE **clear   lifelike**
The opposite is dull

voice *noun*
For different ways you can use your voice, see **talk**

volume *noun*
1 The tank holds a large volume of oil.
OTHER WORDS ARE **amount   mass   quantity**
2 How many volumes are there in the library?
ANOTHER WORD IS **book**

volunteer *verb*
Sam volunteered to wash up.
ANOTHER VERB IS **to offer**

vote *verb*
Who did you vote for?
OTHER VERBS YOU MIGHT USE ARE **to choose   to pick   to select**

vow *verb*
He vowed never to do it again.
OTHER VERBS YOU MIGHT USE ARE **to give your word   to guarantee   to promise   to swear**

voyage *noun*
For other words, see **travel**

vulgar *adjective*
We don't like vulgar language.
OTHER WORDS YOU MIGHT USE ARE **bad-mannered   coarse   impolite   improper   indecent   rude**
The opposite is polite

Ww

wait *verb*

1 Wait there!

OTHER VERBS YOU MIGHT USE ARE   **to halt**   **to keep still**   **to remain**   **to rest**   **to stay**   **to stop**

2 Don't wait: get on with it!

OTHER VERBS ARE   **to delay**   **to hesitate**   **to pause**

wake *verb*

I asked Mum to wake me early.

OTHER VERBS YOU MIGHT USE ARE   **to call**   **to rouse**

walk *verb*

DIFFERENT WAYS TO WALK ARE

to creep   **to hobble**   **to limp**   **to march**   **to plod**   **to prowl**
to shuffle   **to stagger**   **to stride**   **to strut**   **to stumble**   **to totter**
to trot   **to trudge**
to go for a gentle walk: **to stroll**
to go for a long country walk
to hike   **to ramble**   **to trek**
When a baby tries to walk it **crawls**.

DIFFERENT WORDS FOR A WALKER ARE
a person who walks in the street: **pedestrian**
a person who goes for a walk in the country
hiker   **rambler**

wander *verb*

The sheep wander about the hills.

OTHER VERBS YOU MIGHT USE ARE   **to ramble**   **to roam**   **to stray**

want *verb*

You can't always have what you want.

OTHER VERBS YOU MIGHT USE ARE   **to desire**   **to fancy**   **to long for**   **to wish for**   **to yearn for**

war *noun*

THINGS THAT HAPPEN IN WAR ARE:

ambush   **attack**   **battle**   **fighting**   **invasion**   **retreat**   **siege**
surrender

For other words, see **weapon**

warm *adjective*

If something is very warm it is **hot**.
If something is slightly warm it is **lukewarm** or **tepid**.
WORDS TO DESCRIBE WARM WEATHER ARE   **close**   **humid**   **sultry**

warn *verb*

The policeman warned him not to do it again.

ANOTHER VERB IS   **to caution**

a
b
c
d
e
f
g
h
i
j
k
l
m
n
o
p
q
r
s
t
u
v
w
x
y
z

227

wash *verb*
> DIFFERENT WAYS TO WASH THINGS ARE
> **to bath   to mop   to rinse   to scrub   to shampoo   to sponge down   to swill   to wipe**

waste *noun*
Put the waste in the bin.
> OTHER WORDS YOU MIGHT USE ARE **junk   litter   refuse   rubbish**

watch *verb*
1 I watched the ducks on the lake.
> OTHER VERBS ARE **to gaze at   to look at   to observe   to stare at**
2 Will you watch my things while I go for a swim?
> OTHER VERBS YOU MIGHT USE ARE **to guard   to look after   to mind**

water *noun*
> KINDS OF WATER YOU CAN DRINK ARE
> **mineral water   spring water   tap water**
>
> OTHER KINDS OF WATER ARE
> big stretches of water
> **lake   ocean   reservoir   sea**
> small areas of water
> **pond   puddle**
> water that spreads over land that is usually dry
> **flood**
> water which goes along a channel
> **brook   canal   ditch   river   stream   waterway**
> water which rushes over rocks
> **cascade   cataract   rapids   waterfall**
> places where water comes out of the ground
> **spring   well**
> water which spurts out of a hole
> **fountain   jet   spray**
> A place where water seems to spin round and round is a **whirlpool**.

wave *noun*
Big waves are **breakers** or **surf**.
Small waves are **ripples**.

wave *verb*
The flags waved in the breeze.
> OTHER VERBS YOU MIGHT USE ARE **to flap   to flutter   to shake**

way *noun*
1 Sam thinks his way of building a den is the best.
> OTHER WORDS YOU MIGHT USE ARE **method   technique**
2 She does her hair in a pretty way.
> OTHER WORDS ARE **fashion   manner   style**
3 What is the best way home?
> ANOTHER WORD IS **route**

weak *adjective*

1 a weak person.
    OTHER WORDS YOU MIGHT USE ARE **delicate**   **feeble**   **frail**
For other words, see **ill**

2 a weak branch.
    OTHER WORDS YOU MIGHT USE ARE **brittle**   **flimsy**   **fragile**   **thin**

3 weak tea.
    OTHER WORDS YOU MIGHT USE ARE **tasteless**   **watery**
The opposite is strong

wealthy *adjective*

a wealthy businessman.
    OTHER WORDS YOU MIGHT USE ARE **prosperous**   **rich**   **well-off**
The opposite is poor

---

weapon *noun*

WEAPONS WHICH FIRE THINGS ARE

airgun	**bow and arrow**	**cannon**
catapult	**crossbow**	**machine-gun**
musket	**pistol**	**revolver**
rifle	**shotgun**	

WEAPONS WHICH BLOW UP ARE

bomb	**grenade**	**mine**
missile	**nuclear weapons**	**time bomb**
torpedo		

WEAPONS WHICH CUT WITH A SHARP EDGE ARE

cutlass	**dagger**	**sabre**
sword		

WEAPONS WITH A SHARP POINT ARE

bayonet	**harpoon**	**javelin**
lance	**spear**	

---

weary *adjective*

I was weary after the long walk.
    OTHER WORDS YOU MIGHT USE ARE **exhausted**   **tired**   **worn out**

weather *noun*, see next page

weep *verb*

He wept when his dog died.
    OTHER VERBS YOU MIGHT USE ARE **to cry**   **to shed tears**   **to sob**

weird *adjective*

1 What a weird thing to do!
    OTHER WORDS YOU MIGHT USE ARE **curious**   **funny**   **odd**   **peculiar**   **queer**
       strange

2 There was a weird atmosphere in the castle.
    OTHER WORDS ARE *(informal)* **creepy**   **ghostly**   *(informal)* **scary**

welcome *verb*

We welcomed the guests at the door.
    OTHER VERBS YOU MIGHT USE ARE **to greet**   **to receive**

a b c d e f g h i j k l m n o p q r s t u v w x y z

weather *noun*

WORDS TO DO WITH DIFFERENT KINDS OF WEATHER ARE

cloud	**drought**	**fog**	**frost**
hail	**heatwave**	**ice**	**lightning**
mist	**rain**	**rainbow**	**snow**
storm	**sunshine**	**thaw**	**thunder**
wind			

WORDS FOR DIFFERENT KINDS OF RAIN

a short fall of rain **shower**
very heavy rain **downpour**
very fine light rain **drizzle**
mixed rain and snow **sleet**

DIFFERENT KINDS OF WIND

a very strong wind **gale**
a gentle wind **breeze**
a sudden puff of wind **gust**

DIFFERENT KINDS OF STORM

a violent storm **tempest**
a snow storm **blizzard**
a storm with a lot of wind
 gale   hurricane   tornado   whirlwind
a storm with a lot of rain
 deluge   rainstorm
a storm with thunder and lightning **thunderstorm**

WORDS YOU MIGHT USE TO DESCRIBE THE WEATHER ARE

blustery	**bright**	**clear**	**cloudless**
cloudy	**cold**	**drizzly**	**dull**
fair	**fine**	**foggy**	**freezing**
frosty	**hazy**	**hot**	**icy**
misty	**rainy**	**showery**	**snowy**
stormy	**sultry**	**sunny**	**thundery**
wet	**windy**	**wintry**	

well *adjective*

I hope you are well.
 OTHER WORDS ARE **fit   healthy**
The opposite is ill

well-known *adjective*

a well-known pop star.
 OTHER WORDS YOU MIGHT USE ARE **familiar   famous**

wet *adjective*

1 I got wet in the storm.
 OTHER WORDS YOU MIGHT USE ARE **drenched   soaked**
2 The field is too wet to play on.
 OTHER WORDS ARE **muddy   soggy   waterlogged**
3 It was a wet day.
 OTHER WORDS ARE **drizzly   rainy   showery**
 If something is slightly wet it is **damp** or **moist**.
The opposite is dry

whip *verb*

For other verbs, see **hit**

whirl *verb*
The wheel whirled round.
> OTHER VERBS YOU MIGHT USE ARE **to revolve** **to rotate** **to spin** **to turn** **to twirl**

whiskers *noun*
> OTHER WORDS ARE **hairs** **bristles**

whisper *verb*
For other verbs, see **talk**

whole *adjective*
1 We ate the whole cake.
> OTHER WORDS YOU MIGHT USE ARE **complete** **entire**
2 Yasmin dropped the cake but it stayed whole.
> OTHER WORDS ARE **intact** **undamaged**

wicked *adjective*
It's wicked to take food from starving people.
> OTHER WORDS YOU MIGHT USE ARE **bad** **evil** **immoral** **sinful** **wrong**
The opposite is good

wide *adjective*
1 The stream was too wide to jump.
> ANOTHER WORD IS **broad**
2 There's a wide gap between the two scores.
> ANOTHER WORD IS **large**

wild *adjective*
1 wild animals.
> OTHER WORDS YOU MIGHT USE ARE **free** **natural** **untamed**
The opposite is tame
2 wild weather.
> OTHER WORDS ARE **rough** **stormy** **violent** **windy**
The opposite is calm
3 wild behaviour.
> OTHER WORDS ARE **boisterous** **disorderly** **excited** **noisy** **rowdy** **unruly**
The opposite is orderly

willing *adjective*
1 Sam is willing to help us.
> OTHER WORDS YOU MIGHT USE ARE **happy** **prepared** **ready**
2 Jo is a willing worker, too.
> OTHER WORDS ARE **cooperative** **helpful** **obliging**
The opposite is reluctant

win *verb*
1 Jo won first prize.
> OTHER VERBS YOU MIGHT USE ARE **to earn** **to gain** **to receive**
2 The better team won.
> OTHER VERBS ARE **to come first** **to succeed** **to triumph**
The opposite is lose

a
b
c
d
e
f
g
h
i
j
k
l
m
n
o
p
q
r
s
t
u
v
w
x
y
z

231

wind (rhymes with *tinned*) *noun*

KINDS OF WIND

a very strong wind is a **gale**.
a gentle wind is a **breeze**.
a sudden puff of wind is a **gust**.
A **whirlwind** blows round and round and can do a lot of damage.

For other words, see **weather**
A kind of wind you feel if someone leaves a door open indoors is a **draught**.

wind (rhymes with *find*) *verb*
I wound the string into a ball.
OTHER VERBS YOU MIGHT USE ARE **to coil   to curl   to loop   to turn   to twist**

windy, **wintry** *adjectives*
For other words, see **weather**

wipe *verb*
DIFFERENT WAYS TO WIPE THINGS ARE **to dry   to dust   to mop   to polish   to rub
to scour   to sponge   to wash**

wire *noun*
an electric wire.
OTHER WORDS YOU MIGHT USE ARE **cable   flex   lead**

wise *adjective*
If you're wise you won't go out in the rain.
OTHER WORDS YOU MIGHT USE ARE **intelligent   reasonable   sensible
thoughtful**
The opposite is silly

wish *verb*
For other verbs, see **want**

wither *verb*
The plants withered in the dry weather.
OTHER VERBS YOU MIGHT USE ARE **to dry up   to shrink   to shrivel   to wilt**

wobble *verb*
1 Jo wobbled a bit when she first rode a bike.
OTHER VERBS YOU MIGHT USE ARE **to be unsteady   to sway   to waver**
2 The jelly wobbles when you move the plate.
OTHER VERBS ARE **to shake   to tremble**

woman *noun*
OTHER WORDS YOU MIGHT USE
a polite word is a **lady**.
a married woman is a **wife**.
a woman who is not married is a **spinster**.
a woman whose husband has died is a **widow**.
a woman who has children is a **mother**.
a young woman is a **girl**.
The man who plays a woman in a pantomime is the **dame**.

wonder *verb*
I wonder if it will be fine tomorrow.
    ANOTHER VERB IS **to ask yourself**

wonderful *adjective*
We had a wonderful time.
    OTHER WORDS YOU MIGHT USE ARE **amazing** **excellent** (*informal*) **fabulous**
        marvellous **special**
The opposite is dreadful

---

wood *noun*
  1 Dad bought some wood to make a table.
    ANOTHER WORD IS
    timber
    KINDS OF TIMBER ARE
    beams **boards** **planks** **posts**
  2 We went for a walk in the wood.
    ANOTHER WORD IS
    woodland
    A large wood is a **forest**.
    A small wood is a **copse** or **grove** or **thicket**.
    A place where fruit trees are growing is an **orchard**.

---

word *noun*, see next page

work *noun*
  1 Keeping a garden tidy takes a lot of work.
    OTHER WORDS YOU MIGHT USE ARE **effort** **exertion** **labour** **toil**
  2 What kind of work does Dad do?
    OTHER WORDS ARE **job** **occupation** **profession** **trade**
  3 Our teacher set us work to do.
    OTHER WORDS ARE **assignment** **project** **task**

work *verb*
  1 We worked hard all morning.
    OTHER VERBS YOU MIGHT USE ARE **to labour** (*informal*) **to slave away** **to toil**
  2 Does your watch work?
    ANOTHER VERB IS **to go**
  3 Can you work this machine?
    ANOTHER VERB IS **to operate**

worry *verb*
  1 Don't worry; everything will be all right.
    PHRASES YOU MIGHT USE ARE **to be anxious** **to be concerned** **to be troubled**
        to feel uneasy
  2 Don't worry the cat when she's sleeping.
    OTHER VERBS ARE **to annoy** **to bother** **to disturb** **to pester** **to trouble**
        to upset

a b c d e f g h i j k l m n o p q r s t u v w x y z

word *noun*

Different words do different jobs and so they belong to different groups called parts of speech.

THE EIGHT PARTS OF SPEECH ARE

adjective   **adverb**   **conjunction**
interjection or **exclamation**   **noun**
preposition   **pronoun**   **verb**

Words which are the names of people, things, or ideas are nouns. For example: *girl*, *animal*, and *happiness* are all nouns.

A word which you use instead of a noun is a pronoun. For example: *I, you, she,* and *it* are pronouns.

A word which describes a noun is an adjective. In the phrase '*an old green car*' *old* and *green* are adjectives.

A word which goes in front of a noun to make a phrase is a preposition. In the phrases '*near my house*' and '*under the table*' *near* and *under* are prepositions.

Words which show what someone does or what happens are verbs. In the sentences '*Jo ran home*' and '*The rain stopped*' *ran* and *stopped* are verbs.

A word which tells you how, when, or where something happens is an adverb. For example: in the sentences '*Jo ran home quickly*' and '*Put it here*' *quickly* and *here* are adverbs.

Words like *and* or *but* which we use to join words or ideas are conjunctions.

A word like *Hello!* or *Well!* is an interjection or exclamation.

worship *verb*

Jo worships her Grandad.
OTHER VERBS YOU MIGHT USE ARE   **to adore**   **to love**

worthless *adjective*

worthless rubbish.
ANOTHER WORD IS   **useless**
The opposite is **valuable**

wound *verb*

Was anyone wounded in the accident?
OTHER VERBS YOU MIGHT USE ARE
to harm   **to hurt**   **to injure**
THERE ARE DIFFERENT WAYS YOU CAN BE WOUNDED
An animal can **bite** you.
A knock or fall can **bruise** you.
Something very hot **burns** you.
A knife will **cut** you.
You can **break** or **fracture** a bone.
You can **graze** your skin on something rough.
A gun can **shoot** you.
You can **sprain** a joint by twisting it.
A dagger can **stab** you.
Some insects can **sting** you.

wrap *verb*

I wrapped the parcel in paper.

OTHER VERBS YOU MIGHT USE ARE **to cover** **to enclose**

wreck *verb*

The accident wrecked the car.

OTHER VERBS YOU MIGHT USE ARE **to break up** **to destroy** **to ruin** **to shatter** **to smash**

write *verb*

THERE ARE DIFFERENT WAYS TO WRITE THINGS

Musicians **compose** music.

When you are bored, you **doodle**.

You **jot** down rough notes.

People **print** books and newspapers.

When you are in a hurry you **scrawl** or **scribble**.

You can **type** things or use a word processor.

DIFFERENT KINDS OF WRITING

articles for a magazine or paper

diary **essays** **films** **letters** **novels** **plays** **poems** **stories** **programmes** for radio and TV

Another word for a writer is **author**.

DIFFERENT KINDS OF WRITER

a writer of novels is a **novelist**.

a writer for a newspaper is a **journalist**.

a person who writes poetry is a **poet**.

a person who writes for radio or TV is a **scriptwriter**.

a person who writes plays is a **dramatist** or **playwright**.

Someone who writes music is a **composer**.

wrong *adjective*

1 I gave a wrong answer.

OTHER WORDS YOU MIGHT USE ARE **false** **inaccurate** **incorrect** **mistaken** **untrue**

2 It is wrong to steal.

OTHER WORDS ARE **dishonest** **illegal** **immoral**

3 Cruelty to animals is wrong.

OTHER WORDS ARE **evil** **wicked**

The opposite is right

xylophone *noun*

For other musical instruments, see **instrument**

Yy

yell *verb*

He yelled angrily at me.

OTHER VERBS YOU MIGHT USE ARE **to call   to shout**

---

young *adjective*

SOMETIMES THERE ARE SPECIAL WORDS FOR YOUNG THINGS

A person who is not a child but is not yet grown up **adolescent   juvenile   teenager**

A young person **baby   boy   child   girl   infant   toddler**

A young cow or whale is a **calf**.

A young hen is a **chick** or **pullet**.

A young bear is a **cub**.

A young swan is a **cygnet**.

A young duck is a **duckling**.

A young deer is a **fawn**.

A young bird is a **fledgling** or **nestling**.

A young horse is a **foal**.

A young goose is a **gosling**.

A young goat is a **kid**.

A young cat is a **kitten**.

A young sheep is a **lamb**.

A young pig is a **piglet**.

A young dog is a **puppy**.

A young tree is a **sapling**.

A young plant is a **seedling**.

Zz

zero *noun*

OTHER WORDS YOU MIGHT USE ARE **nil   nothing   nought**

zigzag *noun*

a zigzag line.

OTHER WORDS YOU MIGHT USE ARE **bendy   crooked**